"PLEASE LET KNOWING HELP SOMEBODY. PLEASE BEFORE I DIE."

— from Jenny's Journal

Jenny was safe . . . in the many worlds of her mind. People could never hurt her as long as they didn't know that the "others" could take her place. The "others" would experience the rapes, incest, bestiality and orgies; they would see the painted faces and naked bodies that subjected her to ritualistic sexual abuse . . .

The "others" would bear witness to the hours of imprisonment in potato crates and coffins, to the use of acid, heroin, bennies, booze and "magic" potions. They could take her place when she was crucified, when she was cut, when she was violated . . .

The "others" would enter the satanic cult that forced her at the age of ten to become the devil's bride, that ritually killed animals and humans, and made innocent children witness and participate in their acts. And finally, the "others" would help Jenny fight the systematic brainwashing by the cult that tied her to them — until she finally, painfully, broke the chains . . .

SUFFER THE CHILD

"AN EXTRAORDINARY BOOK. . . . I have said many times that if a multiple personality will get treatment from knowledgeable therapists and stay with it they will get well. Jenny seems to be an extraordinary example of this in view of the horrors and the prolonged and terribly destructive abuse."

— *Cornelia B. Wilbur, M.D., psychiatrist for Sybil,*
subject of Flora Rheta Schreiber's classic book, Sybil

"SUFFER THE CHILD is a gut-wrenching book yet one that doesn't drown in misery and hopelessness. I recommend it because it skillfully shows how a life shattered by fiendishly cruel child abuse can be helped to become whole."

— *Hank Giarretto, Ph.D., Executive Director,*
Parents United International, Inc.,
Help for Sexually Abused Children and Their Families

"A COMPELLING BOOK AND AN IMPORTANT PIECE OF WORK. . . . *SUFFER THE CHILD* represents the courageous attempt by two therapists and a patient to overcome the horror of major victimization of a young child, who reported ongoing violence and torture as her treatment unfolded. . . . Judith Spencer is the first to document, in *SUFFER THE CHILD*, the connection . . . between [satanic cult] ritual abuse and the development of a multiple personality disorder."

— *Walter C. Young, M.D., Medical Director,*
Columbine Psychiatric Center, Director,
Columbine Psychiatric Center for the
Treatment of Dissociative Disorders, Denver

"SUFFER THE CHILD may be the best account of multiple personality disorder caused by physical and sexual abuse from an occult group that I have ever come across. . . . You will be shocked and saddened at the stories Jenny tells, yet reassured by her courage and

determination in making herself healthy again through therapy. *SUFFER THE CHILD* IS A BOOK THAT SHOULD NOT BE MISSED."

— *Larry Kahaner, author of* Cults That Kill

"*SUFFER THE CHILD* IS AN EXTREMELY IMPORTANT WORK because it is the first book to relate a survivor's true story of cult abuse. I believe it will become a benchmark for other works on this subject. . . . *SUFFER THE CHILD* . . . celebrates one child's resourceful survival. If you fear to read the truth which Judith Spencer lays bare here, please remember that the real horror is not in these pages, but in our culture which tolerates torture, human sacrifice and cannibalism simply by denying that any of us could be so evil! . . . I THANK JUDITH SPENCER FOR DARING TO SHED LIGHT IN THE DARKNESS."

— *Lynne Lamb Bryant, President, VOICES In Action, the national organization for survivors of incest and child sexual abuse*

ABOUT THE AUTHOR

JUDITH SPENCER is a writer, pediatric nurse and nurse educator, with a master's degree in nursing. Her work with Jenny began when Jenny had been in therapy only a month. With unprecedented access to the therapists' records, including session notes, audiotapes, videotapes, and copies of Jenny's journal, as well as interactions with Jenny and her "others," Ms. Spencer spent five years researching Jenny's story. Jenny's therapy continues to this day. The book has been a part of her healing. Jenny told the author, "When I was little, and Mama would hurt me, the scars healed fast, so no one could see them. *A book will leave a mark that the world can see.*"

SUFFER THE CHILD

JUDITH SPENCER

POCKET BOOKS

New York   London   Toronto   Sydney   Tokyo

An *Original* Publication of POCKET BOOKS

POCKET BOOKS, a division of Simon & Schuster Inc.
1230 Avenue of the Americas, New York, NY 10020

ISBN: 0-671-66852-8

First Pocket Books printing August 1989

10 9 8 7 6 5 4 3 2 1

Printed in the U.S.A.

To my husband, Bob, and our son, Jason,
with love

CONTENTS

INTRODUCTION

For decades I was a multiple woman, known only as Eve of *The Three Faces of Eve*. My alters acted without my knowledge or approval. In my own work, *I'm Eve,* I disclosed that there were nineteen more entities who were part of me. In 1974 my twenty-two personalities unified, and I became a well person. Since then I have devoted my life to sharing my experiences, hoping to bring better understanding to an unknown wilderness of pain, multiple personality disorder (MPD).

Frustration and disappointment have long been associated with my feelings about the concern and response from the psychiatric community. Since the beginning of time, the MPD patient has suffered without proper diagnosis and treatment. Not until the 1980s did the American Psychiatric Association's *Diagnostic and Statistical Manual of Mental Disorders* recognize this painful disorder. I remain distressed that many professionals show no concern for the multiple sufferer.

More than any other organization, the International Society for the Study of Multiple Personality and Dissociation (ISSMP&D) has certainly brought into focus the needs of patients, and has provided an ongoing learning process for therapists. These pioneers have my respect and deepest appreciation.

INTRODUCTION

Over the past ten years I have consulted with many MPD patients, and each time I feel their pain. When I met Jenny, I was not prepared for her calmness. Soon I realized that it was the support of her therapists, Karl and Rachel Alexander, that kept her secure.

Studying her artwork, I felt a stirring anger, and when I received Jenny's letter, I cried. Though she and I had not had the same traumatic experiences, she was suffering the same desperate feeling, struggling with the desire to be free of multiple personality and the fear of the unknown aloneness of being one. In telling her story, Jenny has demonstrated enormous courage.

Judith Spencer is the first author, to my knowledge, to write a detailed account of multiple personality resulting from occult practices. *Suffer the Child* is a moving story, written with compassion and insight. For those who suffer similar abuse, it is a word of hope. For those of us who have been sheltered, it validates, "There but for the grace of God go I."

Chris Costner Sizemore
February 2, 1989

FOREWORD

As you read Jenny's story, be prepared to experience the grimness of child abuse and the perplexity of multiple personality disorder, and set against that, the joy of knowing that Jenny is gaining control of her life. If at first you are skeptical of Jenny's memories of horrible physical, sexual, and emotional abuse, including forced participation in satanic cult worship, that ultimately will enable you to imagine the difficulties Jenny has faced in her search for the real world.

As you begin the story of Jenny, sensitively recorded and compiled by the author over a period of five years, it will be useful to you, we believe, to understand the chronology and nature of our professional work with her. In 1983, when we first suspected that Jenny was multiple, we referred her to the local hospital's consulting psychiatrist from a major medical center. The diagnosis was confirmed, but the psychiatrist reported that because of the complexity of the case, no one from her staff wanted to get involved either as a direct provider of services or as a consultant to us. After making contacts throughout the state, we could find no one in psychiatry or psychology who had experience working with complex multiple personality cases.

We went to the literature to learn about this condition, which we believed was rare. Research articles were sparse at first, but in 1984 helpful papers began to appear in the scientific literature, and we learned that the condition was no longer considered a rarity. We were able to glean enough information from reports by experienced therapists to develop a framework for Jenny's therapy. We learned that if Jenny was willing to participate in intensive psychotherapy, she had an excellent chance for making significant improvement. The goals of therapy were twofold: to help Jenny control her life day by day and to work toward integrating her separate personalities and maintaining them as a unified individual.

In October 1984 the First International Conference on Multiple Personality/Dissociative States was held in Chicago. We were not aware of the conference at the time; however, a support system was developing that eventually became available for our venture into the treatment of multiple personality disorder. At the Third International Conference in 1986 we learned that therapists across the country were working with patients who had cult experiences similar to Jenny's. We knew that we would have to help Jenny face her terrifying memories and help her cope with the rage she would feel when her denial defenses broke down. At this conference two books were released by American Psychiatric Press, Inc.: *Treatment of Multiple Personality Disorder,* edited by Bennett G. Braun, M.D., and *Childhood Antecedents of Multiple Personality Disorder,* edited by Richard P. Kluft, M.D., Ph.D. At last we were able to benefit from the collected knowledge and experience of researchers and clinicians in the field. By the time the Fifth Conference was held in 1988, we had discovered a phenomenal growth in the study of multiple personality. During the conference the International Society for the Study of Multiple Personality and Dissociation registered its thousandth member. As Jenny was beginning her sixth year of therapy, we became members of a regional MPD study group. We had found collegial support that was not available in our early work with Jenny.

In an engrossing narrative style, Judith Spencer presents a clinically accurate portrayal of the development and perpetuation of multiple personality as reaction to "repeated exposure to an inconsistently stressful environment" (Braun, 1986, p. 5). Her account of the polyfragmented system of personalities attests to the duration, frequency, and intensity of abuses that Jenny suffered. More than four hundred personalities have been documented in our therapy. This large number does not represent distinct persons in one body, but is shown to be Jenny's experiences as responses to nearly unimaginable abuse.

The author has succeeded in communicating to both the professional and the nonprofessional reader the complex issues in the diagnosis and treatment of multiple personality disorder. Although an important purpose in itself, you should know also that the process involved in producing the book has contributed to Jenny's continued progress in therapy. The author has been more than an observer of the therapy process. She has served as Jenny's primary support person, providing a safe environment where she could acquire healthy patterns of social interaction. As an active participant in many of the marathon therapy sessions in and out of the office, her support as a nursing professional was invaluable to Jenny and to us.

To our knowledge, there have been no books written about persons with multiple personality disorder in which a nontherapist writer played such an important role in the therapeutic process. Especially during the first few years of our work with Jenny, we had no one but Ms. Spencer to look objectively at the effects of therapeutic interventions on both Jenny and us. Her insight into general human behavior, her acquired knowledge about multiple personality disorder and ritualistic cult activities, and her understanding of the dynamics of psychotherapy provided us with consultative support when our colleagues were not supportive. She served as a sounding board as we evaluated the methods we used. Her candid comments enabled us to learn from our errors. Her positive reinforcement for our efforts enabled us to continue to be optimistic about Jenny's opportunities for wholeness and health.

For Jenny's part, she has let down her walls and broken her silence — bravely and to the benefit of our society. Listen to Jenny, believe Jenny, and perhaps you will be able to believe a child who reports abuse. Perhaps you will be able to shield a child from the devastating effects that occur when stressors are so severe that the only coping mechanism is the creation of multiple personalities.

Rachel Alexander, Ph.D., Psychologist
Karl Alexander, MHDL, Counselor

PREFACE

Suffer the Child is the story of Jenny Walters Harris, who created over four hundred personalities to survive profound child abuse and the bizarre reality of forced involvement in a satanic cult. It is about her growing up in a rural area of the southeastern United States, where being an unwanted girl child gave license to exploit her. It is the story of her struggle as a woman to uncover a single whole identity among her many selves, to redeem a soul she believed irretrievably lost.

My involvement with Jenny's story began over five years ago through a chance meeting with her therapists, whom I have known for some time. They had just begun working with her, and she had expressed a desire to tell her story. My background as a pediatric nurse sensitized me to child abuse and provided a knowledge base for me to understand the origins and mechanisms of multiple personality. Experiences in writing teaching materials and contributing to professional journals as a nurse educator readied me for taking on this work.

A number of books and movies have popularized the notion of multiple personality. Among them, *The Three Faces of Eve* in 1957 and *Sybil* in 1973 and the films based on them had by far the greatest effect in educating the public about multiple personality disorder.

More so than the general public, the scientific community

has been slow and reluctant to accept the reality of multiple personality and to recognize the extent of abuse that underlies the condition. It was not until 1980 that the disorder achieved the status of a diagnostic category of mental illness in the American Psychiatric Association's *Diagnostic and Statistical Manual of Mental Disorders.* While occasional articles, usually case studies, have appeared in the scientific literature, it was not until 1984 that issues of *Psychiatric Annals* and *Psychiatric Clinics of North America* were devoted to the diagnosis and treatment of multiple personality disorder. Many cases of multiple personality have been diagnosed and reported, as courageous, caring therapists have engaged in innovative treatment and research. The definition for diagnosis has been refined as the disorder becomes better understood. The first conference, in 1984, of the International Society for the Study of Multiple Personality and Dissociation further attests to the serious attention being given to the condition.

The relationship between childhood abuse and the development of multiple personality has been well established. Now there is mounting evidence of the participation of many children in satanic cult experiences. A passage from *The Treatment of Multiple Personality Disorder,* Bennett G. Braun, M.D. (ed.), published by the American Psychiatric Press in 1986, is especially relevant:

> Some information, for example forced participation since childhood in satanistic cult worship entailing ritualistic sex, human sacrifice, and cannibalism is so terrifying and overwhelming that it requires the assistance of a trained staff available 24 hours a day to help these patients cope. Dr. Roberta Sachs and I have successfully aided nine patients from different parts of the United States who had experienced such terrifying circumstances, and I know of at least 50 others.

Such evidence has to shake our complacency and force us to acknowledge that abuse is widespread, that young lives are touched daily by physical, emotional, and sexual cruelty. Next, we have to abandon the protective self-deception that makes us believe such cruelty happens only to people we don't know. Then we can give up the delusion that these incidents of childhood have little influence on the course of events when the children become adults.

Even when we accept that child abuse and ritual abuse are widespread, it is difficult to grasp the impact on a single individual. To do so makes the horror too real. We would rather avert our eyes than see how badly a child can be hurt.

Many times as I worked at preparing this book, I wanted to avert my eyes; however, I knew I had to verify the authenticity of events to be sure I imparted only truth in the telling. Still, I found myself not wanting to verify the story so that I could maintain a secret hope that a child had not suffered so. I reasoned that the relevant truth was what Jenny perceived it to be. Without proof I could convince myself that a child's imagination had embellished ordinary happenings, and that common vicissitudes of growing up had been given uncommon blame. But wanted or not, proof came.

During the five years of researching the story, I have extensively reviewed the literature as well as materials and observations relating directly to Jenny, and have found undeniable evidence to corroborate her recall. Writings on the wall of an abandoned house, a scar on her chest, her close knowledge of areas not seen since very early childhood, school records of deteriorating abilities, medical records of injuries, and repeated confirmation of her diagnosis all serve to document her story.

I have attempted to record as accurately as possible Jenny's life as she lived it, or remembers that she lived it. Events prior to her birth are reconstructed based on Jenny's perceptions of the actions and motives of people significant in her life — perceptions based on what she was told by her mother and close relatives and what she heard them tell others. Events of her early childhood have basis not only in what she was told, but also in what she remembers, including her sense of her responses to meaningful and traumatic events. Jenny's memories have been recovered in the context of intensive therapy, aided by hypnosis. She has shown remarkable recall of details as once-scattered bits of remembered information have shaped themselves into patterns of experiences.

PREFACE

Because the story is true, some names have been changed, including those of Jenny and her therapists, the Alexanders, and details of some places and events have been modified to obscure identities and protect the people involved. In some instances, characters in the story represent more than one person in Jenny's life, and some personalities are given the traits of several in order to keep the numbers manageable. With the exception of the primary alter personality, whom I call Selena, the names of the personalities are their own.

The need to maintain anonymity prevented my interviewing Jenny's various teachers, counselors, doctors, and ministers. However, much information concerning her interactions with these people was available in numerous school records, medical records, and mental health records. Descriptions of the actions and opinions of these people are derived from statements in these records. Direct quotations are designated.

Keeping anonymity also meant not informing members of her family other than her husband and children about the telling of her story. Jenny expressed much concern that none of her family be harmed by the telling. Respecting her wishes, I did not involve her children in inquiry, but limited my contacts with them to social interactions. Certainly, information about Jenny's adult life was obtained from the children in a nondeliberate fashion. In like manner, social encounters with her aunt in the house where she lived as a young child, and with another aunt and cousin, yielded important clues about Jenny's childhood.

Jenny's husband was cooperative in supplying information. On numerous social occasions, including a long-weekend trip I shared with Jenny and her husband, he disclosed his perspective of life with Jenny. On two occasions I recorded structured interviews with him.

The primary sources of information were Jenny and her alter personalities, and her therapists. I have been fortunate to be allowed what I believe to be unprecedented access to the unfolding of Jenny's story. My work with Jenny began when she had been in therapy only a month. At that time none of us realized the complexity of Jenny's story or what that meant in terms of the demands of therapy, the impact on her life, and what was required to write about these.

With Jenny's permission her therapists made available to me all their records including notes from sessions, some audiotapes, a hundred and fifty hours of videotapes, photographs, Jenny's drawings, and copies of her journal. Jenny's journal, which was maintained by her various personalities for many years prior to her therapy and continued throughout the course of therapy, provides remarkable insight into her experiences and emotions. Where excerpts from her journal are used, I have taken the liberty of correcting spelling and adding punctuation.

In the portion of the story encompassing her therapy, conversations are, for the most part, reproduced verbatim from recordings, notes made during sessions, or notes made during telephone contact with the therapists or Jenny immediately after events occurred. Conversations early in the story are reconstructed based on my sense of events described to me, and are placed in context according to my observations of the environment in which the events occurred.

My own observations and the rich information in records were enhanced through frequent interactions with the therapists and with Jenny and her alters. When I could spend time in the area, the therapists and Jenny allowed me to be present during therapy, often scheduling marathon sessions when I could be there. I traveled with them to nearly all of the sites significant to her recall and her story.

I kept continual telephone contact with the therapists throughout the five years, making or receiving several calls a week. These calls kept me current with Jenny's progress in therapy, the emergence of alters, and the content of memories. I kept extensive records so that I could place randomly remembered facts in chronological order and track incredible events as they unfolded.

Being with Jenny in aspects of her life other than therapy gave me a broad perspective of her experiences. I spent days with Jenny, not just as a writer, but as a friend. As the story came together, my experiences were profound. I have been astonished, saddened, frightened, humbled, and elated. I know that because of these experiences, I am forever changed. I have, however, not made myself a part in the story, because what is important is what happened to Jenny.

PREFACE

This story could not have been written were it not for trust, the solid trust of longstanding friendship with the therapists, and the fragile trust of Jenny, who had every reason never to trust anyone. I am grateful for this trust.

I am grateful also for the support of caring family and friends who believed in my writing and in Jenny's story before either was proved. I thank especially Frances Henderson, Jan Jarnagin, and Jean Weinhardt for their early comments and support, and for their encouragement throughout the project. I thank my agent, Linda Allen, for her enthusiasm and her constancy. I thank my editor at Pocket Books, Paul McCarthy, for the exceptional capability he brought to his part in this work, and the thoughtful guidance he provided for mine.

Early in my acquaintance with Jenny she stated better than anyone else could her reason for wanting the story told. "When I was little," she said, "and Mama hurt me, she covered the places and the scars healed fast, so no one could see them. *A book will leave a mark the world can see.*"

As I came to know Jenny, I realized how much her motivation arose from her hope that other children need never suffer in secret. The intelligence and creativity she once used to conceal her scars are matched now by the courage she shows in revealing them. Knowing the outcome of Jenny's struggle gives hope for other survivors of abusive pasts. Seeing the process of her struggle may help us to halt abuse of the children of our future.

J.S.

San Jose, California
April 1989

THE PERSONALITIES

The personalities, listed here in alphabetical order, are described as they existed when they first revealed themselves in therapy. For some, times of first appearances and specific purposes are noted in parentheses. The number represents only a fraction of the more than four hundred personalities encountered in Jenny's therapy.

1. ABBY: Age 9, played teacher at the little house near school. (To play)

2. AMANDA: Age 17, a witch, strong, uppity, and untrusting; had knowledge of much cult abuse. (To pull back to the cult)

3. AUNT SUE: Age 84, 5'3", 150 lbs., brown hair with gray; palsied; an old maid and vegetarian; an inner-self-helper who got things from the house when Jenny was locked out, and told her bad things were dreams. (To protect from the mother's abuse)

4. AUTUMN: Age 34, a witch who didn't want to belong to Lucifer. (To reject the cult)

5. AYLA: A pious and religious young woman who knew nothing of the things remembered. (Made 2/87; to allow Jenny to deny her past)

6. BARBARA: Age 34, understood the "black book" the mother used to prove Jenny was evil; heavy German accent; originally from Germany. (To protect Jenny from the Bible)

7. BECKY: Age 7, frightened and tearful; sucked her thumb; able to play when afraid. (A playmate for Lisa)

8. BLAIR: Ugly male creature, three feet tall, with one big distorted eye, a long nose, and horns; shy and ashamed. (To protect Jenny from ugliness)

9. BOB, JEFF, PHIL, and TERRY: Male fragments who helped to discipline Jenny's children.

10. BRIDGETTE: Age 18, came at Grandmother's and Mother's funerals. (To handle practical aspects of dealing with death)

11. CHUNK: The essence of the mother; full of raw anger and fear; said that Jenny was the seed of Satan and must be killed.

12. FLISHA: Age 28, auburn hair, very sophisticated in dress and manner; excellent cook and attentive to the children; played piano, had a sweet soprano voice, and wrote poetry; enjoyed art, crafts, opera, symphony, museums, reading. (Came at age 2; to be a good little girl)

13. GLADYS FAYE: The essence of the mother; fearful and ashamed that she failed to protect Jenny; troubled by headaches and nosebleeds; ashamed of being fat.

14. HILDA: Age 34, angry, strong, tough, and belligerent; showed anger at Michael, Jenny's husband; hated washing dishes. (Came when young to deal with anger)

15. JENNY: Age 34, the birth personality; in her own worlds from age 7 to 34; repressed, quiet, gentle, fearful;

kept hands in fists and had rash on chest when anxious; allergic to wool and onions.

16. JUSTIN: Age 57, 168 lbs., brown hair with graying temples; smoked a pipe; a loving and protective father for Jenny. (Came at age 6; to supply a father image)

17. KATHY: Age 34, 5'4", 105 lbs., pretty with brown hair; talkative and outgoing; used mirrors to help Jenny dress in the morning if no other personality was out. (To help see only pretty things)

18. KAYLA: Age 5, the lost child; the inner core of Jenny who was always there and experienced everything no matter who else was there.

19. KECIA: Age 8; sucked thumb; had doll with music box; a sweet child with some memories of the cult. (To have a childhood)

20. LISA: Age 12, a pretty child with long hair and an innocent, endearing smile; loved to give; enjoyed drawing, coloring, sunny days, and sitting outside in the rain; suspicious of most grown-ups. (Came when very young; to allow Jenny to play)

21. LOUANN: Age 12, knew of demon-calling rituals.

22. MARCIE: Age 31, a gentle, loving, and compliant homebody who gave birth to and mothered the children; wore conservative dresses and little or no make-up; sold Avon products. (Came at age 2; to cry and laugh)

23. MELISSA: Age 10, wore the gown in a ceremony as a bride of Satan.

24. MIND: Jenny's unconscious mind; pretty and delicate with long silky hair, blue eyes, white skin, and fragile hands; the main inner-self-helper or center. (To protect Jenny from memories and feelings)

25. MINDOLINE: A powerful demon with no skin, bloody flesh, horns, cloven hooves, and hair on face, chest, and back. (To possess Selena and teach her to understand the demons)

26. NINA: Age 15, pretty and proper; liked and catered to Michael. (Came at 15; to date and marry Michael)

27. PAM: Age 18, 5'5", 100 lbs., blue eyes, short blond hair; angry, bitter, distrustful, fidgety, hurt by touch; drank and used drugs; had memories of near drowning, abuse in bathroom, blood in bathtub. (To protect from feeling unloved)

28. PENNY: Little girl, sickly; stayed in the corner and hid; depressed, almost catatonic. (To stay out of the way)

29. SANDY: Age 34, a witch, tall with long black hair; only one who wore glasses and was not allergic to wool; felt she was sold to the devil and her soul was doomed; well versed in scriptures and believed in reincarnation. (Came around age 5; to deal with the occult)

30. SELENA: Age 17, primary alter personality; 110 lbs., red hair; wild, free, rebellious teenager who felt no physical pain; wore tight sweaters and tighter jeans and heavy makeup; a prostitute into the drug scene; liked rock music and sang low in a country style; liked junk food and onions; constantly chewed bubble gum. (Came before age 2; to deal with physical pain)

31. THE FATHER: Very old; gray hair and skin, and horns; one of many fathers (priests) in the cult. (To claim Jenny, the birth child, for the master)

32. TODD: Age 6, mute; broke windows; fought everyone at the little house during the lost years. (To be a boy and be loved; to rebel against the abuse)

33. TOLANDA: Age 14; a witch who wanted to belong to Lucifer. (To desire the cult and find approval)

34. **VERA ANN BIRCHAUSEN:** Indian teenager, 5'4", slim, black hair in pigtails, black eyes; father was American Indian; violent and hostile; used alcohol and drugs. (To fight Billy Joe, the cousin who raped her)

35. **WAHNOLA:** Age unknown, mean, evil, and feared by the others; a self-abuser. (To fulfill Jenny's desire to be like her mother)

Who will ever know?
Just as tears are lost in the rain
And rain and tears in time,
We are lost in this dream,
A dream we can't remember.
                              Jenny's Journal

SUFFER THE CHILD

PROLOGUE

The once-pretty little house seemed long abandoned. Once-white paint was now cracked and gray. Round attic windows were broken and stuffed with rags. The shattered wrap-around porch no longer beckoned with respite from the summer sun. The arch of the doorway seemed more to caution than to welcome.

Inside, the house was just as dilapidated as out. Hard-wood floors could barely be seen beneath a coating of grime. The walls, some of tongue-and-groove siding, others of wallboard, were uniformly dingy, the dirt almost obscuring writings and drawings, probably the work of vandals.

At the door to one small bedroom Jenny stopped, unwilling to enter. "That was my room," she said. "Bad things happened there." She pointed to a pair of windows. "We would sit there and cry when it rained. Things were falling apart here."

As we prepared to leave, the writing on the walls again caught my eye — and a chill caught my heart as I read the crayoned scrawls of the childish hand: *I must keep my mouth shut because if I don't I will get in trouble.*

This was not the work of vandals. Nearly every wall in every room of the small house had some writing. But there were no vandals' scrawled profanities or teenagers' declarations of undying love. The writings were those of a child, a child in deep distress. The marks had been made by Jenny over twenty years before. There were signs of playing school — sentences to complete, arithmetic to do, a picture with the colors named, a list of assignments. There were strange faces and fuzzy creatures like those Jenny had sketched just a few months before in the therapists' office. There was a long list of names, many of them familiar, and twice more the quelling refrain: *I must keep my mouth shut . . .*

There were no clues to specific events in the place. Jenny had moved to the house with her mother when she was twelve years old. At fourteen Jenny was admitted to a state hospital, unable to recall more than small bits of the two years in this house. Now, many years later, it would take many hours of work in therapy to uncover the events so fully repressed in those lost years.

Why had the writing been left on the walls? Perhaps her family and the family who occupied the house briefly after them were unconcerned, or were too overwhelmed with other issues to worry that the small dwelling that made a roof over their heads had marks on its walls. Whatever the reason, the house never had more than its original coat of paint. Now it stood empty, falling to ruin with Jenny's silent evidence.

Forbidden to scream, unable to cry out her pain and rage, Jenny took her tears inward, making them crystals to contain the fragments of her life. Like substances that form crystals when exposed to extremes of temperature or pressure, Jenny, exposed to the extremes of her childhood, responded by becoming a multiple personality.

At the time of dissociation in very early childhood, the solution was exceptionally logical and effective. The child, vulnerable in physical size and strength, and immature in psychological resources, could not cope with or successfully confront abuses and traumas perpetrated by the adults in her life. So by a sort of self-hypnosis she delegated the experiences to alter personalities. Other selves experienced the rejection, the pain, the fear, the horrors, the hatred. Then the existence of these other selves was relegated to the unconscious mind by continued self-hypnotic means. In this way the child escaped abuses which if experienced could have led to insanity. (For discussion of the theory concerning the place of self-hypnosis in multiple personality, see Bliss, 1986.)

In the world of childhood, with fantasy and reality freely intermingled and time a fluid commodity, Jenny could accept the inward existence of multiple selves and periods of trance and amnesia as commonplace. The other selves protected Jenny, but as she grew older she paid a higher and higher price for her protection.

The alter personalities once created did not cease to exist when the child was no longer threatened. Instead, they became more complex and demanding as each attended to assigned functions and struggled to make complete an existence destined to be partial. Jenny, relinquishing more and more of now-finite time to other selves, could not hold on to reality and control of her life. She became as an artist unable to complete a single self-portrait, yet compelled to begin a thousand canvases — a sculptor compelled to carve a thousand stones.

Part I

Dark Secrets

I, Sandy, was allowed to dance with the devil
A takeover of my human body and soul by demons
Who force me to speak and act according to the
devil's will.
I'm doomed for hell. Forever lost.
No one to help me.

Jenny's Journal

CHAPTER 1

Cold. Cold. Dear Lord, the stone was cold — as cold as the cellar potato box, as cold as the world when you're born unwanted. Jenny couldn't bear the cold, not again. She had to get away. And when she was gone, the ritual began.

Sandy took her place upon the altar. She trembled, but not from cold. She was afraid. She felt the rough coolness of the granite slab beneath her small naked body. She had seen others lie upon the stone and heard their muffled moans, seen the silver glint of the dagger, a dark glistening of blood. The altar was for sacrifice. Now it was her turn.

She lay still and resigned, and breathed in the smoky smell of the fire mixed with the sweet medicine smell of madonna burning in bowls by the fire. Her heart pounded when she saw hooded figures approach. She could read nothing in the faces sometimes shadowed by firelight, sometimes silhouetted by the full moon. Her breath caught short as one tall figure moved toward her, its hideous goat's head almost brushing her face. Her breath escaped in a sigh as she felt warm oil touch her body.

As the high priest poured the oil, the others began to croon, "Cum-ee-she-la, La-she-na, Pen-she-ee-ah, Cum-eefa." They swayed and moved in an undulating dance about the stone, swirling by the dazzled child.

Sandy knew not to move, not to cry out. She had learned at other times, when she stood near the altar to take part in rituals, that she must wait and accept. She felt now the chill of the night air, saw the circle of trees just beyond the clearing, as naked as she this late in the fall. The chant continued. "Cum-ee-she-la . . ." She kept still, as still as time seemed to be.

The sounds of the chant faded as the high priest began to read. At first the words carried the usual tone of the meetings. Then they took on a different familiarity for Sandy, and she saw that the priest read from a black book. If Jenny had been there, she would have known that it was the same black book the preacher read from in church, and the same black book her mother read from at home. Many times Jenny had heard the Old Testament lines.

A bastard shall not enter into the congregation of the Lord; even to his tenth generation shall he not enter into the congregation of the Lord. (Deuteronomy 23:2)

And a bastard shall dwell in Ashdod, and I will cut off the pride of the Philistines. (Zechariah 9:6)

Jenny would have been even more frightened hearing the words from this unholy man than she was when her mother screamed the words at her. But Jenny didn't hear the words now in this place, and Sandy didn't understand why the words seemed so familiar.

The reading completed, the priest placed his hand upon the child's forehead and intoned, "Spirit of vile little one come forth — to do thy bidding, to be thy servant." He anointed her once more, then wrapped her in white linen.

Holding the child at arm's length in front of the people, the priest presented them with their newest initiate, saying, "Suffer the little children to come unto him, for of such is the kingdom of hell."

The people smiled their pleasure and responded, "All

praise be unto Satan, for he is master of all. All condemnation be unto God, for he is master of nothing."

As strong arms lifted her from the altar, Sandy felt relieved, happy. She had a father. She belonged. She would complete the destiny she had been born to fulfill. But she did not know she would keep Jenny from finding out that the mother who would soon sell her body had already sold her soul.

Sandy sensed danger as the priest placed her back upon the altar. He commanded her to sit up and drink from the cup he held for her. Then he laid the child down and opened the white linen wrap in preparation for completing the ritual. The drug she had drunk made her feel dizzy. She never really saw the blade, but as soon as she felt the first cut of the dagger, Sandy, like Jenny, fled the cold, hard stone.

Selena was not much surprised to find herself among these strangers with staring eyes and painted faces. She knew something bad would happen. It always did for her. And the pain and shame would make wherever she was seem all too familiar. Selena had received no drugs to deaden her responses. She was fully alert. Yet she felt nothing as blood trickled between her legs, drawn by the sharp dagger. She did not taste her own blood placed in her mouth by the smiling priest. And she still felt nothing as men and women touched and entered her nakedness with their hands and strange elongated objects.

Selena knew that the things that were happening hurt, but she felt no physical pain. She knew the acts were shameful, but she felt no emotional pain. That's what she had come for. She felt no pain, but she was aware of all that happened. She even noticed that Jenny's mother did not hold back from taking her part in this sexual initiation.

As soon as the adults tired of tormenting the child, they turned their attentions, now fully aroused, to one another. They moved away from the fire in couples and groups. They danced and drank more wine and more of the drink called madonna, and removed their black wool robes to mingle their bodies in a sensuous frenzy of sight and touch and smell.

Five-year-old Selena was exhausted. She got down from the stone, and staying clear of the light from the fire, huddled at the corner of the barn. Jenny's mother, now lost among the laughing group, would find her when it was time to go home.

Jenny came slowly awake, safe in the dark and the shelter of the barn. She thought about what she had seen. She had caught glimpses of two children on the altar. The children were familiar to her. She sensed kinship with them, but she was not aware that these children were a part of her. Though each in turn inhabited her body while she somehow contrived to leave it, she saw them as separate, distinct in appearance and independent in action. She had seen the one who looked like her many times before and in many places. She was the one who came when there was pain. But she had seen the girl with long dark hair only in this place. She remembered the first time she had seen the dark-haired girl, and the first time she had come here. It had been no more than six months earlier. But that was a very long time in the life of a child.

It was late in the evening when the car pulled into the yard. Jenny was outside, not playing really, just outside sitting on the still-warm grass. She had seen the car before and expected her mother would go in the car and not return until she was long asleep. But this time was different. She jumped when she heard her mother say, "Get in the car."

Without questioning, without even looking at her mother, Jenny climbed into the old Ford among the adults. She heard a skinny lady she had never seen before say, "She's a pretty little thing." Jenny looked at her mother. Her mother smiled, and briefly the child relaxed.

Jenny settled herself between her mother and the strange skinny lady, feeling the steamy warmth of too many sweaty bodies in too small a space. She paid no attention to the talk of the adults, but strained to look out the window and wished she could feel some air on her face.

The old car turned by the stone schoolhouse, and paved road gave way to gravel and finally to dirt. Jenny caught glimpses out the window as they drove into the country. They passed some houses with gardens and plowed fields, but soon there were only pastures with a few cows and horses, and open fields.

Three or four cars were already at the old barn where they stopped. A rusty pickup pulled in just behind them, and clouds of dust on the road predicted latecomers. Adults and children piled out of the cars and trucks. Jenny was glad to be out of the car, outside where she could feel the bit of a breeze, and away from the sharp elbows of the skinny lady whose hands could not be still when she talked. Jenny held back as she saw the other little children do, while the grown-ups and older children got busy.

Three men struggled to drag a large stone slab from the truck and set it on smaller stones next to a fire laid in the center of a clearing. Women stirred some kind of liquid and set bowls of it near the fire. People hurried in and out of the barn until all were dressed in black robes, hoods covering their heads, nearly hiding their faces. The activity, the people, confused Jenny. There were men and women, Negroes and whites. Some had painted their faces white with black around their eyes.

Jenny looked around for the other little children. None ran up to say, "Let's play." None even so much as said, "Hey." She saw a few of them by the trees or just sitting in the grass, separate, silent. They seemed to want to disappear as much as she did. Jenny was glad. She didn't know how to play with other children. And as she had gotten in the car, her mother had said under her breath, "You keep your mouth shut." She knew her mother meant it. It was good to be left alone.

Even if she wanted to, Jenny could not follow what was going on. She caught snatches of words, singsong words, words she had heard her mother say from the black book. She watched the people move around the fire, their motion lit only by the fire's glow and a bright moon. She could make no sense of their doings. She grew more and more weary. Her eyes were very heavy. She couldn't pick out her mother among the robed figures, though sometimes she thought she heard her harsh laugh. She curled up on the warm ground and smelled the sweet grass and wild clover as she let her eyes begin to close.

Suddenly she was on her feet, her attention riveted on one man at the fire. "You young-uns come here," he commanded. "Now!" Children materialized from the trees and bushes around the clearing and walked with her toward the fire, frightened of moving, more frightened of disobeying the man.

When they were close, they could see that the man held a small squirming dog in one hand, a knife in the other. The grown-ups were quiet around the fire and the stone. Almost too fast to see, the knife flashed. The dog yelped, then was limp upon the stone. The man lifted the dog so that the blood flowing from its cut throat would be caught in a silvery bowl.

Jenny was terrified. She wanted to run. She didn't. She wanted to cry. Some did. But they all stood still and watched the dark red liquid fill the small bowl. They all heard the man say, "Now you will know to keep your mouths shut. You don't tell what you see. You don't tell what you hear. You keep still, or you will . . ." His voice trailed off in Jenny's mind. It was not necessary to hear more.

The frightened child thought her ordeal had ended. Instead, it intensified. The man picked up the silvery bowl and held it to her lips and to the lips of each child in turn. "Drink," he said, "and seal your lips, evil spirit."

Jenny tasted the salty sweetness of the blood, the awful taste of killing, the words "evil spirit" echoing in her brain. She would never be pretty to these people. Somehow they already knew of her ugliness. She fled in terror and defeat from the bowl, the fire, the man who knew she was wicked.

This was not the first time Jenny had to escape lest some awful circumstance overwhelm her. Without effort, without awareness even, she called to play the same skill that she had needed to release her from pain and fear when she was very young. Through the process of dissociation, Jenny called forth a separate consciousness, a kind of new being, to withstand what she could not.

Sandy licked the sticky blood from her lips, curious about the taste of killing. With the same curiosity she studied the face of the high priest, looking for his approval as his dictum for silence hung in the air. She would obey. She studied the others around the fire, saw that young women stood in places of honor by the high priest. She knew that she had much to learn, but she would be one of them. Through an act of divided consciousness Jenny watched from her safe place, as the dark-haired Sandy left the fire with the other children and returned to the solitary spot on the grass.

CHAPTER 2

Jenny was five years old when her mother took her, late in the spring, to the meeting of the cult. From that young age, through the cycles of the seasons, the rhythms of Satan worship permeated her childhood. At five, six, and seven years old, with her child's measuring of time, she could not tell when next she'd be called to the car to ride again to a secluded field or barn or to a stranger's house for another secret meeting. But the calls came, and her indoctrination continued with a regularity she could not track.

Jenny came to dread the dusk. She couldn't feel the peace of summer gloamings sweetened by thunderstorms that brought blessed coolness to hot, sultry days, nor delight in the balmy red sunsets of autumn that matched the sky to the changing leaves.

Sandy, whose existence depended on Jenny's terror, welcomed the twilight. It signaled for her another chance to learn and to please the people who could help her become what she had to be. With a singleness of purpose, this child, who had no infancy but sprang suddenly into being at age five, sought her education.

The early years in the cult were a time for learning. Young children were not so much expected to participate in the rituals as they were expected to watch and learn and tell no one of what they saw. They saw a great deal. Animals, older children, and even adults were made to endure physical tortures, cutting, and burning. The little ones had to watch mutely, and sometimes to drink the potions guaranteed to keep them silent.

Jenny wanted desperately to please her mother, and sensed that in the worship of the devil she had a chance. She saw her mother's happiness among these people, saw her settle in at the meetings with an air of belonging. Jenny had never seen her mother so at ease, and like her mother she was drawn by an unspoken promise of acceptance. She tried to pay attention, to do as she was told. She struggled against the fear she felt for this place, fighting for a chance to be wanted so her mother would love her, would be proud of her.

So Jenny went to the meetings that began at dusky dark, and hid among the trees or shrubs that encircled the clearing or in the shadows of the house or barn and watched and hoped she would learn how to be worthy of belonging there. But each time the really important lessons came, and she was called forward with the other small children to approach the altar, terror overcame her, and Sandy was left to learn the precious secrets.

Jenny would start toward the inner circle, eyes focused on the flames from the black candles, trying to avoid the gaze of the giant single eye staring from the black curtain. She would catch glimpses of animals being placed on the altar or see an outstretched hand laid upon the stone or a naked human form exposed in the firelight, but after that first killing of the dog, she never again saw clearly the blade complete its work.

It was Sandy who stood boldly to see other dogs, and then cats, chickens, squirrels, rabbits, and goats killed. She watched the amputation of fingers and nipples, and, sometimes, penises. Many times she saw the ooze of blood as designs were carved on chests or skin was layered from arms and ankles. She listened carefully to what was said. She had a sense of where to stand to have the best view, and she made accurate and important observations: the knife was handled with delicate and deliberate skill; the victims made little or no attempt to resist (the result of heavy doses of drugs and alcohol), and eager adults and reluctant children drank the blood and ate the bits of flesh provided by the sacrifice.

At these times, if Jenny had seen her mother's face, she would have seen the pride she longed to see. As did everyone else, her mother could see that Jenny was special. Of all the children, she was the boldest and the quickest to learn. Gladys Faye Walters had a right to be proud of her daughter.

Gladys Faye herself had no special status in the cult. She was neither bright nor pretty, and while she was accepted as a faithful member and watched over, as were the others, by the high priest and priestesses, she had no hope of finding a place of power in the group. Her daughter showed promise of beauty and intelligence, and Gladys Faye realized she had something the cult wanted. She controlled something of worth. As over and over again the members watched this child stand bravely at the altar and gave their knowing nods of approval, Gladys Faye accepted a mother's credit.

Each time, Jenny felt a terrible sense of defeat. She had again failed to please her mother. She had run away to a safe place and left another to take whatever blame or praise would come. While others still saw Jenny there, Jenny saw a child at the altar who was tall with straight long black hair and olive skin. This dark child had no interest in Gladys Faye's approval. Sandy was unconcerned with Jenny's mother. It wasn't her mother; she had none. She had only to please the father, Satan, and to learn from those who could help her please him.

Sandy learned the early lessons well. She memorized the chants as other kindergarteners did the alphabet. She even began to put meaning to the objects and symbols—the dagger for manhood, the cup for womanhood, and the powerful great eye through which Satan watched his servants and drew them to him.

With her attention fixed on the outward trappings of the cult, the young Sandy was not aware that a perverse logic was being instilled that would create a nearly unbreakable bond. Though never expressed openly and clearly, the premises of Satan worship promised for her an otherwise unobtainable salvation.

Evil ones cannot go to heaven. Those who are evil will abide in hell, a place of burning, ruled by Satan. Those who serve Satan will go to hell, yet they will not burn. Sandy never questioned her place in the cult.

Jenny continued to struggle to deserve her place. She tried to please the others, and through them, to please her mother. But she was not able to deal with what belonging demanded. An especially sensitive child, she felt deeply when she saw others hurt or frightened, and she had long since reached the limits of tolerance for her own fear and pain. More and more she escaped to her inner places of safety.

When she was called to seal her allegiance to Satan, she made her final escape and left surrogates in her stead. Jenny never returned to the cult, but the experiences there were indelibly etched in her memory. Hers was the single mind of all who lived the experiences for her.

The children delivered to Satan in anointing sacrifice were considered ready to serve him. They would continue to learn in his service and were expected to take more and more central roles in the rituals.

At first Sandy did well. She could recite the chants, remember the order of things, and stand without flinching at the altar. But then she began to be placed on the altar herself to learn or serve through pain or sexual submission. Sandy was not equal to these challenges. She could not tolerate pain. She had first come to the altar to taste the blood of sacrifice, and had returned to receive anointing. She had fled the altar when the pouring of oil was followed by sexual attack, leaving Selena to the debasement and the pain.

Over and over again Selena found herself finishing what Sandy had begun. She smelled her flesh burn, felt the blisters rise and tasted the salty fluid as they burst, while the man deftly tilted the candle to let the wax fall again on the tongue Sandy had so obediently extended. Or she saw the areas made raw as flesh was layered from the arms Sandy had placed on the altar.

The members of the cult did not see that alter personalities, other children, responded to their bidding. They did not see Sandy's long dark hair or Selena's confident expression, features much apparent to Jenny, who watched the others succeed in her stead. The cult members saw a single child named Jenny, and they became more and more impressed with her. They had known from the start she was smart. Now they sensed she had something more than brains. They began to suspect that she had some special powers.

They had never seen a child quite like her before. She was a standout among the children. Small for her age, she looked almost cherubic, with strawberry-blond curls framing a pretty, round face. Her fair skin did not freckle, but turned golden in the summer sun. And her skin could not seem to be marked. Burns or cuts healed almost instantly, leaving scars so faint they could barely be seen.

She was always clean — as if she just stepped out of a bandbox. She wore pretty little dresses and knee socks and black patent Mary Janes. She looked special.

They had never known a child to give so little trouble. Except for the first time she was brought to the meeting, she never seemed to be afraid. She did what she was told and more. At times it seemed she enjoyed it. She never pulled away or screamed in pain. She just watched when they cut her or poured the hot oil. She never turned away from them, and she never cried out to them.

Even with the sedating drugs they were given, the children always fought at first, and they stayed afraid. Fear kept them quiet. But Jenny Walters did not fight and was not afraid. It was as if she willed herself to be silent.

They began to pay particular attention to Jenny. The high priest took notice of her and included her more than the other children in the rituals. The members watched and talked among themselves. Yes, they concluded, it was likely this child had powers. It was important to direct her early and to keep the powers under control.

By the time she was eleven years old, Sandy had already been honored by being allowed to hold the cup while other children were made to drink the mixture of drugs and human fluids. The honor was given to celebrate her cutting with the dagger. Not flinching at the task, she had cut skin from the man's ankles as well as any adult could have. The priest knew she was ready for more important things. These would take place at the autumn high mass.

The evening of the high black mass was cool, cold almost, and the fires seemed to draw the robed figures to them. Sandy was invited to sit among the adults and to drink the drugged wine with them. All the children were staying close to the fire tonight.

As the evening advanced, preparations for the special service continued. The black curtain was suspended behind the black-draped altar. Black candles were set to burn beside the inverted cross and the always-watching great eye. A nude woman was placed upon the altar, and the high priest and priestesses moved to their places to begin the ritual.

The brass bell was rung, and the people began to croon and chant. Pseudo-scriptures were read, blaspheming God, extolling Satan. The priest held on to the words, presenting them to the people like individual gifts. The people, already under the influence of alcohol and drugs, returned the gifts with echoing resonance. To them the rhythmic sounds and firelit sights were almost stupefying. The people became subdued as the high priest moved to the altar.

The high priest caressed the woman's face and breasts. Then, concealing his actions, he injected her with a drug to sedate her further. He continued to explore her body with his hands, now exaggerating the moves for the benefit of the observers. He entered her first with the tip of the dagger, then with his hands. He prolonged the sensual play. He presented first a symbolic phallus, then his own for her to fondle and take into her mouth. She offered no resistance to these acts, nor to his final act of coupling.

The people became increasingly aroused. They were eager to begin their own parts in the sexual celebration, waiting only for the signal from the priest. But the high priest did not release them, not yet. He waited for the priestesses to take their places and for the high priestess to replace his robe for him and then to stand ready to serve at his side.

Sandy had moved with the others to the altar when the ritual began. She repeated the chants and paid her usual careful attention. She watched the priest as he performed the ritual acts. But mostly, she watched the priestesses. She had the most to learn from them. She had little interest in the submissive woman on the altar, and did not really watch the priest as he moved with her.

Even so, she didn't notice the two priestesses coming toward her until they were right in front of her. She followed quietly as they led her between them to stand behind the altar. She was accustomed to being singled out for special lessons. She stood ready to learn.

Sandy drank the bitter liquid from the proffered chalice and looked carefully at the woman who lay before her. Sandy didn't know many people in the cult. She had no desire to know them. She kept to herself. But this looked like the skinny lady who sometimes rode in the car with them. Sandy looked down at her and felt a little sorry for her. She didn't know why.

Sandy waited expectantly to see the ritual concluded. The drugs were taking effect. She fought to stay awake. She could no longer focus on details. She wanted to be done with this.

The priestesses who stood next to her seemed to transform. The high priest himself now stood on one side of her, the high priestess on the other. Somehow Sandy had come to be wearing a black wool robe like the others. She didn't know where it came from, but she was grateful for its scratchy warmth.

Through the static of narcotics, Sandy heard the voice of the high priest. It took another beat before she realized he was talking to her, and still another before she realized what he said.

"Kill her."

The words hung amid the noisome music in her mind. She knew she must obey. She felt the hilt of the dagger placed in her hand, strangely strengthened by the feel of the familiar cold object. She raised the knife above her head.

A few moments earlier she could not see details. Now she could see nothing else — pink flesh, closed eyes, a pretty mouth, naked toes, curly brown hair between white legs, and such pink, pink flesh. Sandy could not move her arm to complete the act.

Selena's head spun with confusion. She stood with the knife poised. She closed her eyes, trying to make sense of where she was. As if guided by someone else, her hand came down. She saw the pink flesh, the soft hair, the eyes open in startled accusation. Then she saw the dark red, warm, flowing blood. An awesome internal scream pierced the mind noise to make its mark of evil on Jenny's soul.

Part II

Origins

Little girl of two
Losing someone she loves,
Locked behind the doors
Afraid of the dark,
Afraid of the pain that waits.

Little girl of five
Still not sure of life,
Locked behind the doors
Afraid of the dark,
Afraid of the pain that waits.

Little girl of nine,
Look how time has passed.
Locked behind the doors
Afraid of the dark,
Afraid of the pain that waits.

Little girl of twelve
Now slowly losing her mind.
Locked behind the doors
Afraid of the dark,
Afraid of the people outside.

Jenny's Journal

CHAPTER 3

"I don't want it! I'll kill it!"

Whump! Whump! With her big hands doubled into tight fists, the distraught woman unleashed her anger on the flicker of movement in her expanding abdomen.

Up to now, Gladys Faye had been fairly successful at ignoring her pregnancy. Of course she had known about it right away. She'd had a child before, for God's sake. But that was over ten years earlier. She was married then. But they had come to a parting of the ways. She didn't even use his name anymore. She had long since adjusted to being single — a decent job in the mill, welcome to live with her son in her sister's house, and attention enough from men, more than enough.

How could she have been so stupid, so unlucky? God is sure to punish you for your sins, and she was in for a lifetime of it. She should have gotten rid of it as soon as she missed the first period. But she had lulled herself into a childish fantasy that the dark, handsome Donald Poehlman would marry her, and she would actually have a house, and with her son, Lloyd, and the baby they'd be a real family. She simultaneously denied to herself that she carried his child.

Even at quickening the pregnancy was not apparent. Any weight gain was insignificant compared to her already sizable girth. Her loose-fitting cotton print dresses concealed the truth from others as well as she hid it from herself.

Gladys Faye had always been heavyset. When she was young, her round little face prompted people to say, "She'd be a pretty child if . . ." By the time she was three, and had changed from a round, plump baby to a square, chubby toddler, her uncle Cleatus dubbed her Chunky. The sobriquet stuck, and when she became an adult, family members were as apt to call her Chunk or Chunky as they were to use her Christian name.

Right now she hated that stupid, fat nickname and hated her looks. She was furious with herself for even thinking that Don would marry a fat, ugly thirty-two-year-old. She would be stuck with his bastard child just because she wasn't slim and pretty.

"I have to get rid of it, Mama. I don't want it. I can't stand it," she pleaded, staring helplessly at the neat gray bun, the only visible part of her mother's lowered head. The older woman calmly kept rocking. She was careful to conceal a smile as she thought about how young people want to act today. Why, it had never even crossed her mind to think about whether she wanted her babies. You took your babies when and if God gave them to you. She had reared them all, too, except for Claudette who got the pneumonia when she was just three weeks old. Surely Gladys Faye could rear two young-uns, when she had managed very well herself with ten.

There was no sense in getting worked up about not being married either. There were already two grandchildren who didn't have fathers to legalize their names. The name Walters worked just fine for them. As far as she could tell, nobody in the family looked down their noses at them either. At least they didn't have the nerve to do it in front of her. The Walters name could serve all right for this baby too.

Gladys Faye would have the baby as God planned. Anything else was unthinkable, a sin against God, against the commandments. Gladys Faye knew that. She just needed to be reminded. She was always so excitable, would get hysterical over the least little thing. She'd settle down directly and love the baby once it got here — like every mother does.

The aging matriarch looked up and reached out with soothing words and supporting arms. "We'll see this through together, Chunky, hon," she said. "Just simmer down." As Gladys Faye slumped at her mother's feet, the little woman quietly and slowly reminded her daughter of the truths she'd learned many times over at New Hope Baptist Church.

Gladys Faye was almost as afraid to displease her mother as she was to compound her sin. Yet when the baby moved within her, she was overwhelmed with the need to be rid of it. Each flutter reminded her of the man who had used her and turned his back on her. And it renewed her anger at herself for letting this happen when she was more than old enough to know better. The anger festered within her as relentlessly as the pregnancy progressed.

Gladys Faye held her breath and gulped down the glass of oily liquid. She nearly gagged at the heavy smell of turpentine, but she drank the whole dose. Within moments Gladys Faye felt deathly ill. She went pale, breaking out in cold sweat. But the waves of nausea, the vomiting, the spasms of diarrhea, could not dislodge the developing fetus. The unborn child, however, was given notice, through a kind of visceral language, that the world would be forever hostile.

As desperate as Gladys Faye had been to rid herself of the unwanted child, she had no intention of making herself that sick ever again. She resigned herself to having the baby.

As she neared term, she became physically ill and grew more and more uncomfortable. She had gained entirely too much weight. Her feet and ankles swelled unmercifully in the hot, humid afternoons. But worst of all were the blinding headaches that struck two or three times a week. She dragged about, looking pale and puffy, and finally quit her job to stay most of the time in bed. The bed rest would not lower her rising blood pressure. She had to go to the hospital four or five times during her last few months for shots to control it.

The whole family was as relieved as Gladys Faye when her labor finally began. Some twenty hours later, at 12:03 A.M. on an October 30th morning that would become a warm Indian summer day, she was delivered of a healthy six-pound six-ounce girl.

At the hospital no one was surprised that Mrs. Walters showed little interest in her newborn. She was surely exhausted from her toxic pregnancy and her prolonged labor. So the nurses took care of Baby Girl Walters while her mother relished the much-needed rest and attention.

The family seemed not to notice Gladys Faye's indifference. They were happy to have a baby in the house. Mamie had never had children, never been married, though she was proud to be aunt to the Walters clan's sizable brood.

The family turned to Mamie when they were short of money, or in need of a place to stay, or wanted a baby-sitter for a few days, or were just after some advice. After Papa died so young — a stroke when he was only forty-three years old — Mamaw had nearly broken, and the spinster Mamie had stepped naturally in as the eldest sister to be the central figure about whom the doings of the family revolved.

Mamie tended garden and kept up the pretty, dormered, two-story white house with a smokehouse out back. She had had the place built in the summer of 1949, when the war shortages were no longer such a problem. The place was just far enough out of town to be peaceful, just close enough so she could get to her job easily, second shift in the mill.

The house and its table seemed able to expand so that there was always a place to sleep or something to eat for anyone in the family. The brothers and their wives and the sisters and their husbands came by often with the kids on a Saturday afternoon or Sunday after church. They'd stay for dinner of ham and redeye gravy and fresh collards, or some white corn or mashed potatoes and sliced tomatoes from the garden, and they'd visit some with Mamaw. Then, too, there was an abundance of aunts, uncles, and cousins by blood and by marriage who stopped by often and always kept in touch.

With the new baby in her arms, Mamaw was in her element. As the family came to see the new arrival, Gladys Faye was delighted with their approval and the gifts and attention they showered on her. She even liked the name, Jenny Lynn, that her mother insisted was right for the pink, pretty, perfect baby girl.

Gladys Faye phoned Donald Poehlman. Maybe when he saw this beautiful baby he'd see things differently. He came to the house one Sunday after Thanksgiving when Jenny was about six weeks old. As he lifted his daughter from her grandmother's arms, he saw himself reflected in her shining eyes. Her fragile fairness contrasted with his dark features; still, he knew it was from him she got the flawless skin and the soft curl in her baby hair.

Gladys Faye followed quietly as he walked with the baby to the living room and motioned her beside him on the faded Duncan Phyfe sofa. "Faye," he said, "she's sure pretty, but it don't change nothing. I can't marry you. You know it as well as I do. But I want to do right by her. I'll send you something along the first of every month."

Gladys Faye knew now for sure she was beaten. "Don't come around here again," she told him.

Jenny's father got up from the couch without a word. Avoiding Gladys Faye's stare, he walked with his small bundle back to the rocking chair by the kitchen stove and put Jenny again in her grandmother's arms. As the old woman sat by the hour and rocked and sang to her, Jenny basked in the warmth.

Although the checks came regularly every month, and she cashed them just as regularly, Gladys Faye never again spoke a word to Donald Poehlman. And he never again saw his daughter.

Jenny's care fell naturally to her grandmother, and both the infant and the old woman thrived on it. By the time Gladys Faye recovered from childbirth, the routine was established. Mamaw bathed and changed the baby and gave her bottles, and often took her in the yard for sun and fresh air. Gladys Faye went back to her job in the mill. Every payday she'd buy an outfit for her baby. She nodded and smiled when someone in the family or someone at church would say, "You sure take care of Jenny. You dress her up just like a doll baby."

Still, Gladys Faye's resentment toward the baby would build. Jealous of the attention the baby got from Mamaw and the others, Gladys Faye withheld attention herself.

One day when Jenny was about five months old Gladys Faye went to get her up from her crib. Finding the baby soaked, she began to change her. Jenny squirmed away from her mother, and the diaper pin entered her soft flesh. "Be still, you stupid little brat," Gladys Faye muttered as Jenny screamed her protest. Then she clutched her daughter to her, whispering, "I'm sorry, baby. I love you."

A few days later Gladys Faye took Jenny to the jewelry store and had her ears pierced for tiny gold earrings. A few months later Gladys Faye bought her a baby ring engraved with delicate roses and attached by a tiny chain to a matching bracelet. Gladys Faye had hurt the baby again, but the pretty things would make up for that.

Jenny's first smiles were for her grandmother. As soon as she was old enough to recognize her, Jenny always quieted when she saw the gold-rimmed glasses, the soft gray hair.

Mamaw purely doted on the baby and was just beside herself the few times the infant was ill. When a cold turned into pneumonia just before Jenny's first birthday, Mamaw made a steam tent over the rocking chair from her good quilts. She sat with the baby for days, soothing her, holding her upright to make her breathing easier. Mamaw wouldn't lose another baby to pneumonia.

When Jenny was well, Mamaw began to sew for her along with taking up her quilting again. The little dresses and sunsuits she made put the store-bought ones to shame. Mostly she used blue fabrics. They brought out the color of Jenny's eyes. Gladys Faye still bought something new every few weeks. She began to tend toward the blues too.

Once as Mamaw sat sewing a little gingham dress in the

upstairs bedroom, the almost-two-year-old Jenny toddled around playing with toys. Jenny saw the cup on the chair arm. "Wa-wa," she chortled, and had a taste before her Mamaw could stop her. Mamaw couldn't help but laugh at the awful screwed-up face and at the sputtering and spitting. Jenny had gotten hold of Mamaw's snuff cup. She'd have been sick, too, if she hadn't spit it out so fast.

Mamaw hugged her and settled her with a real drink of water. Mamaw nearly gave up her snuff after that. And Jenny never forgot that taste. Years later she would taste it whenever she thought of her mamaw and blue dresses.

Within the month Mamaw was dead. She went out to pick beans while Jenny was napping one afternoon. The heart attack took her without warning.

As her mother lay in state in the small, tidy living room, Gladys Faye lifted Jenny up to the coffin. "Tell Mamaw bye-bye, baby." Gladys Faye choked. "We won't see her no more."

Jenny saw the gold-rimmed glasses, the gray hair, and reached her little hands to her beloved mamaw. She touched her mamaw's arms, and felt the awful cold.

CHAPTER 4

Her mother's death had a profound effect on Gladys Faye. Her usual labile moods stabilized into a long and deep depression. She moved about in a daze, sometimes hardly aware of her surroundings. Her flowery print dresses, bright red lipstick, and rouged cheeks contrasted clownishly with her dour face and muted existence.

The family knew how much Chunk was grieving. All of them missed Mamaw, but Chunk had been the closest to her. It would just take more time for her to get over it. They all knew how high-strung Chunk was. Maybe she blamed herself; maybe she thought taking care of the baby was too much on Mamaw. For sure, something was preying on her mind.

Gladys Faye stayed home from the mill and put what little energy she had into taking care of Jenny. She stayed in bed a lot. The headaches, not as frequent as during her pregnancy, still plagued her. Her patience was short, her temper quick.

Gladys Faye let the baby cry too much, hardly ever picked her up or played with her. But Mamie made excuses for her. Chunk was grieving, and the baby was fretful, since Mamaw had spoiled her. But she had her own problems, her own life. Chunk was lucky to have had Mamaw for as long as she did.

She'd had no more sense than to have that baby. Now she'd have it to raise.

More and more frequently Gladys Faye had to hurt the child. She would leave the baby wet and cold in the crib, then scream at her for wetting, when finally she came to her. At first it was enough to complete the punishment with the diaper pins. Then she added another twist to the abuse.

The child needed to be taught about men. To do this, Gladys Faye restrained Jenny in her crib. With subdued determination she explained clearly enough for anyone to understand, "All men are the same — bad. They only want to hurt you. And when they do, this is how it feels." Gladys Faye brought the wire kitchen whip down again and again between Jenny's outspread legs.

Cut, bruised, and bleeding, Jenny cried in pain and terror. Gladys Faye, no longer subdued, raged at her, "You wicked bastard." She filled first the child's vagina and then her rectum with icy water from the enema bag hanging at the foot of the crib.

Suddenly Jenny was safe from harm. For almost two years the child had endured the hurts. Pushed now beyond endurance, she found release. Selena lay in the crib feeling nothing as the blood-pinkened water drained from her small body. The cold water controlled the bleeding. Jenny controlled the pain.

Gladys Faye quieted nearly as quickly as the child did. She cleared away the mess, and diapered the child as she crooned, "I love you, baby. I'm sorry," then left her, as usual, alone.

As long as Mamaw had lived in Mamie's house along with her and her children, Gladys Faye was able to come and go as she pleased. With Mamaw gone, staying home with the baby really cramped her style. Mamie would watch Jenny for brief periods, but she made it clear that the baby was not her responsibility. Gladys Faye could tolerate the mornings when the others were around. But when her twelve-year-old son, Lloyd, was still in school in the afternoons, and Mamie went off to work, Gladys Faye felt trapped.

On a Friday afternoon when she was alone in the house

with Jenny, Gladys Faye took her down in the basement to sit in the cool to shell the black-eyed peas for supper. As Gladys Faye's hands worked the peas, her eyes fell on the two big boxes on the ledge.

The old boxes had been there so long, she hardly ever noticed them. About four feet square and short of two feet high, the boxes were made from rough two-by-sixes. They sat on cinder blocks to let air circulate above the red clay earth. The wood boxes, gray with age and permeated with the smell of earth, still kept potatoes dry and cool year after year. It was almost time now to dig potatoes, so the boxes were empty except for a few yams and russets.

Gladys Faye methodically finished with the mess of peas. Then, without ceremony, she picked Jenny up, carried her to the ledge, and dropped her into one of the boxes. "Keep still," Gladys Faye said, and brought down the heavy wooden lid.

Jenny screeched in terror and clawed at the box, reaching toward the slits of light between the boards. Gladys Faye smiled as she noticed how well the thick boards muffled the small voice. She walked up the stairs, put the peas on low to cook for supper, fixed her makeup, and took her regained freedom to town.

Jenny's initial panic became a sustained hysteria. She screamed and tore at the box until her small fingers bled. Finally spent, and cold and wet, she wept soft snubbing sobs and curled up in the dark until she slept.

When Jenny awoke she didn't feel the sting of her fingers made raw or the cramping of muscles in the too-small space. Selena had come to take the pain.

Gladys Faye was careful to return before Lloyd got out of school. She cleaned Jenny up, put salve on her hands, and had her in bed well before Mamie came home from work.

Once her anger had found vent, Gladys Faye was helpless, without Mamaw's restraining presence, to stop the flow. She managed only to keep it enough in check to conceal her acts of violence on the child.

The situation presented a disturbing paradox. Gladys

Faye must have experienced a general relief of tension when she got away from the restricting care of the child, and a specific release when she did things that hurt Jenny. Yet, she knew it was wrong to hurt an innocent child. Somehow she had to resolve the conflict. Gladys Faye could do so by fitting logic to her disordered thoughts.

Given the times and her upbringing in the South's Bible Belt, Gladys Faye had to associate her problems — poor health, restrictions on her life, loss of her mother, rejection — with her obvious sin of adultery. To relieve her guilt and its accompanying self-hate, it made sense to place the blame on the growing, enduring evidence of her sin. With that twist of thinking, the bastard, Jenny, became for Gladys Faye the evil child who required constant discipline and who deserved repeated punishment.

During this time of upheaval for Gladys Faye — the sustained grief at her mother's death and a flagging ability to cope with her child — her family watched helplessly as she sank deeper into despair. Only her cousin, Rose, and Rose's husband, Billy Joe, offered a solution. The timing was right for them to take Gladys Faye to a meeting of the cult of Satan worshippers. Gladys Faye was at first reluctant to go. Billy Joe had tried to get her to go before and she had had no interest. Now she didn't have the energy to turn Billy Joe and Rose down when they coaxed her with an "Aw, come on with us, Chunk. It'll do y'all good." Anyway, it was something to do to get out of the house.

Gladys Faye related immediately to the happenings of the cult. She liked the way they accepted her right off, giving her a share of the wine and taking her into their inner circle. Here was refuge for a sinner such as she, where you didn't need to ask for forgiveness, and you didn't need to fear punishment. Here her bastard child would be welcomed as the true spawn of Satan. Here Gladys Faye would be valued as his faithful servant.

The cult gave Gladys Faye a grotesque confirmation of the necessity for her actions against the child. Thus validated, her attacks intensified. She brought home to Jenny what she learned at the dark meetings and looked forward to the time when Jenny would go for her own lessons. With the influence of the cult, the abuse became more vicious and took on the reality of the devil. Gladys Faye combined her Christian teachings with satanic ones and turned them all on Jenny.

Gladys Faye would make the child sit down with commands to keep still while she read from the Bible. Jenny's fear would escalate with the changing timbre of her mother's voice until at last Gladys Faye would scream the damning words at her, "Bastard—spawn of Satan," and throw the large black Bible at the defenseless child. If Jenny failed to keep still, she was tied in her chair for another reading.

Gladys Faye often tied Jenny in her red rocking chair after she finished with the lessons. Gladys Faye would admonish the child to silence with threats such as "The devil will get you if you don't keep your mouth shut" or "I'll cut your tongue out if you tell this." Then Gladys Faye would read from the black book so Jenny would understand what being a bastard meant. When Jenny could no longer listen to the fearsome lessons, Barbara came to hear the readings.

Gladys Faye seemed obsessed with concerns over urine and wetting. When she figured Jenny was old enough to be potty trained, she began to beat her for wetting her panties. Jenny tried to stay dry, but it was hard when she was in the box or when her mother made her stay outside for hours.

When the beatings failed to break the child of wetting, Gladys Faye resorted to pushing Jenny's face into the toilet to teach her. Jenny became afraid to go in the bathroom, and was even less able to stay dry.

When three-year-old Jenny wet her brand new panties with the pink lace, Gladys Faye dragged her to the bathroom. She put the child on the commode and demanded that she urinate there. When Jenny was unable to "pee" for her mother, Gladys Faye made her watch as she urinated into a glass herself. Then the mother made the child drink the warm yellow liquid. For a moment Jenny gagged at the repulsive fluid. Then she watched Pam drink the urine. It would be years before Jenny would use a commode again. Pam used the bathroom and dealt with what Gladys Faye did to her there.

Pam to deal with bathroom things, Barbara to deal with the black book, and Selena to come when there was pain were still not enough to cope with her mother's vacillating behavior. More splitting was needed. The next time Jenny was put in the potato box, Flisha came. Flisha could be the good little girl Gladys Faye wanted. Flisha had no feelings of being evil, no fear of Gladys Faye. Like a little lady, she could be quiet and still and patient. She never wet her panties, and she would come to like the pretty, frilly dresses and lacy panties Gladys Faye put on her, and to like to hear the motherly "I love you."

Jenny felt continually on guard. She was afraid to move around much, for she was apt to get knocked down, then get kicked for crawling. She was afraid to play. Laughing at something like television cartoons could bring a slap to still the laughter, and more slaps to stop the crying. Even smiling at a soft kitten or a pretty flower could set off her mother.

To keep her guard up, Jenny gave over her capacity for laughing and crying to still another fragment of herself. Marcie, like Flisha, was not afraid of Jenny's mother. Marcie was clever and practical. She, too, was a good little girl.

Fragmenting into alter personalities provided vital protection but added confusion to Jenny's life. Now she could predict her own behavior no better than she could predict her mother's. She thought all children found themselves places without knowing how they got there, or got blamed for doing things they never even thought about doing. It was very hard to be a child.

Many times Jenny watched a little girl, who looked a lot like her, smile as her mother pulled a ruffled dress over her head, pulled up her knee socks, and buckled her Mary Janes. A few minutes later Jenny couldn't understand how she came to be wearing that little girl's clothes. She better take them off. But when Jenny took the clothes off, rather than being praised, she was slapped or screamed at for being bad and stupid. Jenny would escape, leaving Marcie to cry at the injustice or Flisha to placate the mother and ask again to be made pretty.

Just as Jenny saw them, she heard the voices of the children who lived inside her. But she was as separate from them as she was from her brother and numerous cousins whose brief periods of playing with her always ended with their calling her names and leaving her alone.

Jenny needed to play, perhaps more than she needed the company of other children. However, she was too constrained to stay involved in childhood's activities for long. Lisa came to play for her. Lisa loved cartoons — Bugs Bunny was her favorite. She loved to color with crayons and to draw with a pencil. She liked to rock in her little chair, to roll in the grass in the sun, and to run and play in the rain.

For both mother and child the world was topsy-turvy. Neither could make sense of the actions of the other. Jenny experienced a mother who was hugs and kisses when other people were around but who could even then lapse into profound indifference. When the two were alone, her attacks were sudden and terrifying.

Gladys Faye experienced a child who would sometimes reach out to her and sometimes cringe away. When the two were alone, Jenny would react to the same situation sometimes with tears and trembling, sometimes with quiet acceptance, and sometimes with stubborn defiance.

Both adult and child reached the same conclusion. Jenny was wicked, evil. How else could you explain her behavior? Why else would she deserve to be treated this way? Gladys Faye had to justify her own actions. Jenny, with the pure logic of childhood, justified them too.

When the mother drew her daughter to her to tend or to threaten, she did not suspect that Jenny was, by the age of three, already split into several personalities. Nor could Gladys Faye have guessed that before she was done, Jenny would require many more selves to cope with her life.

Jenny seemed to want to fit herself to the mold her mother fashioned. After her grandmother's death, Jenny was withdrawn, sullen, unresponsive. She had given little notice to her mother, her aunts, uncles, and cousins before; now she gave even less. She could not be soothed or amused by them. Leery of people, she seemed attracted only to sounds, colors, and textures. Jenny would play for hours with quilting scraps or bits of paper. She would sit on the ground to stroke the earth, and to explore the rocks and flowers and grasses. She would stay by the radio or the piano by the hour, for as long as either was played, entranced by the rhythm of the music.

For all the adults in the family, Jenny was a child hard to figure. She would no sooner get the thing she cried for, reached for, or whined for than she no longer wanted it. The food she liked one day, she spit out the next. She fought sleep, crying with fretful restlessness to the point of total exhaustion. Although she would often smile to herself, she could not be coaxed by them to smile. When family pictures were taken, the camera unerringly recorded the unhappy face of the shattered child.

The family looked neither for cause nor for remedy. They simply accepted the withdrawn, erratic behavior, and explained to anyone who asked, "That's just Jenny — always was a strange child, a difficult young-un."

CHAPTER 5

Jenny did not think herself or her circumstances strange. She would become aware when she was older of how different she was from other children. But as a four-year-old, and even into her early school years, as far as Jenny knew, she was like any other child. She knew she was often bad and had to try very hard to be good so her mother could love her. She thought all children had to try so hard.

At least Jenny was beginning to have some success at being a good girl. She had been sick, real sick. But once she got out of the hospital after a kidney infection and surgery, her mother stopped hurting her for a time.

Jenny was even able to get away from the crib she hated. Once she could stay dry at night, Gladys Faye took Jenny with her to sleep in the double bed. Jenny was delighted with the new closeness. With her little feet propped on her mother's ample belly, Jenny slept warm.

She was faring better, too, with staying dry during the day. If Mama made her stay outside too long, and she had an accident, Aunt Sue would sneak inside to get dry panties for her so Mama wouldn't know. When Aunt Sue got caught, Jenny was startled to be the one punished, while Aunt Sue left without defending her. Still, Aunt Sue didn't get caught much. Jenny didn't know that she, in the guise of Aunt Sue, was her own resourceful rescuer.

To Jenny, Aunt Sue was as real as the other aunts and uncles who moved in a constant flow through Aunt Mamie's house. Mamaw had reared six boys and four girls, including Gladys Faye. Now most of them were married and had children of their own. In typical southern style, many adults and children had double names. On top of that, pet names endured over the years.

Uncle Russell might stop by to borrow the canner for Aunt Alma. "Hey, Bubba," Mamie would ask, "how is Blue doing putting up her tomatoes?" And so it went. Jenny heard her relatives called first one name and then another. There was no way for the little girl to keep them straight.

The pictures in the living room didn't help much. There were pictures of all the boys in uniform — James, Lance, Royce, Russell, Junior, and Joe. There were wedding pictures and baby pictures and vacation pictures. Sometimes Aunt Mamie would tell Jenny about the people in the photographs, and Jenny would try to sort them in her mind. Aunt Mamie's real name was Margaret, Aunt Myrt was really Myrtle, Uncle James was J.D., Uncle Duke was really Lance, and Uncle Cleatus was her mother's uncle too. It did not seem out of the ordinary to Jenny for there to be so many people in her life, and so many names.

Jenny kept her distance from the family, and they from her. Left alone, she could give in to her creative and sensitive nature. She was a child who could be totally absorbed by objects or events. She could be engulfed by the transporting song of a bird or bathed in the cool life-giving green of a single leaf.

As she lay quietly on the country lawn of grass, clover, and weeds, her imagination turned the clouds overhead to animals, flowers, and dragons. She moved among the clouds, stroking the animals, making bouquets of the flowers, and running with glee from the playful dragons.

All things for her were imbued with life. The creek at the edge of the yard spoke to her, and she answered. Jenny learned from trees about life in the rain and sun, and about the nurturing earth. She learned from rocks the secret of their everlasting stillness. With all her senses she experienced the world. She touched colors, envisioned sounds, and followed her curiosity wherever it led. Already as scattered internally as the airborne seeds of the ubiquitous dandelion, Jenny was most herself when she was alone outside on the warm, sweet grass in the sun.

When things happened that made the others come, Jenny escaped the pain and fear and found safe places to be in her own worlds in her mind. At first she glimpsed the safe worlds only, while she watched her other selves in this one. As time went on, Jenny retreated farther into her own worlds of colors, sounds, and beauty.

She reached for beauty in the real world too. By the time she was four, she was picking out tunes on the piano. She mimicked songs she heard and made up melodies of her own. When Gladys Faye showed no interest in Jenny's musical talent, Aunt Mamie took it on herself to see that talent developed. Mamie enrolled her in piano lessons when she was five and drove Jenny every week to Mrs. Wright's house in the country for instruction. Jenny never had to be made to practice. She sat at the keyboard, her hands too small to reach an octave, and played the music as long as she was allowed. Flisha loved music, too, especially the scales and classical pieces. Flisha came to practice sometimes.

Jenny was clever and independent. As much as she could, she steered clear of her mother and took care of herself. She didn't wait either for Mamie, who slept late in the mornings. Jenny learned to push a stool to the stove and cook mush and fry eggs. If Jenny had trouble, Flisha or Marcie helped her. By the time Gladys Faye got home from third shift, Jenny had eaten her breakfast and was dressed. Gladys Faye went off to bed and left Jenny alone for much of the day.

Gladys Faye found a sitter to keep Jenny some afternoons. Jenny liked Miss Kress, who was in her seventies and had kept children around there for years. Miss Thelma Kress prided herself on how well she got on with children, but she just couldn't get close to Jenny Walters. Miss Kress let it go when Jenny let the cows out and killed two chickens with the hoe and then lied about it. Miss Kress sensed the child was troubled and hoped she would settle down. A few weeks later when she caught Jenny tormenting the kittens, and Jenny, with a frazzled, frightened kitten still in her hands, denied hurting the animals, Miss Kress decided she was just plain mean and refused to care for her any longer.

Jenny didn't know why she was sent away from the woman who was much like her mamaw. Jenny had seen another little girl do the things she was accused of, but she had learned it didn't help to say so. She only held firmly to the truth that she didn't do it. Wahnola had come to earn her mother's love for Jenny by becoming like her. Wahnola teased and hurt the animals. Unaware of Wahnola within her, Jenny was left with the consequences of her meanness. The next afternoon Jenny was back in the potato box.

Jenny didn't resist being put in the box anymore. She went in quietly, and lay down and listened to the others with her in the box as they played a game they called "keep still." First she heard Flisha and Marcie, then Selena as her arms and legs began to ache. Jenny moved in and out of her worlds until she felt soft fur against her leg. The creature could have been there by chance, but Jenny suspected that her mother had put it there to cause her terror. At the sharp, quick bite of the rat, Jenny screamed and screamed. The sound traveled no farther than the cold basement walls. For a moment the box was empty except for Jenny and the little creature huddled in the opposite corner. Then Selena was left with the pain.

Jenny's need for love and acceptance compelled her to continue to reach out to her mother, although Gladys Faye was becoming increasingly unreachable. The obese, hypertensive woman suffered frequent blinding headaches and sudden nosebleeds. Periods of anxious activity alternated with dolorous lethargy.

When her mother was agitated, Jenny hurriedly obeyed commands to stay out of her sight. Jenny went to her special place by the creek, or hid under the couch or in the crawl space under the side porch. On rainy days she could stay dry and warm against the brick foundation as she played in the powdery dirt there. Sometimes Lisa played games of pretend. Most times Marcie played "going away" and always kept her dolly warm as she rode an imaginary train to pretty places where people loved her.

When her mother looked sad, Jenny was touched. She tried making pretty faces for her mother out of colored paper. Before she could finish, Gladys Faye grabbed the faces and ripped them. Jenny saw the tears from the paper eyes mix the colors all together. The color feelings — red pain, blue warmth, pink softness, black deadness — all mixed too.

Once Marcie picked flowers to make Jenny's mother feel better. Her little arms full of dogwood blossoms, she brought them proudly to her. Marcie might as well have defied Gladys Faye the way Selena did. Coming in when she was told to stay out usually earned Selena a beating with the broomstick or having her hand slammed in the door. Gladys Faye's response to the flowers was more direct; she used them to beat the child.

After these incidents, anger welled, but Jenny did not express the feeling, didn't even experience it. Jenny had been taught at home and at church that it was wrong to get angry. Faced with repeated abuse and injustice, she created another to feel the rage. Safely compartmentalized, Hilda kept the anger.

Hilda's keeping the anger did not entirely mitigate the power of the emotion. Wahnola, emulating a mother who repeatedly threatened, "You'll be just like me," turned her need to hurt on Jenny. She caused Jenny to bang her head and to bite herself until she bled. Gladys Faye was quick to tell the household that her daughter did things to hurt herself.

In the ensuing weeks Gladys Faye increased her perverted attentions toward Jenny. Troubled by nosebleeds, Gladys Faye focused on the cult's fixation with blood. "Blood ties you to the devil. Bleeding proves you are the devil's child," Gladys Faye intoned along with regular Bible readings.

Gladys Faye prepared a special bath for Jenny by adding

chicken blood and red food dye to icy water. When she carried Jenny into the bathroom, Jenny expected that as before, her feet would be held in burning hot water. This time she saw that the tub was filled with red liquid. The mother explained, as she lowered Jenny into the tub: "This is the blood of evil spirits, where you belong. The blood must be cold so the spirits won't die and can live within you forever." Jenny was numb with fear and cold when Gladys Faye wrapped her in a towel and took her to her chair by the fire.

A few days later Gladys Faye completed her private ritual. She placed Jenny on the kitchen table. A quick stab with a kitchen knife cut the small vagina enough for it to bleed freely. Gladys Faye caught the blood in a shallow pan and transferred it to a cup. Her face distorted with intensity as she held the Bible open and commanded Jenny to write her name. Jenny dipped her finger in the blood and printed the scrawl of a five-year-old. Gladys Faye slammed the book shut and gave it to the child to hold. Jenny clutched the heavy book and sat in the corner and listened to the words echo. "Now you are sealed forever in the book of bad and evil."

Part III

Escape

I remember the moment it happened.
I remember when everything went wrong,
And I couldn't put it right again.
It happened in a space called BOX.
It was so fast — too fast for me.

Jenny's Journal

CHAPTER 6

Jenny held tightly to her mother's hand as they approached the front steps of the elementary school. Ever since the few weeks of kindergarten, Jenny had looked forward to starting "real" school. Kindergarten had been fun, with cookies and Kool-Aid the first day, and songs and coloring on other days. Now she'd have a chance to learn to read and write.

Involuntarily Jenny drew in her breath and pulled back when she eyed the stain encircling the base of the pale gray stone building. Not recognizing the marks as red earth kicked up on the stones by season after season of rains, Jenny's mind flashed to cultic scenes of red stains on granite.

"Come on now, don't start acting up," Gladys Faye commanded. She piloted the child to follow the others to the auditorium. Gladys Faye had changed from her cotton work dress to a Sunday one and had taken special care in choosing Jenny's dress. Gladys Faye was determined that Jenny not look like the ragged country hicks or the grubby "white trash" who went to Hamilton School. She was also determined that Jenny not embarrass her with any of her strange doings.

Jenny and Gladys Faye pulled down maroon horsehair

seats in the front row and waited Jenny's turn to be called to the stage. Already the stage was filled with crying children, comforting and reproaching mothers, and frantic nurses completing the legally mandated inoculations for the start of school. When Jenny's turn came, Gladys Faye was relieved to see her calm and obedient. Several mothers remarked about the well-behaved child as Selena quietly bared her arms in turn for the vaccinations.

The next day Jenny boarded the big yellow school bus alone when it stopped right in front of the house. When she got to school, she panicked. She had no idea how to find the classroom Selena had been shown the day before. Jenny stood immobilized while children hurried by in the hallway. Miss Thomas, the first-grade teacher, spotted her, and taking her quietly by the hand, led her to the right place.

Miss Thomas, sensitive to the child's distress, took Jenny on her lap as she began the day by reading a story to the children. Jenny had never been read to at home. She felt really special — the story was meant just for her.

The soles of Jenny's new shoes made a satisfying click on the wood floor when the teacher gently nudged the child from her lap. Jenny made her way to the vacant desk and climbed into a seat too large for her, although scaled to suit most first graders.

Jenny explored the smoothness of the oak desktop, which was interrupted by small irregular grooves of childish markings and by a long straight notch which held a fat black pencil. Jenny tested the pencil in her small hand, eager to put it to work.

At the teacher's direction, all the children lifted desktops to discover crayons, creamy lined paper, bright construction paper, and shiny scissors. Jenny could scarcely believe all these things were meant just for her use.

"Now," Miss Thomas said, "y'all make a picture for me of your favorite things." Jenny chose a soft blue paper from among the stack in her desk and began at once to draw a schoolroom, a plumpish teacher, and a little girl holding a big box of new crayons. She watched proudly as Miss

Thomas put a bright star in the corner and tacked her pretty picture up for all to see.

School was fun for Jenny. She loved to draw and color, to listen to stories, and especially to play the blocks or the triangle in the rhythm band. Only reading circle was hard. Jenny didn't like being so close to the other children and having to read aloud in front of them. At first the reading was merely echoing the teacher's words. Still, it was hard for Jenny. But she forgot about reading as soon as it was time to practice printing. She could copy exactly the letters Miss Thomas put on the blackboard, and was almost always rewarded with a "That's good, Jenny."

On the playground Jenny shied away from the line of children waiting to be picked for dodge ball, and from the huddle of giggling girls. She retreated to the low back steps of the school to play alone at pretending school. She'd be the strict but caring teacher for a row of imagined pupils seated on the bottom step. Invisible pupils who did well graduated to the second step, but slackers had to stay on the first. At pretend recess Jenny, as surrogate for the imagined class, transformed the steps into a jumping arena with fabulous prizes for successful jumpers clearing both steps in a single leap from the granite side piece.

On days she didn't play school, Jenny wandered around the edge of the playground, sometimes firing the missiles of high heads at supposed intruders. The high heads, like miniature cattails, grew in profusion in the school yard. Jenny had learned from her brother, Lloyd, to bend the fibrous leggy stem of the common weed, trapping the ovoid head of seeds, and leaving a workable loop to snap the fuzzy projectile free. She'd watch the elliptic track of the missile, then ready another to better the distance of the first.

Sometimes Jenny simply used a stick to mark patterns in the spots of ground foot-worn bare of grass and weeds. Other times she looked for four-leaf clovers in the patches scattered around the playground, avoiding the honeybees attending the sweet blossoms.

After a few weeks Janice, another child who stayed apart

from the group, sidled over to Jenny on the playground. Janice was in Miss Thomas's room too, but Jenny had never spoken to her. Janice's hair was scraggly; her clothes were ill-fitting, and her legs were scarred from untended sores, impetigo probably. Jenny knew her mother would not approve of her being around this "trashy" girl. Still, she warmed to Janice.

Soon they were playing school together on the back steps, trading turns being teacher and pupil. They played whole recess periods jumping from the steps and landing in giggly heaps in the red dirt. Janice introduced Jenny to the tummy-tickling pleasure of spinning around the metal support posts of the covered walkway to the cafeteria, pretending to be airplanes coming in to land. Jenny taught Janice how to shoot high heads, and the two would stockpile ammunition to fire from ambush at unsuspecting targets.

Aside from her obligatory appearance on the first day, Gladys Faye was completely indifferent to Jenny's schooling. She consistently rebuffed Jenny's efforts to show her papers or to print the alphabet. Jenny did not persist long, but went back to her pattern of steering clear of her mother. While she longed for someone to notice her new skills, Jenny settled for being left alone.

Most mornings, her aunt was still asleep while Jenny got her own breakfast and dressed for school. Gladys Faye, arriving home from the third shift just before the school bus came, usually went off to bed without so much as acknowledging her daughter. Sometimes she threw offhand reminders for Jenny to be a good girl at school. On rare occasions she'd call Jenny to her for a morning surprise. Invariably the surprise was a frosted cherry tart from the snack cart at the mill. Jenny ate half of the sticky pastry and pocketed the rest for recess or after lunch, always thanking her mother profusely for the treat.

After school, with Mamie at work and Gladys Faye asleep, Jenny was often unable to get inside the house. She was afraid to wake her mother, so she played in the yard or by the creek and hoped her mother would open the door before it got too cold or dark. As autumn moved toward winter, many days it was both dark and cold before Jenny was allowed inside. On those days Jenny sought refuge in her hiding place under the side porch. When it rained, the hiding place offered little relief from the cold and none from her fears of what lurked in the dark.

Experiences in the church and the cult continually renewed in Jenny a sense of fear and dread. She went every Sunday with her mother and aunt to New Hope Church, and knew she was as bad a sinner as any the preacher decried. She heard the preacher and longed to be born again and washed whiter than snow in the blood of the lamb. She just didn't know how that could happen. She listened as much as she could to the sermons and to the words of the hymns. She liked to hear the choir sing, especially the songs of rejoicing, but the black robes they wore made her feel threatened.

She felt threatened, too, whenever she was near the preacher. He spoke nicely enough to her when her mother shook hands with him coming out of the church. "Good to see y'all, Sister Faye, and how's our pretty little Jenny today?" Reverend Ellis queried, patting Jenny on the head. His practiced smile didn't affect Jenny's sure knowledge of how much he disliked her. There was no smile that day last summer when he called her a bastard, a child of the devil.

That day in Bible school, Barbara had to come out to listen to the black book as the teacher read from the Old Testament. The reading completed and refreshments served, Barbara was confronted with a religious picture Jenny had been coloring. Not knowing what to do, Barbara simply took a black crayon and began to mark through the picture. When the teacher chided Jenny (in the guise of Barbara), Selena came to her defense by ripping the picture and sassing the teacher with "Mind your own stupid business."

Reverend Ellis walked up just in time to punctuate the incident with his reprimand. "Be still, you unruly brat." In a single moment Selena picked up the cup of Kool-Aid, threw it on the preacher, and escaped, leaving Jenny to hear his condemnation.

Condemnation in the cult continued, deliberate and studied. The first full moon in October of her first year in school, Jenny found herself in the old Ford for the usual ride to the cult meeting. The ride became longer than usual. Jenny fell asleep in the car, and evening deepened to night. She awakened to being jostled by her mother's stripping off her clothes and wrapping her in a filmy white cloth. As Jenny came fully awake, she felt a piercing chill and realized she was alone in a bright, stark white room. The walls of the room seemed to shimmer in swirls of frigid air.

At once several people robed in white entered, and a man began to speak. "White, the symbol of purity, surrounds us in this place."

"White for purity, saith Amature," echoed the robed people.

"But this child is impure," Amature said accusingly, "a bastard child, the spawn of Satan." He tore away Jenny's white wrap, causing her to shake uncontrollably from fear and cold.

Selena came as soon as the beating began. Amature struck the child repeatedly. He watched her eyes swell nearly shut and her lips begin to bleed from the assault. As the bitter cold air reached through their wool robes, Amature and the others repeated the chant of the single word "impure."

A single figure, robed in black, entered the white room, interceding for the helpless child. "Give to me the impure child to take from this place," Gladys Faye recited. She wrapped Selena in a soft black shawl and took her in her arms. Gladys Faye carried her child with uncharacteristic tenderness into a pitch-black room.

Selena forced open her swollen eyes to see first the flickering flames of a circle of black candles, then the golden red glow of the fire just lighted. A circle of people, all clothed in black, moved forward, petting and warming the child. Someone soothed her lips with ointment, then offered her a steaming posset to drink. In the warmth Jenny returned in time to hear, as Selena had heard repeatedly, "Impure bastard child, seed of Satan, this is where you belong."

Until she started school, not having a father had not seemed important to Jenny. At school when she heard the other children talk about their daddies, she thought about her own. She knew little about him. The few times Gladys Faye talked about him it was with such hate and anger, Jenny expected she'd be afraid of him if ever she saw him. Gladys Faye had said he was an artist, that he was smart, though "not as smart as he thinks he is." Once she told Jenny, "Don't need to think he'll ever come see you. He has a wife and a whole houseful of kids." Jenny couldn't bear to think of his being with other children. Over the school year she listened to children talk happily about their fathers. Gradually she came to think of her own as special, a man who loved her, but who had to go away.

In preparation for the Father's Day art project, Miss Thomas asked the class to tell about their fathers' jobs. When Jenny's turn came, she fell silent. She couldn't think fast enough, didn't know if "artist" was a kind of job, like farming or working in the weave room at the mill. Margaret Ann, who knew Jenny's family from church, was eager to fill the silence. "Jenny ain't got no daddy," she reported, proud of her considerable knowledge.

"Well, it's no matter," Miss Thomas said, trying to smooth over Jenny's discomfiture. "Jenny can make her card for a special friend."

The bell rang for recess. On the playground Jenny ran from the mean little girls who ridiculed her with a singsong "Jenny ain't got no daddy. Jenny's a bastard child."

Jenny knew it was bad to be a bastard. She had been called that word many times. Now for the first time she realized the word meant not having a father to live with you.

After recess Jenny began her art project along with the rest of the children. Miss Thomas was pleased to see that she didn't seem to be upset by the awkward incident earlier. Jenny took special care with her card. She drew a picture of a man and little girl with presents, and lettered HAPPY FATHER'S DAY in bright bold crayon. The next day, Friday, she put the card in the blue construction-paper envelope she had made and lovingly took it home.

On Sunday morning Gladys Faye found the handmade greeting on the kitchen table and threw it in the trash. She walked into the living room to find Jenny smiling and gently rocking back and forth on the sofa, her arms firmly entwined across her chest as she stroked her own small cheeks and shoulders. Jenny seemed oblivious to her mother, and her calm and happy expression gave Gladys Faye the impression that Jenny was being held on someone's lap. Gladys Faye walked back into the kitchen to leave her odd child alone.

Jenny, however, was not alone. Justin had come to be the father who lived with her. He was tall and dark, graying slightly at the temples, very distinguished. He was very happy with the beautiful Father's Day card. He gave his daughter a great big hug.

Jenny wished that Justin could be with her all the time to protect her, but at best he could come only sometimes to comfort her. She had some respite at school. At home Gladys Faye's cruel attacks continued. Jenny sought refuge in her own worlds. Gladys Faye intensified her assaults, increasingly frustrated in her attempts to make the child respond.

Gladys Faye's anger flared when she saw Jenny's faraway look. The child was standing by the living room window, staring out at the torrents of rain. The storm had been a particularly fierce one. By now only distant flickers of blue and low rumbles remained of the almost blinding, jagged streaks of lightning and the shattering cracks of thunder that had preceded the downpour. As the rain continued, puddles, which had formed all over the yard, became small ponds. The rutted dirt road by the garden became a roiling lake, the water the color of rust.

Jenny, scared by the lightning and thunder, had been transported to her crystal world by the first drops of rain against the window. Peering into the raindrops, Jenny watched the light reflected endlessly in rainbows in the crystal facets.

"Come here, Jenny." Gladys Faye's words were soft. Jenny returned reluctantly to the real world, quieted from the storm's turbulence to a gentle rain. Gladys Faye silently led Jenny outside. The sky was brightening, the air becoming chilly as the last few drops of rain fell. Gladys Faye picked up Jenny, walked directly to the flooded road, and threw the child into the muddy water. As Jenny struggled, screaming, she gulped great mouthfuls of water. Gladys Faye pushed her back under each time she struggled to the surface. When Jenny's lungs seemed almost ready to burst, Selena came.

In the same instant the assailant became rescuer. Gladys Faye stared in horror. "My God! What has happened to my baby?" She clutched the deathly pale child to her as Selena went limp in her arms.

"Don't die, baby, don't die," Gladys Faye gasped while struggling up the steep back steps. She frantically rubbed the too-white face and clammy little arms until color returned and the child could sit without support. Then she pulled off the soaked, mud-stained dress and wrapped soft towels around the child and put her in her little chair. Selena shivered, aware at some level of how close this woman had come to killing her, sorry somehow that she had failed.

Jenny became increasingly unable to distinguish the real world from the worlds in her mind. At school the second-grade teacher became concerned with what she saw as constant daydreaming.

The ringing of the telephone awakened Gladys Faye at two o'clock in the afternoon. "I thought I ought to call about Jenny. She is not paying attention in class, seems like her mind wanders. Today she was just sitting and staring. When I asked her what she was looking at, she said, 'pretty things,' and gave me the strangest look. I figured you'd want to know, Mrs. Walters. Maybe you can talk to her."

Gladys Faye held her temper long enough to thank the teacher, then seethed with anger that her sleep had been disturbed because that stupid brat was doing her weird stuff at school. Jenny walked off the school bus straight into her mother's fury.

The whirr of the drill was interrupted by Gladys Faye's rantings as she held the instrument only a fraction of an inch from Jenny's eye. "You won't see pretty things when you're dead, you stupid bastard. How can anything as ugly as you find something pretty to look at? I'd drill out your brains, too, if you had any." Selena came out with the sting of the drill tip touching her eye. She heard the final, "This should be the last I ever hear about your stupid pretty things." Gladys Faye stopped short of blinding the child, although for several days Jenny stumbled into things, as if at times she could not see.

Being put again into the potato box was the event that triggered Jenny's flight into her own worlds to stay. At seven she was nearly too big to fit in the box. She felt the furry movement of rats in the box with her, as she had felt once before. This time Jenny did not abandon Selena with the rats. It was easy enough to catch the rats, even in the dark, with them crowded with her in the cramped space. Jenny grasped a squirming rat in each hand, and with silent determination squeezed her fists until the hapless creatures were still. When her hands relaxed, *Jenny Lynn Walters was gone.*

Gladys Faye returned to free Jenny from the box, not realizing that she would never again touch the child to whom she had given birth. Jenny had given over her entire existence to alter personalities.

Some personalities were as clear and distinct as photographs: practical and level-headed Marcie, proud and sophisticated Flisha, and feisty and resilient Selena. Others were as nebulous as impressionistic paintings: Sandy, the child of Satan; Barbara, strongly religious; Justin, a comforting father; Hilda, angry and indignant; Lisa, a happy child; Aunt Sue, a protector; and Wahnola, an internal abuser. Scores of other personalities, some surreal, some startling in their realism, would eventually take their places in response to relentless abuse in the real world while Jenny stayed in safe worlds in her mind.

CHAPTER 7

"Jenny, honey, come up here."

Lisa reluctantly put down her dolls in the living room and climbed the stairs. Gladys Faye was applying final touches of mascara to already garish makeup. Lisa sat on the bed, fingering the soft tufts of the chenille bedspread, while Gladys Faye modeled for her. Lisa stared appreciatively at the black skirt, split up the side, and the blouse, shiny with metallic thread and a cluster of sequins. Enough of the late afternoon sun remained to stream briefly through the dormer window and spotlight the private show.

"Ain't I pretty, baby?" Gladys Faye asked coaxingly.

"Yes, Mama," Lisa agreed, "you sure are pretty."

Satisfied with her primping and the child's approval, Gladys Faye sent her away. "Go get ready for bed now. Sleep in Aunt Mamie's room. Don't come back up here tonight."

Lisa gave no argument, but got her nightgown and went downstairs. She couldn't resist returning to her dolls, and became so engrossed in play that the sound of the man's voice coming from upstairs startled her completely.

Marcie found herself in the clutter of toys, the nightgown wadded on the floor. It was dark outside, and light in the living room was dim. She knew it must be past bedtime.

Worried that there'd be trouble, Marcie grabbed the night-gown and her teddy bear and hurried upstairs.

Marcie opened the door and stopped in her tracks at the sight of the naked man in bed with her mother. The man turned his dark face from Gladys Faye's breasts and withdrew his huge hand from her thigh. He screamed at the child as he struck a forceful backhand blow, "Whatcha lookin' at? Get outta here."

Marcie made a stunned retreat, stopping just long enough to retrieve the bear, which had fallen to the floor when she was hit. Once downstairs, she carefully pulled the plastic button eyes out of the bear, so he could never be hurt for looking at bad things.

Child enough still to see life in all things, Marcie's sensitivity urged her to protect her friend. She did not expect what happened next. As she looked at the damaged teddy bear face, she saw blood begin to stream from where the eyes had been. She clutched the dear toy to her until she was sure he was dead, her own tears blending with his crimson ones. Conquering for the moment her fear of the dark, she carried him gently outside. Leaving the circle of light from the porch, she walked down the backyard steps to the edge of the woods. She dug a hole in the earth kept soft by the cover of leaves, and buried him where he'd be safe. Marcie returned to the house, and not bothering with nightclothes or covers, curled up on the sofa and went to sleep.

Gladys Faye paid no attention to her daughter's going outside in the dark nor to her returning. As long as the child stayed out of her way, Gladys Faye left her alone.

Marcie, of all the alter personalities, was the most like Jenny. She was as quiet and sensitive as Jenny had been, but not as withdrawn. Marcie could laugh and cry, and was open to other people's feelings as well as her own. She liked to play with other children, and even tried to initiate friendships. But except for Janice, her friend from first grade, the children tended to leave her alone. They saw Jenny Walters as strange and moody. Their opinions were reinforced every time Flisha snubbed a child Marcie spent time with, or Selena got too rambunctious on the playground, and later Marcie wanted to play, acting as if nothing had happened.

Switching of personalities was controlled in large part by circumstances in the environment. Much of the time the system was orderly. For instance, Flisha might get up, fix breakfast, and get herself on the school bus. Marcie might come out for a reading lesson or to play at recess. Selena would usually come if there was trouble. Those around her were not aware of these internal changes; they noticed only brief periods of staring or inattention.

The rub came because the system was not always orderly. Certain events or sights or sounds or smells could trigger switches. The smell of a flower or seeing a puppy could attract Marcie. Pop music or talking about parties or boys interested Selena. Flisha was drawn to art and classical music. Minor personalities could respond to triggering events. Sandy might react to a star as a satanic symbol. Hilda might show anger at a perceived injustice. The personality in control at a given time could not always prevent the appearance of another, nor could the one in control summon the help of an alter personality at will. Sometimes the controlling personality resisted relinquishing control, at other times it gladly gave way to another.

For each of them, existence was discontinuous. Each experienced longer or shorter periods of lost time while others were in control. Awareness of the others was variable. Sometimes a personality could know the thoughts and actions of another. Other times there was no such awareness. All the personalities answered to the name Jenny. All experienced finding themselves in places and situations without knowing how they got there. All learned to bluff through the situations until they could orient themselves.

For her teachers Jenny Walters was a real enigma. They wondered how a child who seemed to be catching on well to a lesson could become so totally confused. They saw wide swings in artistic and musical and academic ability. To her frustrated teachers Jenny seemed to be bright enough, just not willing to pay attention and apply herself.

The teachers' frustration was nothing to compare with that of the personalities struggling to keep up and learn in school. Each of the personalities tried to make sense of the scattered bits of information in the interrupted lessons. Together they managed to complete enough work to stay up with classmates, but they could not bridge irreparable gaps left in the learning, nor could they prevent the damage to Jenny's reputation.

While Jenny's reputation suffered at school, she gained status in the cult. With Jenny gone to her own worlds, there were no instances of hesitation or expressions of fear as there had been when Jenny still tried to participate. With Jenny gone, Sandy and Selena were unfaltering in their ability to withstand the cult's continual tests of obedience.

Cult leaders who witnessed the extraordinary performances were compelled by what they saw to use this exceptional child to their advantage. They involved the Walters child more and more in rituals to enhance their powers in controlling the forces of evil. They used her as a conduit for the passage of spirits in their service.

The most important rituals for conjuring demons were reserved for large regional meetings of the cult. High priests and their assistants spent days in preparation, cleansing with special oils, burning incense, combining herbs, to ensure success in calling up the demons, and, more important, ensuring control over them once they were summoned.

In the ritual the priest assumed complete control over the one through whom the demons passed. The demons called forth to complete a task, to destroy an enemy, or to assist an ally had to be returned from whence they came. If not controlled by those who called them, the demons would be loosed on the world, their energy squandered, or, worse yet, turned back against the ones who sought to exploit their power.

On the long drive to take part in the ritual, Gladys Faye admonished her eight-year-old daughter: "Now, Jenny, do what you're told tonight and don't be asking no questions."

Sandy nodded assent. "Yes'um, I'll listen."

Satisfied, Gladys Faye returned to the adult conversation; Sandy, to watching the passing countryside. They arrived at the churchyard at twilight. The whole carload climbed out on the gravel parking lot. Sandy saw some familiar faces, people she had seen at other big meetings. She was happy to see Patty get out of the car that pulled in next to theirs. Patty was about her age, and Sandy had seen her a number of times at meetings. They had become friends, whispering together while they watched the adults from a safe distance. Selena liked Patty too.

Before they could escape to watch from the edge of the woods, they were led along with the other children to the center of the cemetery. The man leading them took them directly to a large gravestone made of a block of polished rose granite resting on a rough base and topped by a flattened pyramid of rough-cut stone. "Y'all stay here until you're told," the man ordered, "and hear now what I say."

The children huddled near the distinctive headstone and heard the man intone, "By this stone, mark this place. By this stone, mark this place. By this stone, mark this place." Sandy touched the rough granite and traced the triangular symbol of Satan with her fingers while listening to the threefold command.

She looked around the graveyard in the fading light. Many of the stones were old, the marble blackened by mold, inscriptions almost obliterated by weathering of the stones. Tall, peaked stones projected above classically rounded ones. A life-size marble statue of an angel stood on a granite pedestal, silently watching over the scene.

There was little time for the children to contemplate their position. Cult members began to emerge from behind the church building. All wore hooded black robes. Some held candles as they approached in single file, their feet making crunching noises on the gravel parking lot. Murmuring a low chant, the group walked a triangular track around the graveyard, then crossed it to inscribe a pentagram. They completed the protective symbol by forming a circle around the tracks of their march, enclosing the children within.

As the ritual began in earnest, the presiding priest directed attention to the angel-topped stone. "By the power of Satan, we scorn the angels."

"Scorn the angels," the group echoed.

"Elohim, Adonay, Jehovah, release the spirits to us."

The children did not catch the significance of the name carved beneath the angel, but the adults did. "Minnie Skoff," the inscription read, "Dec. 1842 – Oct. 1908." In bold letters SKOFF was repeated on the base of the stone, forming a target for mockery by the devil worshippers, who responded readily to the opportune symbolism.

A man separated Sandy from the other children. Without speaking, he took her hand and led her to a grave specially selected for the ceremony. As Sandy stood obediently waiting, she could just make out in the candlelight the word FATHER engraved across the open book of marble atop the old marker. Two robed figures, their whitened faces obscured by hoods, removed Sandy's clothes and laid her on the grave. Binding her wrists with ropes, they secured her small arms above her head, around the base of the stone. Sandy raised her head to drink the bitter sedating drug they offered, then lay still, her head touching the unyielding stone. She watched a circle of white powder be sprinkled around her, then a second like circle be inscribed around the grave. She winced at the near smell of some foul substance.

The high priest approached and began his chant that would prepare her for the ritual. "Dagon, Besheva, Abaddon, hear us. Come now peacefully, visibly, without delay." To make way for the demons, the priest touched or entered each body orifice of the child with cold, hard instruments.

At the biting pain of these "Satan's rods," Selena took Sandy's place. The priest's voice became more insistent, his thrusts at the child more violent as he first beckoned the spirits, then demanded they appear. "In the name of Baphomet, I curse your reluctance. Appear now, I compel you."

The priest raised the child by her hair and made her drink again. Selena felt as much as heard the thundering petitions of the priest and the murmuring repetitions of the circle of members. The gentle rumbling of the sounds within her chest gave way to violent trembling. She felt her body lower into the dank, putrid dirt of the grave. It seemed to Selena that she was screaming, but all who could hear were gone away. As a function of her drugged state and in response to the demands of those who held her in their control, she saw the leaping fires of hell as the demons began their journey through her. She recoiled, but could not escape the horrid deformed faces, skulls with hanging flesh, unspeakable ancient things which materialized from her mouth, her eyes, between her legs. As if the things could not find swift enough exit, her flesh began to open for them in great gaping craters to exude the torrent of terror.

Exposure in the chill night and the effects of the drugs hastened the stupor that released the child from awareness. She did not regain consciousness until long after she and her mother had returned home. The experience seemed to Selena almost like a dream. But she knew it was real, as real as the blood she still tasted from the wounds left in her mouth, as real as the rope marks still on her wrists. Bad as it was, Selena was glad that it was she and not Patty who had been put on the grave. Patty seemed to fight so much, to bleed so much, to scream so.

At home, circumstances for Jenny were changing, none for the better. (Jenny was in her own worlds from age seven. Reference to her by her birth name serves as reminder that all the events happened to a single mind and body, however fragmented that mind became in its own defense.) For years her mother's abuse continued, relentlessly telling her she was unwanted, ugly, stupid, evil.

Gladys Faye's hatred and anger for the man who had used her sexually and abandoned her were repeatedly ignited by the child. Gladys Faye saw Donald Poehlman when she looked in Jenny's eyes. She saw him in the child's small, agile hands. She knew it was he who gave Jenny the musical talent to pick out tunes on the piano, the artistic skill to draw her pretty pictures. As Jenny grew, so did Gladys Faye's resentment of the pretty, clever child. Denying any extension of herself in the child, Gladys Faye saw Jenny only as the product of her father. She took satisfaction in seeing her daughter become big enough to be used by men as she herself had been.

Jenny was at times excluded from her mother's bedroom. She missed the warmth of going to sleep next to Gladys Faye's plump belly. She'd go to sleep alone, usually in Aunt Mamie's bed. When Aunt Mamie got home from work, she'd crawl in beside Jenny, scolding if Jenny tried to cuddle up to her. Sometimes she'd send Jenny back to her mother's bed, vacated when Gladys Faye left for the midnight shift.

From Aunt Mamie's bed Jenny often heard men's voices along with her mother's from upstairs. She didn't go investigate, not since the time Marcie had walked in on the hateful man.

Marcie was nearly asleep when she heard her mother call, "Jenny, come here, honey, right now." Marcie had heard men talking upstairs earlier. She was afraid, but she had to respond to Gladys Faye's insistent "Get up here, I said."

Gladys Faye and one of the men were talking so intently they didn't notice Marcie's silent entering. In a few minutes the man turned to look at Marcie and smiled. "Well," he said, "she really is a pretty little thing, Faye. She'll be just fine." Marcie watched the man hand Gladys Faye money before he reached for her. Gladys Faye smiled approval and turned her attention to the other man.

Marcie wanted to run away, to scream, to stop the man from carrying her across to the bed. She kept still, knowing that what her mother might do could be worse that what the man might do. Too, it felt good to hear the man say she was pretty; it felt good to see her mother smile.

The man was gentle enough as he removed the little nightgown and began to pet her, cooing, "Sweet little thing, my doll baby." But he got rough when she pulled her hand back from the warm, smooth skin of his penis. Marcie could not deal with the shame and hurt. Even for Selena, it was hard to endure the frantic pressures of the man forcing entry on the eight-year-old child.

When the spent, sweaty man moved off her, Selena crawled to the head of the bed, away from the bloody stain.

She clutched a pillow to her and huddled in the corner, feeling sick to her stomach. The sick feeling was all mixed up with a child's desire to please her mother, with hate for a mother who had sold her for money.

The mixed feelings found focus in fear. She worried that that man would come again, or that other men would come, and her mother would turn her over to them. Many nights she hid in the attic crawl space. She crept in through the little square door where the quilts were stored and squatted on the wooden joists, careful not to step on the ceiling Sheetrock. Her brother, Lloyd, had told her once that if she stepped there, she would fall all the way to the basement.

She stayed very still and listened until she heard the men leave her mother's room and heard her mother go to work. Still she crouched there, imagining the men might come back. Only after she heard her aunt come in from work did she dare go to bed. The actual time between her mother's leaving for work and her aunt's coming home was about an hour. To the child, the time of her peril was endless.

Hiding made her feel safer, but did not really protect her once her mother involved her in prostitution. Selena endured what the men who paid Gladys Faye did to her. It was worse when there were two men at once. Every time when it was over, Selena crawled with her pillow to the corner of the bed, alone with the sick feelings.

There were periods when Jenny was not left alone. The perennial ebb and flow of extended family through Mamie's house meant there was often a houseful of adults and children. Adults used the beds in shifts, and the children were put on quilt pallets on the floor. In warm weather they even set up beds in the basement, especially when Rose and Billy Joe moved in with their two girls and two boys.

All of Rose and Billy Joe's children were younger than Jenny. Anna, their oldest, looked to Jenny to take the lead, and she followed, although she was often baffled by Jenny's moodiness.

The apparent mood changes were the manifestations of the various alter personalities. Marcie was happy to have children in the house. Flisha found them dirty and unruly. Selena liked having somebody to boss around.

The one unifying feature was fear. When the children were left alone, Jenny would terrify the others. Certain she heard someone trying to break into the house, Jenny would run to hide, often finding Anna huddled next to her in the attic. The children imagined there were monsters in the woods behind the house. "Booger woods," they called them. Jenny told them a headless man lived there. All any child had to do to end play in the backyard was to point toward the woods and claim to see something moving. Squealing in terror, the children raced for the back steps and the interminable climb to safety.

The night monsters Jenny feared were becoming increasingly real to her. She had been told often at cult meetings that demons were placed in the woods to catch children who ran away. She had heard members speak of the dangers of demons called up by someone who couldn't control them. Whatever monsters her cousins imagined, Jenny was seeing glimpses of demons from the grave.

Daytimes, it was easier to play. A favorite of the girls was to make mud pies in the basement. An open shower supplied the water to moisten dirt scooped up from the ledge beside the potato boxes. This day, Lisa and Anna were making special mud cakes with blue soap powder frosting for a tea party. The boys were playing with toys on the basement floor. It was Saturday, and the adults who had gone into town returned too soon. Lisa heard them upstairs. She knew she'd be in trouble if Aunt Mamie saw the mess, so Lisa left the mess to Selena. There was no time to wash the mud down the drain; besides, Aunt Mamie would hear the running water. Selena found a simple solution. She made the little boys eat the soap-topped mud cakes.

Selena was in trouble often enough. Like the time Sandy put red food coloring all over her two-year-old cousin, Brian. As any child would, Sandy imitated the activities of the adults. She made play of the things she witnessed in the cult. The other children didn't understand about the ritual, and got so scared, they ran to Aunt Mamie. Aunt Mamie got pretty mad. Selena took the spanking.

Jenny's playmate cousins came and went. When Billy Joe got enough money together, he moved his brood to a small rental house nearby. A few months later they'd be back at Mamie's, repeating this cycle for several years.

None of Jenny's alter personalities liked Billy Joe. Marcie managed to be tolerant, but Flisha thought him crude and repulsive. Even Selena was intimidated by his coarse manner and his sharp, dark features. She had heard said he was part Cherokee Indian, and thought that accounted for his wild nature. Indians were known to be savages.

Selena was scared when Billy Joe walked in on her in the bathroom. She had been enjoying her warm, sudsy bath. She liked the slick feel of the smooth porcelain tub, the sweet smell of the soap. Her pleasant time was cut abruptly. "Come here to me," Billy Joe said. He lifted her roughly from the warm tub to the cold linoleum floor. Pinning the child with one hand, he opened his trousers with the other. Selena smelled the liquor on his foul breath as he slurred, "Keep your mouth shut, or I'll cut your tongue out." Selena saw the switchblade beside her head. She did not protest.

After Billy Joe left her, Selena bathed again, wanting to feel clean. Other men had done those things to her, but that was something Gladys Faye wanted. At least the men wanted her, said nice things to her. There was nothing good in what Billy Joe did to her. There was a special outrage in his rape of the nine-year-old girl.

CHAPTER 8

In almost every aspect of her young life, Jenny was treated as an object. Like a toy, like a pretty, pliant doll, she was manipulated to suit the whims of her family. None of the adults who should have nurtured her did so. Those she had every right to trust either inflicted harm or failed to protect her from it.

The rape by her cousin was just one in a series of abuses by him. Unrestrained, Billy Joe drew Jenny into his version of drugs, sex, and violence. He introduced her to drugs soon after the first sexual attack. Periodically he gave her a handful of pills, insisting that she take them to make her feel good. Selena took the pills and discovered she did feel better, and was better able to tolerate Billy Joe. Billy Joe further insured her compliance with threats with the knife and threats to take to school the pictures he made of her. Selena did the sexy things and posed as he directed.

Often out of work, Billy Joe lay about Mamie's house. When Flisha practiced the piano, he sidled up to her on the bench. He held the knife to her throat and made her play the pieces while he played with her. Flisha lost herself in the beauty of music to escape his ugliness.

When Billy Joe moved his family to their own quarters,

Jenny was sent to spend weekends with her cousins. Selena usually went. She got a kick out of the night raids the children were sent on to steal coal for the heater. The bucketful of coal the children could filch from the neighbors was enough to burn in the stove a whole day. Each night Billy Joe had brightly colored pills to reward the giggling children, home again, black-handed.

Billy Joe and Rose took the older children with them to parties. If Jenny was visiting, she went, too, and shared in the drugs and revelry. At times things got rough. Shooting up drugs put an edge on Billy Joe's temper. Selena heard the loud quarreling just before she saw the familiar switchblade and Billy Joe's laying open the man's chest. She heard Rose yell, "Run!" They got in the car just as Rose got the engine started, but the angry crowd tipped the car in the ditch, pulling Billy Joe out to beat him. Rose yelled again, and again the children ran. The last Selena remembered was running into the woods with people running after her. She woke up at home in bed. No one ever talked about the wild weekend, or about any of the other times she spent with her cousins, Rose and Billy Joe.

Not knowing who in her family to trust, Jenny trusted none of them. Some of the many aunts, uncles, and cousins might have given her the closeness she needed, but she pulled away from their closeness. As far as she knew, every present, every hug, had a price.

Summertimes, Uncle Cleatus, Jenny's great-uncle, and his wife, Aunt Ramona, loaded the bunch into their old pickup, the children on old bus seats in the back, and headed out for some time at the beach or the mountains. Fumes from the old truck engulfed the children. Jenny fought down car sickness by chewing on lemon slices and crushed ice, and waited to see if the rolling hills gave way to hazy domed peaks of the Appalachians, or to the limitless flatlands bordering the Atlantic.

The vacationers camped under a tarp beside the truck or rented a cabin to spend several days hiking, fishing, and swimming. Uncle Cleatus was known to pick at the children. "Leave them young-uns alone" said laughingly by the others just egged him on. He scared the children with tales of sharks in the ocean, snakes in the trees, and monsters in the dark. He chuckled at their shrieks when he dangled them from a pier or from a ledge or swinging bridge, and threatened to release his hold.

Some of Uncle Cleatus's antics were secret. When he took Selena into the river and threatened to hold her under unless she stroked his penis and took it in her mouth, he told her she must never tell. Selena didn't know if the old man did the sex things with other children. She kept his secret.

Wintertimes, Uncle Cleatus played Santa Claus for the children at Aunt Mamie's house. Selena recognized the old man in the red suit and beard. She looked at the snowy scene of the little village under the Christmas tree and thought about summertimes.

What started out as vacations many times were preludes to cult activities. Cult members used parks, campgrounds, and tourist attractions as places to convene and conduct rituals. They sometimes traveled for hours to reach prearranged sites.

Mornings, they browsed in souvenir shops or took in the sights. They topped off lunches of southern Bar-B-Q with treats from the Old Tyme Ice Cream Shop. Afternoons, they explored roadside stands. They cooled off in the shade of rusted tin roofs after sampling honey or selecting the best basket of apples from the rows of sweet-smelling fruit.

The children romped among the statues and novelties in the yards of the shops. Gray cement birdbaths, white plaster of Paris swans, black boys waiting wide-eyed to hitch horses, and long-legged pink flamingos inspired fanciful play.

At dusk play ended. The children were made to wait in crevices under overhanging rocks or in shadowy corners until they were called. The places of daylight fun and beauty became dark and scary. Always opportunists, the cultists made use of available resources to add to the power of their rituals. Things such as a rock formation called Devil's Head, a curiosity billed as the Bottomless Holes, even cemeteries near the campgrounds provided sites for ceremonies.

At these gatherings Jenny, usually as Sandy or Selena, was used in a variety of ways. In sight of the waterwheel of a picturesque grist mill, she was secured to a grave for spirits to be called. At a beautiful mountain stream she was tied with ropes and lowered into icy, black water to meet "the father." Nearly drowned, and numbed by cold, Selena saw the Satan she was told to greet.

Obedience was required at all times in the cult. The children, especially the females, were reviled, then tested. Failure to meet the test meant swift, severe punishment. They were taunted with names: "Unworthy, vile, unclean vessels." They were made to do sexual things with animals, then ridiculed for the acts. Afterward the animals were killed, and the children made to eat the flesh of the sacrifice.

The children were made to endure "the boards." They had to sit or squat on boards spiked with nails and not move for hours. They were confined in cages and made to eat spiders, drink urine. Live cats, the skin torn from their faces, were thrust into the cages to add their bloody leers to the degradation. In perverted sexual ceremonies the children had to remain passive while squirming snakes were put into their mouths, vaginas, rectums.

The purpose was to debase, not to harm the children in ways that could be detected, not to kill them. Bites or other injuries were promptly treated by one of several doctors who were members of the group. The children were cared for and readied for still other tests.

The hardest test was to watch someone else be hurt. Sandy was about nine when she tried to watch a man cut his own throat. The man, half-crazed from drugs, obeyed the command to take the dagger from the altar and tilt his head forward to make the cut. Blood poured from the vein he pierced. Sandy bolted, running in her bare feet wildly through the woods before she lost awareness. The people caught the child almost immediately and brought Selena back to the gory scene. For punishment she was made to take embers from the fire and burn her arms and hands. To show her obedience she had to cut her own arms with the same dagger the dead man had used.

Cutting done by the high priest or his designates removed skin in thin layers from wrists or ankles to be eaten by the members in acts of communion. All sacrifices of human flesh were done in formal services before the black altar. Other acts of atrocity were not so solemnly conducted.

Cult members socialized in small groups at ad hoc meetings. The basement at Mamie's house was a frequent meeting place. With Mamie at work, men and women sneaked in through the basement doors for the evening, leaving before the working woman got home. Gladys Faye was proud to play hostess and to offer her daughter for the amusement of her friends.

Amusement usually involved sexual play among themselves and with the child. As the evenings wore on, conversation dwindled. Dancing and drinking, men and women in pairs and groups responded to their arousal. They passed Jenny among them for everyone, both men and women, to use.

Robes, white made-up faces, and animal masks added to the sinister atmosphere. Often the people tormented Jenny as part of an extemporaneous ritual. They stripped her, wet her in the open shower, and rolled her in the red dirt of the basement ledge. "The dirt is going in so deep it will never come out," they told her.

When they were done with her, the child was allowed to go upstairs and wash herself. Selena was left with cold, lonely, dirty feelings that would not wash away.

Gladys Faye was as aloof toward Jenny at these basement meetings as she was at regular cult gatherings. Giving her daughter over to the cult was complete, without limitations. In Satan worship Gladys Faye was a faithful member. Her offering was final. Abuse by the cult was of no apparent concern to Gladys Faye.

There was enough of her own abuse of Jenny to occupy Gladys Faye. Her abuse took place in incidental occurrences as well as in deliberate attacks. She did not always intend to hurt her daughter; she just did not intend to be inconvenienced by her. Gladys Faye had limited physical, emotional, and financial resources to cope with the child she never wanted in the first place.

Confining Jenny gave Gladys Faye freedom to leave the house with little effort and no cost for child care. When Jenny got too big to fit into the potato box, Gladys Faye either chained her to a metal support post in the basement or put her in a big wooden crate behind the garage. Not sure if the crate would contain her, Gladys Faye added tales of horrible monsters in the woods to discourage escape.

Locking Jenny out of the house gave Gladys Faye uninterrupted time to sleep in the evenings before work or to entertain men in her bed. Gladys Faye seemed to give it no thought when the lockouts extended into hours of darkness or included times of freezing temperatures and rain or snow.

Gladys Faye did not always push Jenny away from her. When it was convenient, she drew the child to her. Taking Jenny to her bed was just such a convenience. Gladys Faye found sexual release in caressing Jenny and exploring her body with fingers and objects. She would make Jenny reciprocate the acts and remain silent about them. Whether excluding Jenny or misusing her, Gladys Faye responded to her own needs, unwilling or unable to consider the needs of the child.

Many incidents of abuse were spontaneous, reactive, the result of Gladys Faye's inability to cope. Gladys Faye was physically ill much of the time. Her headaches were nearly constant, sometimes getting so bad she had to go to bed. Worse yet, nosebleeds emphasized the dangerous nature of her condition. She knew high blood pressure ran in the family. Both her mother and father as well as some aunts and uncles had died of strokes or heart attacks. Although she stayed under a doctor's care and took the prescribed medications in great number, she never felt well, and she feared she would die.

Gladys Faye would have had trouble coping with any child. Jenny's constant trials of her patience led to thoughtless brutality. If Jenny came inside when told to stay out, Gladys Faye mashed her hands in the door. If Jenny sassed,

Gladys Faye slapped. If Jenny talked to herself, Gladys Faye dragged her across the basement floor until she hushed.

Jenny's behavior was so often bizarre, Gladys Faye could not hope to understand it. She was baffled by the child's range of moods, unpredictable acts, and unbelievable self-centeredness. However, she in no way saw herself as cause of Jenny's behavior.

While not understanding her, Gladys Faye was jealous of her child. In contrast to plain, plump Gladys Faye, Jenny was pretty and dainty. Jenny became sensuous, attractive to men. She developed uncommon power in the cult. Gladys Faye alternately relished the reflected glory and despised the shining child.

Hate for Jenny took awful form in premeditated, diabolically creative abuse. In persistent diatribe Gladys Faye railed against the child. "Stupid, worthless, of no more use than the rats in the basement, crazy, evil spirit, spawn of Satan, devil's child," Gladys Faye called her. "Hating you is what makes me the way I am," Gladys Faye accused her. "You'll be just like me, never anything more," she prophesied.

That Gladys Faye gave thought to her torture was evidenced by such things as her having a special electrical instrument made for shocking Jenny in her vagina, and her choosing pyracantha branches for switches. The thorns added sharp stings when the branches lashed bare legs. She put the child's feet alternately in hot water and ice water to produce maximum pain. For years, starting when Jenny was about four, Gladys Faye told her, "Someday you'll bleed from below, and know you have always belonged to Satan." Gladys Faye had time to wait to be proved right.

Gladys Faye waited at other times too. She allowed Jenny to keep the gold bracelet attached to her baby ring for years. Then Gladys Faye ripped it from her arm to stomp it into a shapeless blob because Jenny thought it was pretty.

Gladys Faye didn't protest when Mamie cleaned out the old smokehouse to make a place for Jenny to play. In the little house, which seemed huge to a ten-year-old child, she could draw and color and write and keep her precious things without worrying about her mother finding them. She began a journal, keeping her writings and simple poems in a spiral notebook. Gladys Faye left her alone in the playhouse for months before she made the raid to ridicule Jenny for her "stupid art" and to destroy her treasures.

When Gladys Faye made her raid on the playhouse, Jenny was safe in her own worlds. Lisa ran away at once. Marcie cried helplessly at being yelled at and tried to gather up and restore the torn-up poems and pictures. Selena couldn't stand to see Marcie hurt. She yelled back at Gladys Faye. Hilda made a brief appearance, trying to tear up even more things in her fury.

Gladys Faye smiled to see her too-smart-for-her-own-good daughter lose her precious pretty things, and lose control. It pleased her to see Jenny grovel and cry, impotently trying to fight back.

The smile faded as Gladys Faye saw the little girl regain her composure, and even look pleased with herself. Flisha couldn't help but smile with satisfaction. She knew that with all her hate, Gladys Faye could not stop them. She couldn't get to Jenny; Jenny wasn't even there. There were too many others for Gladys Faye to stop. There would be more writings, more drawings, more pretty things, more than Gladys Faye or anyone could destroy.

Part IV

Shattered

Looking through my crystal eyes, but where am I?
Am I in my worlds or the one they call real?
I can't see or feel, or do I feel?
Are things really real; are they sure or am I?
Are not my worlds real and theirs not?
I know nothing much of their world, and I'm
afraid.
As I even write, I'm not sure if it's my hand
Or someone else's.
Is it me who thinks or someone else?
Who am I?
Or is there a me?

Jenny's Journal

CHAPTER 9

Jenny was ten years old when the bleeding started, bleeding her mother had told her would mean she belonged to Satan. Marcie discovered the stain in her panties in the rest room at school during recess. When she didn't return to class, Mrs. Marks, her fourth-grade teacher, went looking for her. She was not hard to find. Her sobs, echoing off the cold green tile, could be heard in the hallway. Unsuccessful at calming the child huddling in the corner of the rest room, Mrs. Marks half led, half carried her to the school nurse's office. Still, the hysteria continued.

After what seemed a long time, the crying stopped. However, the nurse could see the child was still extremely upset. Selena had come out to help Marcie, but even she could not contain the fear and sense of desperation the bleeding caused.

The nurse could rationalize Jenny's behavior as being the result of her starting her period so young. Jenny Walters was a tiny little thing, but she was filling out early. She had been wearing a bra for close to a year already. It must be hard to deal with growing up so fast. Intending compassion, the nurse called Jenny's home and asked her aunt to come take her home.

Gladys Faye was upstairs asleep after her night shift in the mill. Aunt Mamie didn't ask Jenny any questions. The nurse had explained what the problem was. Muttering something about, "Mighty little kid to be falling off the roof," Aunt Mamie showed Jenny how to fit the belt and pad. "Don't worry about it, honey," Aunt Mamie said, "you just got the curse."

Developing early gave Jenny plenty of problems at school. Boys whistled at her and flirted with her. Girls made fun of her. The worst tease was Margaret Ann. Jenny had had no use for the little busybody ever since Margaret Ann embarrassed her in the first grade about having no father.

"Falsie, falsie," Margaret Ann flung at Jenny every chance she got. Flisha was able to ignore her, but the taunts could reduce Marcie to tears.

One day on the playground, Selena had had it with the little twit. Margaret Ann had Marcie crying, and a crowd of children had gathered to add their laughter to Marcie's humiliation. Selena brought the crying to a stop and raised her head to look Margaret Ann straight in the eye. Selena reached her hands to her own chest, ripped open her blouse, and tore off her bra, releasing very real, very well-developed breasts. The children dispersed in shocked, albeit impressed silence, and the yard monitor led Selena to the principal's office.

"What in the world were y'all thinking of out there?" Mr. Bascom wanted to know.

Undaunted, Selena responded with her own question. "Hell, if you had tits and somebody kept calling them falsies, wouldn't you show them?"

Mr. Bascom smiled at the red-faced, feisty little girl. Yes, he reasoned, he probably would show them. "Go on back to class," he told her.

Mr. Bascom was her teacher the next year in sixth grade. Selena always liked him.

As Jenny neared her teens, the teachers at Hamilton School noticed disturbing changes in her. They had seen her as moody, as she ranged from compliant Marcie to prissy Flisha to rebellious Selena. They had seen her arrive at school one day in a sundress, smacking bubble gum, and the next, dressed in a modest blouse and skirt and acting like a miniature adult. What concerned the teachers now was not Jenny's changeability, but, rather, her lack of it. Jenny presented a uniform visage — quiet, sullen, withdrawn.

Jenny, too, saw evidence of her distress. But while the teachers saw external behavior simplified by depression, Jenny viewed internal structures complicated by dissociation.

The birth personality remained in her own worlds, a complex network of places for her internal existence. These mind places varied in proximity to the real world. Jenny moved among them, staying in worlds farthest away when most threatened, coming close when it seemed safe.

Jenny's world nearest the real one was her crystal world, where brilliant, fragile gems drew in light in single rays and gave it out again multiplied in the spectrum of color. In her crystal world Jenny could see her own and the others' faces reflected in the facets of a beautiful crystal top. The others she saw were different from herself, yet somehow the same. Seeing them kept Jenny from feeling alone. Being watched by Jenny kept the others from being alone. A precarious balance of mutual interdependence kept the complex system of personalities functional.

When Jenny was twelve years old, the balance was very shaky, the result of excessive dissociation into alter personalities required to deal with events continuously threatening to overwhelm the system. Each alter, however well developed, served a limited and specific function, and each had a finite capacity for performing that function. For Jenny, the problems of abuse at home and in the cult were limitless and endless. She could respond only with an endless supply of limited solutions.

The alters arose in response to traumas, and the traumas of abuse at home and in the cult persisted. A general theme seemed to direct both the mother and the cult in their abuse. Both sought to corrupt and control the child. Both were creative in the endeavor. While many episodes of physical, sexual, and/or emotional attacks were much like other such attacks, many added new elements, as if variations on the theme might reach parts of the child not yet touched.

More creative than her abusers, Jenny responded to each nuance. She made alters to deal with every aspect of abuse, and to use a whole range of approaches in the process. Resistance, tolerance, cooperation, espousal — each was tried.

Resistance ranged from open defiance, which brought on more abuse, to inward insistence that she (or he, depending on the gender of the alter) did not belong to that mother, to those people, or to Satan as was claimed. Tolerance of the abuse was accomplished by alters who either did not feel the pain, physical or mental, or if they felt it, were not affected by it. Some alters were able to cooperate, to do or be what they perceived was expected. Whether directed by the mother or the cult leaders, these alters tried to please. Among them they could be bright or simple, quiet or outspoken, pretty or plain. Some would go so far as to imitate the abusers, to aspire to be like the ones who sought to control Jenny's life. When the range of endurance of these alters was exceeded, Jenny created others.

As Jenny created new personalities, reflections in the crystal top increased, each revolution displaying another array of faces. To a point, new faces were a comfort to Jenny. But when the number of personalities increased even more, the reflections multiplied like those in fun house mirrors. Jenny became disoriented and was forced to leave her crystal world for worlds more distant, more secure.

All the personalities felt the effects of Jenny's pulling away. They felt abandoned and became anxious. They turned the anxiety back upon themselves, and all became depressed. Most of the time, either Flisha, Marcie, or Selena was in control. With deepening depression, control was given over to a whole cadre of alters whose frequent switching added to the anxiety and general confusion.

Jenny had been creating alters since early childhood. It became problematic when stresses came more rapidly than the existing system could cope, or when new alters appeared in such number as to unbalance the system. The personalities varied in strength and persistence. Some developed considerable influence; others remained fragmentary. With great creativity and specificity, Jenny used the whole range of alters to meet the demands at home and in the cult. In all the experiences, Jenny just wanted to be a child, to be capable and loved.

Lisa, the child who played, was joined by Becky, who sucked her thumb and hugged her feather pillow, and who could play even when she was frightened. Aunt Sue, the chief protector, had help from others who watched and remembered and helped them all believe the bad things happening were dreams.

Selena was always a part of the sexual abuse because of the pain, but others came to help her with such things as the lesbian acts or the disgrace of being sold. The most persistent was an Indian, Vera Ann Birchausen, who helped to deal with Billy Joe's advances.

Marcie and Flisha were helped in their dealings with Gladys Faye by Penny, who hid in corners to avoid trouble by staying completely withdrawn. Todd came to please the mother by being the boy she seemed to want.

A lot of children came to help with the tortures of the cult. Some could tolerate the time on the blocks or other tests of obedience. Autumn tried to resist the cult, but Tolanda wanted to belong to Lucifer.

More than children came to respond to the cult. Mindoline, a hideous demon, came after Selena's first experience of being placed on the grave, to watch over her lest she become weak.

The cult experiences combined with personal events to create unbearable turmoil for the child. Beginning her period at age ten brought undeniable physical proof of being Satan's child. She had been taught to believe that once she was Satan's, she would always be Satan's, that there was something inside her that could never be changed, no matter what. For her there was no salvation except in whatever mercies the devil showed those who obeyed him. God would forever fail her, forever turn from her. God's church was a place of the enemy, a place where taking communion would mean certain death.

At age eleven Jenny's obedience to Satan was affirmed by Selena in the ritual killing. At age twelve Flisha was received into New Hope Church through the rite of baptism. In front of the whole congregation, dressed in a white robe, she was immersed by Reverend Ellis in the cool water and blessed in the name of the Father, the Son, and the Holy Ghost. At night Marcie tried to say bedtime prayers, but faces came, horrible faces, to remind her to be silent. In fear she kept silent and let other alters take control.

When Selena was able to regain control, she was determined to end the turmoil and depression. Taking a knife from the kitchen, she walked with it to the playhouse. The adults in the house paid no attention to her leaving. She made a final entry in the journal she had begun when she was ten years old, and put the knife to her wrist. She felt nothing as she watched blood begin to seep from the wound. Aunt Sue's struggle for control succeeded in time to keep the knife from making more than a scratch.

A few days later Selena swallowed a handful of aspirin. Gladys Faye rushed her to a doctor in town. No treatment was needed beyond making her vomit and watching that her breathing did not deepen excessively. Once he determined her condition was stable, the doctor asked her why she took the pills.

"Mama gives them to me sometimes to help me sleep," Selena answered in monotone.

"Is that all? You just wanted to sleep?"

"I wanted to get away from the bad things."

"What bad things?"

"At home, the bad sex things," Selena said, taking a risk, her voice still dull and steady. She would not tell about the cult things.

Gladys Faye saw the doctor's concern and gave a look that silenced Selena. Gladys Faye explained that Jenny had been withdrawn since she was around two, and her aunt locked her in her room. "Since she was four or five, she just seems to live in a little world all her own."

The doctor voiced his concern about Jenny's withdrawal and about her being upset by sexual matters. "Well, I reckon one of her cousins could have messed with her," Gladys Faye admitted. "So much goes on around that house, I can't keep up with it and work in the mill too." The doctor recommended she get Jenny out of that house.

Jenny did not expect that anything would change because of her revelations to the doctor. Rather, she expected that her mother would expound on problems of her own childhood, after belittling Jenny with: "You think you have it bad. Well, you don't know nothin'." Gladys Faye told Jenny repeatedly of bad things in her background.

Gladys Faye had developed early, as had Jenny. In school, girls who were jealous had ridiculed her, but the boys had liked her plenty. When she was around ten, three of her brothers lured her into the barn to take turns with her, one demonstrating his sexual abilities while the others called encouragement.

Until they had done the sex things with her, Gladys Faye's brothers had at best ignored her. They were prone to berate her, telling her she was fat and ugly and that no one would ever want her. She was scared of them when they ganged up on her.

From the way Gladys Faye talked, Jenny suspected that somehow it pleased her that her brothers wanted her. She said she did not like being forced by them, but she seemed to like knowing her soft breasts could excite them and the warm place between her thighs could make them feel good. Perhaps knowing this gave her a sense of power in a situation where otherwise she would be powerless.

The boys continued to use their sister sexually for several years. From the first, they warned her not to tell. Lance went so far as to say he'd kill her if she told. They needn't have bothered with their threats. Gladys Faye would never tell. Rather, she lived in fear her father would find out, or that somehow magically he already knew what his evil children were doing.

Papa had been a religious man. He taught Sunday school every week and made sure his family was in attendance any time the doors of the church were open. He quoted scripture nearly as well as the preacher, and he routinely enumerated his children's sins, sins bad enough, he told them, to send them straight to the fires of hell. Redemption seemed unlikely for children who piled sins on sins even when their good papa told them how bad they were and administered stern discipline.

As a child, Gladys Faye kept the sex things secret from her parents. Good girls didn't talk about such things. As a mother, she spoke about them with her daughter, but was not willing to help her understand their meaning.

Jenny's teacher had called Gladys Faye just a few days earlier, concerned about Jenny's depression. Now the doctor was showing concern too. To be a good mother, she had to respond to their concerns.

Gladys Faye told the family about the little place she found to rent across the street from Hamilton School. She did not tell them that the house was provided by the cult. The white frame house had a pretty wraparound porch and an arched doorway. Four tall Lombardy poplars lined the dirt driveway, sprawling elephant ears grew by the front steps, and two peach trees in the side yard were already big enough to bear. There was space for a garden in front of the woods of hickory, gum, and pine trees, like the garden and woods at Mamie's house. Jenny's brother, Lloyd, was married and on his own. Jenny could have her own room. No one could say Gladys Faye Walters didn't do right by her children.

CHAPTER 10

"Don't go in. It's the gateway to hell."

Marcie's thought was so strong that it was as if she heard the words spoken as she walked up the low front steps to the arch of the doorway of their new home. Shielding her eyes from the bright sunlight, she tried to see beyond the shadows of the covered entry to tell what the inside was like.

"Get in here and help me put this stuff away." Gladys Faye's voice overrode the one in Marcie's head. Marcie hurried in with her arms full of boxes and bags. She walked past the oil stove in front of the living room fireplace, through what must be a dining room, to put her bundles on the linoleum counter in the kitchen.

Beyond the kitchen, a tiny bathroom opened off an enclosed back porch. A hallway led from the porch to two small bedrooms. When she finished in the kitchen, Gladys Faye indicated the nearest bedroom. "Put your stuff in there." A pair of windows overlooking the garden spot and a door to the other bedroom interrupted the tongue-and-groove siding of the walls. Marcie put her underwear and things in the drawers of a small dresser. Her other clothes would have to go in the big wardrobe she had seen in the hall. She sat down on the familiar single bed brought from Aunt Mamie's and looked out at the scraggly weeds in the overgrown garden. She was happy to see Queen Anne's lace among the thistles and rabbit tobacco and broom sedge. The white frilly bloom of Queen Anne's lace was a favorite of hers. She used it to make little hats and parasols for her dolls when she played going-away. The game came real for her in the move to this house. Marcie hoped the voice she heard was wrong, that this place would be safe and warm like the places in her game.

For Flisha, the move meant leaving the piano and giving up lessons after nearly seven years. Aunt Mamie had faithfully seen to the lessons since Jenny was five years old. With Jenny gone to her own worlds, Flisha had taken up the lessons entirely, and showed much talent as well as love for music. Flisha would miss the piano, being able to play only whenever they visited at Aunt Mamie's.

In the quiet of the little house, Jenny returned from more remote worlds to her crystal world. Her closeness to the personalities operating in the real world helped to calm the switching of alters and to stabilize the entire system. Everyone was better able to function. Jenny's teachers saw her as less withdrawn. Her mother saw a settling of the volatile mood swings and self-destructive behavior.

The episode with the aspirin had scared Gladys Faye. Jenny had done things to herself in the past, like banging her head against the wall and cutting herself. But this time she really tried to kill herself, and the doctor knew it. Gladys Faye had to be careful. If she hadn't stopped her, Jenny might have talked too much.

As a mill worker Gladys Faye could barely support herself and her daughter. Her medical bills alone were considerable, and rearing a child was costly. She had been told Satan would provide for those who served him. She had been given drugs, liquor, transportation, fellowship. It was time to test the promise further. She turned to the high priest with her problem. She was delighted when a house was made available to her. She didn't think about what might be expected in return.

In many ways Gladys Faye wanted to do the right thing by Jenny. She knew she was hard on the child sometimes; she had to be for Jenny's own good. She had to teach her about the world and about men. Gladys Faye alternately felt afraid for Jenny and afraid of her. She had seen the change from the sparkling innocence of a child's eyes to the dull meanness of a viper's eyes. She had heard Jenny scream in terror one day when closed in the cedar chest to keep her out of the way, and the next day laugh as she hid in the same chest when she played games with her cousins. Gladys Faye admired, was even jealous of, Jenny's power in the cult of the devil, but had begun to have a nagging fear that the little girl's power could be coming from a possession by demons. Gladys Faye hoped that moving would keep things from getting out of hand again.

Gladys Faye was reassured by the quiet of the little house across from the school and the calming of Jenny's behavior. The period of calm was, however, short-lived. With access to mother and child unhampered, the cult began almost at once to conduct regular meetings in the little house and in the old barn some distance behind the house. In the house, sexual activities entertained old members and enticed new ones. In the barn, animals were used sexually and in sacrifice. Young, pretty Jenny was often the central attraction in the acts of sex and in the acts of bestiality.

Activities were the same as had gone on in Mamie's basement — drugs, minor rituals, sexual perversions. But in this house there were no limits, no need to stop before Mamie came home. There was no time of the day or night for Jenny to be safe.

There were no limits either on the men who paid to use her. There was no place she could hide. The men came and did their sex things to her and left the money for Gladys Faye. Again and again Selena endured the sex and huddled in the corner of the bed with her pillow to watch Gladys Faye collect the money.

After one of many episodes Selena looked at the money lying on her bed where the man had left it. He had touched her and called her pretty and said, "You're my little kitten.

Someday you'll be a real tiger." The man had been gentle and open in his need for her. For the moment at least, Selena had a sense of value, a way to feel in control. She reached for the money and tucked it away for herself.

One evening, after a few months in the little house, Selena found herself tied and hanging in the doorway to her room. Several men steadied her. Another man jammed a heavy wire into her. She recognized the wire as an opened-out coat hanger and the men as some she had seen in the cult. Selena felt the sharp pressure of cramps and the gush of blood, out of control, before they let her slump to the floor.

The usual trips to the mountains with Uncle Cleatus and with friends of Gladys Faye continued. If their route took them near enough, they stopped to visit with Mavis or to take her with them to the meetings. Mavis was a gray-haired, sharp-tongued old witch of whom Gladys Faye was clearly fond.

Mavis would sit in her old cane-bottomed rocker, looking for all the world like she was holding court as she laughed and joked with her visitors. At times her voice changed, becoming almost menacing, and the words were not words that made any sense. While her daughter timidly pulled away, Gladys Faye always had plenty to say to the old woman and plenty of time to listen to her. Sandy tried to follow their conversations, but something about Mavis intimidated her. Mavis even intimidated Selena, although Selena had a faint sense that Mavis had once been kind to her, a long time before.

The mountain trips went on, but the visits to Mavis stopped abruptly. Selena was shocked when she heard the reason. She overheard Gladys Faye telling what happened.

Some cult members had gone to see the old woman, and as they gathered around her rocking chair, her voice had become low and indistinct. All at once Mavis and the chair were afire. The fire didn't seem to start anywhere; it just suddenly was. In the instant the flames leapt around the old woman's head, the onlookers saw demons grimacing their terror, while the smell of burning flesh filled the silent room.

Selena detected a catch in Gladys Faye's voice as she finished her telling.

On the way to the next mountain meeting, Selena could not put Mavis out of her mind. Once at the meeting, Selena was again shocked by a happening she could not understand. She began to scream when she saw the skinny lady among the others. The lady was supposed to be dead. Selena had seen the knife in her own hand, had seen the altar run red, had tasted the salty warm blood. That was two years before, now the "dead" woman stood there among the group.

The high priest heard enough to understand what Selena was saying. He hushed her screams. "Don't concern yourself with what your eyes see. You touched her flesh, tasted her sacrifice, when you gave her up to honor Father Satan. It was only her spirit you saw tonight. See, it is gone now."

Selena looked back among the group. The woman was gone. Selena searched the faces as long as she could, until the drugs and wine made her not care that she had to check, had to make sure the skinny woman she saw was not real.

Selena's mistrust of the cult and the high priest showed itself the next time she was used in a ritual for demons to be summoned through her. The high priest drank the prescribed potion, made the required symbols, spoke the words, and commanded the demons to appear.

Selena saw the demons rise through her, but rather than watching them move to follow the directions of the priest, she saw them turn back on him. They caused him to fall to the ground and writhe and mutter insensibly. The priest could have had a seizure or reacted to hysteria, but the people looked for no other cause. They knew the child on the altar had been disobedient to Satan to foul the will of his high priest.

A few days later the group converged on Gladys Faye and Jenny in the little house. They put the child in the old cedar chest Gladys Faye had brought from Mamie's. The high priest sprinkled her with powders of sulfur and asafetida. The people threw live chickens on her to punish her and cleanse her wavering will. The powders burned her eyes, and the frantic chickens clawed at her skin. Selena felt sick to her stomach from the smells, like rotting, dying things, as she lay in the confinement of the coffinlike box.

Considering the child to be sufficiently chastened, the cult proceeded with their plans for her. In spite of all she had so far endured, the new abuses in which she was a helpless object produced intolerable terror. She knew she could not resist them. Even Selena, the strongest, had failed. Her only defense was in more splitting, splitting so tumultuous that none of the major personalities could maintain control for long, nor could they maintain awareness of the activities of the alters. For the major personalities, only bits of time were available. More alters were created, and they along with those already in existence vied for, then hurried to relinquish, control. For Jenny, for the whole system of personalities, great segments of time were lost to awareness, nearly two years, in fact.

Jenny pulled back from her crystal world to more remote ones. She went to Henry's world, where nothing ever got hurt or died in the little village like the one under Aunt Mamie's Christmas tree, except there was no snow. Everything was fresh and green and warm. Henry and Maud were good to her. They held her and told her she was sweet and pretty and a very good girl.

Her jade world was more felt than seen, a place of green smoothness. Her color world was a happy melody of visions. When things got really bad, Jenny left these pleasant worlds for her world of forgotten blackness. There she could feel only aloneness. There she lost all contact with her alter selves.

Away from the house and from the cult, Selena managed a sort of existence, a try at growing up. Adolescent, but physically mature, she turned her attentions to men.

At twenty-six, Tony was twice her age, but Selena knew she was in love with him. He was leader of a five-piece band that played in roadhouses and at weekend parties. He let Selena sing with them at times. She dressed as sexily as she could and stood with them in their matching western shirts with the pearlized snaps, and sang the country songs low and slow.

She made up her mind to marry Tony. When she asked Gladys Faye to sign the papers to let her marry underage, Gladys Faye pitched a fit. "You can't marry him. You'll not ruin this family and have blue-head babies like him," Gladys Faye railed. Gladys Fay knew, as did everyone in the county, about Tony's birth defects. She forbade her daughter to see this man not good enough for her, and kept her more at home.

At home, neither Flisha nor Marcie could hold things together. Most often Marcie would awaken, but before the soft morning mist could give way to a warm humid day, others came. Kathy could look in mirrors and was able to get ready for school in the mornings.

While Jenny had trouble getting across the street to school, over a score of young child alters came to play school in the little house. Abby was always the teacher. Using the walls as her blackboards, she gave assignments in art and spelling and language and arithmetic. She listed the roll on the wall of the front bedroom and called the children in turn to fill in blanks, color pictures, do addition.

Many of the children talked to themselves and drew pictures of things only they saw — fuzzy creatures, little people with no arms or faces. One child printed on the wall in bold red letters the reason for the profound scattering: *I must keep my mouth shut because if I don't I will get in trouble.*

Some behavior was more bizarre, more disturbing than the writing on the walls. Becky dragged her pillow around and sucked her thumb. Todd tried to break glass, which looked to him like the water the mother had tried to use for killing, and which reflected only ugliness.

Wahnola resurfaced and renewed self-abuse. Over a period of months, she banged her head, ingested bits of rat poison, clawed at her eyes, set her hair on fire. Penny hid as much as she could in corners and under things, becoming depressed to the point of immobilization.

From the time Jenny was twelve until she was fourteen,

she lived in the little house that was a hell for her. Through the alter personalities, she lived the hell in discontinuous flashes of experience and emotion. She fought down awful waves of nausea, feeling the sulfur-yellow color of the dining room walls in sweaty, weak-kneed helplessness. She knew self-disgust as she saw her body grow fat like her mother's. She glimpsed unknown new rituals, saw a multitude of black robes, heard the cries of babies. She could only regress, withdraw, scatter, suspend her existence in lost time.

CHAPTER 11

Jenny's eighth-grade teacher could not ignore her frequent and prolonged absences from school and her withdrawn behavior when she was in the classroom. He was struck by her episodes of staring into space, by her confused expressions, and her cocking her head as if listening intently but failing to respond to her own name. When she returned to school after yet another two-week absence, and wrote a note saying she was afraid of going crazy, he sent her immediately to the school counselor. After attempts at discussion with the child, the counselor contacted Gladys Faye and insisted that Jenny be taken that day, at once, to the county mental health clinic.

At the mental health clinic Penny scooted under the table and could not be coaxed to come and sit on the chair. As she cowered, she heard the adults talk about the state hospital. She was afraid she would be locked up forever like Great-uncle Arthur had been. She had heard Aunt Mamie talk about how the old uncle was crazy and had to stay at the hospital until he died. If she stayed under the table, they couldn't make her be crazy.

James Mooreland, a social worker with the clinic, prepared a summary of information for the state hospital. He wrote of the school counselor's concern with Jenny's note about going crazy, and of her talk of a "world of her own." About her interaction with the clinic staff, he wrote, "She appeared to derive pleasure out of telling us about her thoughts, as though she used her stories as attention-getting mechanisms, but in other ways she appeared to be unable to distinguish the fantasy qualities of this 'other world.'" Mr.Mooreland recommended hospitalization because of Jenny's behavior and her thoughts of suicide, noting she was a "very disturbed girl," and that she had a "rather unsettled childhood."

On the long drive to the hospital, Penny huddled by the back window of the sheriff's car. Her mother was in the backseat with her but did not try to make her talk. The roads seemed familiar. Selena would have recognized much of the area. Penny had only a vague sense of familiarity with the Appalachian roads the child had traveled many times before. She hardly saw the beautiful spring green of the forests of pine, hickory, and other hardwoods, interspersed with the bold white blooms of graceful dogwoods and the pinks, whites, and purples of rhododendron and mountain laurel.

She was led from the car to the doorway of a huge brick building surrounded by others just as imposing. Penny retreated, leaving Selena struggling to orient herself. The glare from the polished terrazzo floors and the echoes of voices off the cold, enamel-painted walls were harsh and threatening. Penny reappeared to hide under the metal examining table, making it clang stridently as she scurried for its protection. She would not so much as glance at Dr. Edwards, the physician who saw her on admission.

Finally Marcie responded to Dr. Edwards's calm, persistent persuasion and crawled from under the table and straightened her dress, ready to answer the doctor's questions. Acting in Jenny's stead, she told of her own worlds, where she could be happy. She told how she loved animals and the mountains. "But," she said, "the animals always get killed some way."

Subdued but cooperative, Marcie admitted to hearing

voices at times and complained of much discomfort, "like a knot in my stomach so bad my legs draw up." Her slow speech and quiet, deliberate manner were consistent with her mother's description of her recent deep depression.

Dr. Edwards's patient raised formerly downcast eyes to face him squarely and report in a matter-of-fact tone that she had had some terrible sexual experiences. Not to be outdone by Marcie's candor, Selena added her own information. She said she had been raped by a cousin when she was younger, and that one of her uncles still tried to make out with her. Selena went on to tell about her boyfriend, Tony, and her hopes to marry him.

In interview with the doctor, Gladys Faye used essentially the same story she had told the doctors after Jenny's suicide attempt at age twelve. She explained that Jenny had been withdrawn since one of her aunts locked her in a room when she was two. She acknowledged, as she had before, that Jenny's cousin may have messed with her, but she had moved Jenny away from the household where that took place. She defended Jenny as a good girl who didn't drink or use drugs and who dated schoolmates only with supervision. She denied that Jenny had an older boyfriend, but emphasized she had an active imagination.

Gladys Faye talked about Jenny's love of the church and her interest in the piano and in dancing. (When Jenny had told her mother she wanted to dance, Gladys Faye had laughed at her and told her she could no more dance than the rats in the basement.) She admitted Jenny didn't care much for school and that she spent much time alone. She said the illness began a few months before, when Jenny became sullen and had crying spells and trouble sleeping.

On physical examination Dr. Edwards found all within normal limits, remarking only on a questionable menstrual history and breast tenderness that suggested the need to rule out pregnancy. Concluding the examination and the intake interviews, Dr. Edwards noted his impression that fourteen-year-old Jenny Walters suffered from delusions and hallucinations. She was probably suicidal, but lacked the necessary insight to see herself as mentally ill. He entered a tentative diagnosis of schizophrenic reaction and assigned her to a locked ward.

The very nature of Jenny's illness militated against detection. The alters' ability to switch smoothly, to respond unfailingly to one name, and to feign familiarity in a new situation gave the impression of a single, albeit disturbed, personality. Moreover, Jenny's characteristic of accelerated healing with very little scarring eliminated or markedly diminished clues that could have signaled the physician to suspect abuse.

Selena went with the nurse without protest after saying a perfunctory "good-bye" to Gladys Faye. The walls of Ward 7B were painted the same pale green as the lobby and the admitting area, and the same worn wooden benches lined the hall. Selena noticed several patients in the hall as they got off the elevator, and more in a large room the nurse called the day room. Some were dressed in street clothes, but most wore pajamas or cotton gowns and gray robes.

The nurse showed Selena to a room with four beds. The windows were covered with wire like heavy chicken wire, the same as the window in the door the nurse had closed behind them when they entered the ward. Selena thought she might never get out of this place, but she felt safer here than she had anywhere for a long time.

In the safety of the hospital, the system of personalities quickly regained equilibrium. With unfailing intuition for survival, the personalities adapted to the expectations of the hospital staff to present eventually the very picture of improved mental health the staff wanted to see. The nearly catatonic Penny, who had to hide away, was no longer needed. Other minor personalities receded and no longer surfaced to manifest their characteristics. The major personalities regained control and were able, for the most part, to constrain the several child personalities.

The hospital frightened the children. Their school-playing ended; they came out at night in turns to cry to go home or to play a little. Abby, the erstwhile teacher, used the hospital pens and pencils to draw some pictures and make some lessons, but no one came to work the problems she composed. She was careful to hide herself and her papers away from the nurses.

The other child personalities were also subdued. Missing her own soft feather pillow, Becky managed to find comfort in the hard, heavy hospital one. She often fell asleep sucking her thumb. None of the children betrayed Jenny by being seen by the hospital staff.

The doctors and nurses watched Jenny Walters improve rapidly. Her sullen behavior changed to cooperative, even pleasant interchanges with the staff and other patients. Drugs were discontinued after two weeks, and Jenny was permitted freedom to go outside on the grounds, to shop at the commissary, and to go to occupational therapy to work on crafts. The freedom was balanced with expectations to help care for other, more disabled patients and to take her turn at kitchen chores.

Marcie was compassionate and gentle with the old men and women. She helped to feed them and to change their beds. She talked to them even if they didn't answer her at first, or ever. The old people who still had the capacity to respond were responsive to her, interrupting their otherwise endless reveries to smile at her or to eat the same old institutional food as if it were a special treat. Others had long since given up any semblance of human contact. Even with them, Marcie felt warm and giving, their gray heads and gold-rimmed glasses educing barely conscious memories of a beloved grandmother.

Marcie didn't mind the kitchen chores either. When she was little, she often helped Aunt Mamie. Although she thought Flisha was better at cooking, Marcie could make a passable meal and could keep as clean a kitchen as anyone could want.

Marcie saw Hilda come sometimes just to wash the dishes. Hilda was indignant at the task, but persistent in completing it. She grumbled her anger at being put upon by the senseless repetitive chore.

The situation presented to the staff was typical of a vacillating teenager. Jenny Walters was sometimes rebellious, sometimes compliant in her relationship to authority figures. Most days Marcie was pleasant and cheerful, but she could not conceal, nor could she explain, the sadness she felt when it rained. When afternoon thunderstorms rattled over the mountain ranges, Marcie moved away from the other patients to stand by the window to see her tears duplicated by raindrops on the panes. To her, the universe wept its sadness, and she wept with it. The staff could explain her sadness as to-be-expected homesickness. They had no more awareness than the child of buried memories of being locked out after school in the rain, of being nearly drowned in a rain-flooded road, of sitting by the windows of her bedroom not knowing why she wept with the rain.

Selena did not care much one way or the other about the rain. She simply preferred that the days be clear so she could be outside. The grounds were well kept. Broad, green, gently rolling lawns were shaded by huge oaks and adorned with beds of vibrant flowers in circular and semicircular patterns. Miles of cement walkways connected a complex of buildings that comprised a community larger than the little town close to her home.

Group outings were fun. There were shopping excursions into the nearby village. Selena usually bought makeup and bubble gum at the First Rate Drug Store, then joined the others at the fountain for strawberry ice cream. Periodically groups went for hikes on the mountain trails or for horseback rides. Just getting out was great. The sweaty smell of horses and the rich leather smell of tack were added bonuses to her glimpses of a real childhood.

Selena's favorite place was the big white gazebo. Whenever she could, she spent time there just sitting on one of the built-in benches. The pattern of concentric boards which formed the ceiling fascinated her, a pattern as complex yet as orderly as the personality structure of which she formed a central part. Selena, however, spent no time in introspection. She considered the nearly panoramic view of hills and gorges, verdant in early summer foliage, and dreamed of meeting suitors in this special, pretty place.

It was enough to face reality in the therapy sessions. Much of the time she let Flisha handle it. Flisha remained controlled and calm as she talked with Dr. Edwards, neither confirming nor denying his questions about sexual experiences. She admitted she was not always happy; for instance, she loved the piano and missed it when they moved away from Aunt Mamie's house. Her poise suggested she had risen above whatever unfortunate events may have disturbed her childhood.

Selena was more candid, slightly seductive in her behavior toward the doctor, though the difference from Flisha was not dramatic enough to suggest more than a range of moods. Selena talked about being sexually abused and about her aunt and her mother being hard on her. She disclosed enough about her past that when Dr. Edwards presented her case at staff conference, a diagnosis of dissociative reaction was made.

Her improvement was seen as resulting from her being able to talk in the hospital over a period of time about her traumas. Conferences with Gladys Faye reassured the hospital staff that the home situation was improved as well. Dr. Edwards discharged Jenny after nearly three months of hospitalization.

Dr. Edwards and the staff had come very close to discovering the truth about Jenny. They may not have realized that her "improvement" was as much a function of her dissociative capabilities as was her illness. The system of personalities was able to function so well in the hospital situation that the extent of her fragmenting was not recognized.

During the time in the hospital away from her abusers, Jenny was able to return from more distant worlds to her crystal world. The faces in the crystal top decreased in number as the alter personalities stabilized in their functions, and sensing Jenny's nearness, calmed from frantic switching to almost studied cooperation. Though the gap of nearly two years remained, time, remembered time, resumed for Jenny Walters.

Part V
Safe Places

I sit here watching the shadows of trees at play
Dancing up against the side of the house.
One moment they're here; the next they disappear,
But what fun they have playing the shadow game.

The same is with life. It's a shadow game.
One moment we're here; the next we disappear.
So be very careful, friend, of the shadow game you
play.
For as you know, the shadows can change so very
fast
And they're not what they seem, or what you need
to play.

                                        Jenny's Journal

CHAPTER 12

Jenny's life changed considerably following her return from the state hospital. The physical abuse by her mother, having diminished somewhat as Jenny grew older, stopped altogether. Blows which had heretofore punctuated Gladys Faye's angry outbursts no longer materialized with her anger. Gladys Faye could still be upset, but she limited her responses to verbal attacks on Jenny, as she did to anyone who crossed her.

Jenny was slow to accept the change in the long-established pattern of abuse. She continued to expect both the spontaneous and the premeditated assaults by her mother. But after some time of bracing for blows that did not come, she allowed herself to feel less afraid of her mother. Jenny could not account for the change, although she was fully aware that it was not her own influence that caused Gladys Faye to show this new restraint.

Gladys Faye seemed generally more content at home than Jenny could ever remember her being. She had started dating Grady Camp on a regular basis. Gladys Faye had known Grady, a churchgoing Christian man, for several years. He had shown no interest in marriage, but of late he had been especially attentive to her and faithful. When Grady was around, Gladys Faye was more settled.

Just as Jenny had expected that her mother's abuse would resume where it left off with her return from the hospital, she expected that the cult abuse would also resume. But it did not. No one came to the little house to engage Jenny in occult or sexual activities, nor was she taken to the hidden but familiar places for sexual or sacrificial rites. It was as if for Jenny the cult never existed. Gladys Faye did not speak of the change in her own behavior or the lack of the cult's presence. Jenny did not dare to ask questions.

As far as Jenny knew, her mother's contact with the cult was also broken. Jenny could not be sure, but as a month passed, then another, without any signs of cult activity around her, Jenny came to believe that somehow that dark secret life was over.

Jenny would be going to a different school. Hamilton School went only to the eighth grade. She would go by bus to Markham Junior High in the south part of the county to begin ninth grade. At a new school she could be like anyone else, unafraid that someone — a teacher, a classmate — would suspect old secrets.

Within days of entering junior high school, Jenny realized that she would not be treated like everyone else. Word of her stay in the state hospital had found its way to the new school. She heard students say "crazy," and saw them circle their fingers at their heads, being not quite careful that she not hear or see them.

Jenny was miserable. None of the personalities could, or even wanted to, cope. School was too difficult. She had been thought stupid in grammar school. Now she was called crazy. Flisha was distressed by the treatment at school and disgusted. Marcie was distraught. Selena was disinterested. There was little hope that any part of Jenny would be able to manage the schoolwork or to find friends in this new school.

Janice, her only friend from Hamilton School, was assigned to different classes and a different homeroom. Being with Janice at lunchtime was the only thing that kept Jenny from being at a complete loss with her situation.

Janice was Selena's best friend, although Janice knew her only as Jenny. Selena was aware that Janice's reputation at Hamilton School followed her to Markham too. The teachers shunned her, and the students called her loose, fast, whore. Selena didn't care. She had known Janice since first grade, when they played apart from the other children. She didn't hesitate when Janice asked her to double with her on a blind date.

Janice was just dying to date Mason Martin. But Mason had quit school and gone to work, so Janice's mother wouldn't let her date him unless she doubled. She asked Jenny to come along as date for Mason's best friend, Michael Harris. Michael had quit school, too, and was working. Selena didn't know anything about Michael Harris, and didn't care to know anything. She was glad for a chance to get dressed up and get out of the house.

Michael closed his eyes hard and shook his head, afraid the vision would vanish. He could not believe his luck. Standing in the arch of the doorway was the prettiest girl he had ever seen. And he was about to take her on a date.

He had known Jenny Walters even before she went to grammar school. Well, more knew of her than knew her. She probably wouldn't remember, but he did. He had stayed at the same baby-sitter's and had played with her a few times before Jenny got in trouble with Miss Kress for turning the cows out and tormenting the kittens. Jenny hadn't come to stay with Miss Kress anymore, but after that Michael watched her all through school.

Michael was a year older than Jenny. He came from a family that knew how to keep its place. He figured a girl as well off as Jenny Walters was not likely to have anything to do with him. She was always dressed so pretty, always looked so neat and proper. His worn shirt, overalls, and brogans marked him a poor, dumb country boy. He had been held back a year, so they were in the same class in the eighth grade. But Jenny never acted as if she knew he existed. Even if he had ever gotten up the nerve to talk to her, she probably would have just laughed at him.

He figured she was probably smart. He never was good in school, just barely managed to scrape by. 'Course that didn't make much difference now. He had a steady job, had ever since his daddy let him quit school.

All the boys had to go to work as soon as they could. Their daddy's disability check wasn't nearly enough to keep up a family with five kids even before Grandma came to live with them. Daddy hadn't worked since a car he was fixing fell on him. He could get around all right, but he sat at the house mostly. Even if he didn't work, no one forgot he was head of the household. He let his boys know he would still whip them in a heartbeat if he thought they needed it.

With closed eyes Michael remembered the pretty little schoolgirl. When he opened his eyes, he saw a grown-up woman waiting for him. Sparkling glitter in her upswept blond hair reflected the rich blue of her dress. The color repeated in the depth of her eyes as she smiled at him. The whole effect was stunning. Michael Harris knew he was looking at the woman he would marry.

Michael remembered nothing of the movie they saw, not even the title. He barely remembered going for burgers and Cokes with Mason and Janice, or that they had set up this double date. The details of the date meant little to Michael. He remembered only that Jenny said yes when he asked if he could call her again.

Selena agreed to his calling, although she did not care much for Michael. When he called for a second date, she let Marcie deal with him. Not wanting to hurt Michael's feelings, Marcie agreed to go out with him.

Michael would never forget that second date. This time he went alone to pick her up. She looked just as pretty as before. She wore a modest sweater-and-skirt outfit and seemed more subdued than when he first met her. He was reassured that here was someone he could take home to meet his mother.

After treating Jenny to supper at the fish camp, Michael drove his old car down a rutted dirt road for a little privacy by the woods. He turned off the engine and the headlights but left the radio playing softly. He found his date respon-

sive to his kisses and the play of his hands. He slipped a
hand beneath her sweater to unhook her bra and release the
soft breasts he had been caressing.

Her screams were sudden, piercing, almost paralyzing
Michael with their show of absolute fear. "There—
there—I see him there!" she shrieked, pointing into the
maw of the road entering the woods. Michael watched
Jenny's face turn deathly white and beads of sweat stand
above her lip.

As soon as Michael could regain enough composure, he
switched on the headlights. The pale beam illuminated only
the red dirt of an empty road and the wiry tangle of
underbrush beneath bare trees.

Michael's frantic efforts to start the old Pontiac, with the
battery depleted from playing the radio, merely flooded it.
As the old car defied further efforts to get it started, he saw
that Jenny was going to vomit, and that her nose was
beginning to bleed. Michael tried desperately to calm her.
"What is it?" he asked with as much authority as he could
muster.

"The headless man," Marcie gasped, "the headless man."

After what seemed like an eternity Michael got the old car
started and drove in lurches back to the main road. He
pieced together her sputtering explanation that they had
parked at the far end of the "booger woods" which bordered
her aunt Mamie's property. Michael drove to a little all-
night café. With paper towels from the men's room, he
helped her clean herself up. When she had some color back
in her face, he drove her home.

Michael believed that Jenny had seen a ghost, but he had
no intention of risking upsetting Jenny's mother with the
story. Gladys Faye had seemed to like him well enough the
first time he met her. Affable by nature, Michael worked at
charming her with compliments and mild flirtations. They
would need her consent to marry underage. He didn't want
to have to go against her. He had been raised to respect his
elders. He was pleased when Gladys Faye made no issue
over Jenny's disheveled appearance when they came in late
from their second date. They told her that Jenny had seen

something and got scared. Gladys Faye didn't press for details. She just thanked Michael for taking such good care of Jenny. Michael could get along with Jenny's mother.

His own mother presented another matter altogether. She was against his even dating Jenny Walters. When she learned he was going out with the Walters girl, she spoke against her. "She thinks she's so high class," his mother argued. "We can be sure she ain't our kind anyway." But even her throwing it up to him that people said Jenny had been in the crazy house could not dissuade him. He could see for himself Jenny wasn't crazy.

Believing in ghosts was not the only thing Michael had in common with Jenny. She liked school no better than he did. "Nobody likes me there," she told him. Michael was proud to be the one to protect her from stupid people who didn't understand such a pretty, nice girl.

Both Jenny and Michael were reared in the church. Although both had a fundamentalist perspective, Michael's Pentecostal background was more strict than her traditional Protestant one. He learned fierce loyalty to the faith and to his family. Faith, he believed, could save you in the next world and in this one. He put no store in doctors, knowing prayer and fellowship were all that were necessary to heal the faithful. He believed, as did most of the people he knew, that women should be obedient to their husbands, that husbands should protect their wives.

At first he had some concern about Jenny's Christian upbringing. Although she wore a dress, not forbidden slacks, on their first date, the dress was flashy, and she wore heavy makeup. In her favor, though, she toned down the makeup by the time they went out again. Too, he was impressed by the fact that she showed respect for her mother and the fact that her mother seemed to like him.

Michael was not aware that Gladys Faye's positive response to him presented a dilemma for Jenny. He offered the immediate opportunity for marriage, but nobody liked him besides Gladys Faye. Marriage was a way to get away from school and the stigma placed on her there, and it was a way to escape the control of her mother. Selena, Marcie, and

Flisha all saw the need to get away. Marriage was a good plan. It had been only a few months before that Gladys Faye had put a stop to her marrying Tony. Flisha and Marcie had liked Tony, and Selena thought she loved the country singer, but Gladys Faye said he wasn't good enough for her daughter.

After the scene about Tony, Selena had made up her mind not to marry anyone. As tolerant as Marcie was, she found Michael too coarse in manner to see again, and Flisha wouldn't consider going out with him at all. He was good-looking, of medium build, with softly curling brown hair and brown eyes. He was outgoing, he had a job, and he had his mind set on marrying. But Flisha found him lacking in education and refinement.

Jenny solved the dilemma in her usual fashion. A new alter, Nina, came to court Michael, leaving him unaware that he never even met the real Jenny Walters. Nina supposed she loved Michael. She knew she wanted to please him and to become his wife. To fill the role, she took her cues from Michael.

Four months after their first date, Michael Compton Harris and Jenny Lynn Walters were married. He was sixteen; she was fifteen. Jenny's mother bought her a pure white wedding dress, lace over organza. Michael dressed in his only dark suit.

For the wedding Nina wore her hair in a French twist. She agreed to a touch of lipstick only at Aunt Mamie's insistence. She looked sweet and pretty in the traditional white dress. She asked Michael to pin on the gardenia he had brought her. The gardenia was left behind when Flisha came out and replaced it with an orchid corsage Gladys Faye had bought. Flisha knew it was best to placate Gladys Faye. Nina did not resist. Although his feelings were hurt, Michael didn't force the issue with his pliant, blushing bride. He held her hand in silence as they drove to the justice of the peace across the state line.

Michael's mother refused to go to the wedding, still protesting the union. His father went along to sign the papers. Gladys Faye went along, too, the happy and proud mother of the bride. Her boyfriend, Grady Camp, completed the wedding party. All in all, Michael was pleased with the way the day went.

Unaware that Jenny had been a victim of abuse, unaware of her involvement in the cult, unaware that Jenny was other than what she seemed to be, Michael took his new bride home to his parents' house for a few weeks. His mother resigned herself to a situation she could not change and welcomed them and treated Jenny cordially as a daughter, while the couple waited for the deal to close on the trailer they bought.

Gladys Faye agreed to be cosigner of the papers with them only after Michael and Jenny agreed to park the used trailer at Mamie's house instead of on the two acres in the country that Michael's family offered them. Michael's land had a well and a septic tank, but Gladys Faye was adamant that they stay near her. When Michael and Jenny moved out of the house into the trailer, Gladys Faye moved from the little house with the arched doorway back in with Mamie.

At the time of her marriage to Michael, things were better for Jenny than they had been since her grandmother died. Too, she had a whole system of personalities to accommodate to the demands and routines of married life.

CHAPTER 13

Friday night. Michael assumed they'd be going out with
Grady and Gladys Faye as usual. Most every weekend they'd
go somewhere, if only to get something to eat at the fish
camp or a steak house. Michael liked being with Grady.
Also, when Grady was around, it was easier to be with
Gladys Faye.

Gladys Faye was changeable, as nice as pie to you one
minute and would bite your head off the next. If you let it get
to you, she could embarrass you to death being loud-
mouthed or laughing her horsey laugh. She was big as a
house and she'd wear those bright flowery dresses, and have
a Marlboro cigarette always hanging out of her mouth.
Michael never said anything. After all, she was Jenny's
mama. And she usually acted pretty decent around Grady.

Michael looked forward to the weekends. He worked hard
running a cutting machine that could cut over a hundred
pieces at a time to be sewed into baby clothes and women's
underwear. He didn't earn much over minimum wage, but
the work was steady, and he got overtime whenever he
could. He expected when he got home from work to find his
supper on the table. He had a wife to take care of him.

He had let Jenny quit school right after they got married. She worked as a clerk at the dime store in town. She worked only part-time. She kept up the trailer and cooked good meals, and she was ready to go anytime he said go.

Nina tried to be the consummate housewife. She was content to be at home, concerned only with pleasing the man whose place it was to take care of her and support her. She was content to dress as he said, think as he said.

Nina dressed in simple cotton dresses. She wore no jewelry, no makeup. Quiet, she seldom spoke unless Michael spoke first to her. She was up to fix his breakfast and pack his lunch, and hurried to pick up after him once he left for work. When he got home, she sat with him and rubbed his tired feet.

As much as Nina was compelled to please Michael, she could not handle sex with him. She petted him, pampered him, was even warm to him as she let him caress her. But whenever sexual activity heated up, Nina ran. Only Selena could deal with Michael's lovemaking. Michael did not seem to mind that his usually docile wife became daring in the bedroom.

This Friday evening Michael found Jenny lying across the bed when he got home. "Y'all go on, Michael, with Mama and Grady," she said. "I'm too tired to go anywhere."

"Aw, you're just wore out from working at the store. You need to get out of here awhile." Jenny acquiesced, but she didn't feel like eating and begged to come home as soon as they finished supper.

Over the next several days Jenny grew weaker and was unable to keep much food down. Michael was the first to see the yellow developing in the whites of her eyes and on the palms of her hands. Eventually the jaundice involved her whole body.

"You've got to take her to the doctor," Gladys Faye was waiting in the trailer to tell him. "I heard Dr. Bradford is good in Statesboro."

"We don't need no doctors, not my family." Michael stood firm. "If we have faith in Jesus Christ, she'll be all right. Go on back to the house, and I'll take care of her."

Michael called members of his church to come to fellowship with them and to pray for a healing. They took turns for days, calling on God, laying on their hands, and speaking in tongues. Jenny got no better.

Gladys Faye sailed into Michael. "My baby coulda died, and you woulda left her lying there. She was almost too weak to get to the car with me helping," Gladys Faye chided him. She had defied him by taking Jenny to a doctor. "Dr. Bradford put her straight in the hospital. She's got hepatitis. It's real serious."

Michael made no effort to defend himself, to say that the hospital was against his raising, to say that he was afraid he couldn't pay for doctors and hospitals. He saw the fire in Gladys Faye's eyes and didn't dare protest.

Michael felt out of place in a hospital. He felt like a traitor in the enemy's camp as much as he was intimidated by the place. He went to visit Jenny as little as he dared, mindful of Gladys Faye's sense of his duty. He spent his time after work with his buddies messing with cars and motorcycles.

After weeks in the hospital in isolation, Jenny still had to spend months at home in bed. Gladys Faye and Aunt Ramona took turns tending to her while Michael was at work. When he got home, there was no one to rub his back or scratch his tired, itchy feet. He ate supper at Mamie's house, then went off with his buddies.

Michael was worried. This was their first Christmas together, and his wife was sick in bed. He could barely make the payments on the trailer every month, and the doctor bills were piling up day by day. Of course he wasn't any worse off than most people he knew. His family had never owned a home. His daddy wasn't able to work. His mama did the best she could with the little they had. Of all the children, Michael had done the best. He had a pretty wife, a steady job, and a place of his own to live. All he had to do was hold on to what he had.

It was not easy. They barely got by from payday to payday. Michael hid his money in a drawer and had Jenny make all their credit payments in cash. Every month he gave the cash to Gladys Faye for the trailer payment. She kept the papers on the trailer in her name.

When Jenny was finally better, they had some good times. Michael came home to a supper of potatoes and beans, or maybe fried bologna sandwiches. After supper they'd go for a ride. They'd just mess around town, cruising the main drag. If they ran into some of their friends, they'd pick up the challenge of a street race. The threat of a ticket just added to the excitement of squealing tires and roaring engines. Mostly the police left them alone. Except for an occasional warning about his loud mufflers, Michael stayed out of trouble with the law.

Nina had trouble with things outside home. She would go to ride with Michael, but when they ran into friends and started in with the cars or racing, she gave way to Selena. Selena loved the excitement of racing and the fun of being with friends.

Michael always kept a hot rod of some kind running. He loved cars and spent hours with his head stuck under a hood. His wife didn't seem to mind. She went along and would sit in the car doing needlework or reading while he tinkered at a friend's garage. At home Selena pitched in to help work on the cars. She progressed from passing tools to helping him replace transmissions and rear ends. When Selena couldn't keep up with Michael, Justin, the male alter who had come to be a father for Jenny when she was six, came out to help fix carburetors, rebuild engines, even do body work.

Michael considered himself lucky. On most issues his wife never crossed him, but went along with his ideas. He could come and go as he pleased, hunt and fish whenever he wanted, and go out with his friends as much as he liked. His wife didn't get in his way, but she was there to be with him when he wanted her.

Michael was surprised when religion came to be a point of contention between them. After all the prayers and attention from his church while she was sick, Michael figured that once she was well, she would turn to his Lord. But she went back to her old church, and Michael suspected that she put on makeup and jewelry at times.

Although Nina tried to go along with Michael, Marcie wanted to hold to her old church. Flisha hoped to improve her situation. Without letting Michael know, when she could, she attended the big First Baptist Church in town. Selena had no patience with any of it. She surely couldn't go along with Michael. She couldn't believe anybody would expect a wife to agree to no doctors when you got sick, no makeup, no jewelry, no slacks, no shorts. No fun as far as Selena could see.

Hell, Selena wasn't married to Michael. Let Nina listen to him. Selena would dress and act as she pleased. She waited until he left for work in the morning to change out of the stupid, drab dress Nina wore, and to put on her face. Since she had no desire to be around the house when Michael got home, she left Nina alone in the afternoon to clean her face and get dressed properly for her husband. Michael didn't push the issue about the rules of the church as long as he saw her behave as a proper wife.

Michael had some concern, though, about the store she seemed to put in magic and such. He didn't pay that much attention, but she was always reading in some book or having the place stunk up from burning incense or candles in the trailer.

The first time he saw her actually work a spell, she talked the fire out of a burn. He wanted to put lard on her hand when she blistered it on a burner of the gas stove. She snatched her hand away from him and held it close to her as she looked dreamy-eyed and chanted something like, "The sun is hot; the moon is cool," over and over again.

Michael didn't let on that he prayed for Jesus to heal her. He was still surprised the next day when her hand showed only a slight redness instead of the blistering burn. Maybe it hadn't been as bad as it looked at first.

He had seen her get rid of warts for sure, though. Jenny cut the wart on his thumb four ways, crisscross. Then she cut an onion the same way and dripped the blood from the cut wart into the onion. She buried the onion in the drip line of the house. It rained. In a week the wart was gone.

Maybe there was no harm in what she did. A lot of people could get rid of warts. His grandpa had been able to talk them away. Still Michael wanted Jenny to put her trust in the Lord, to turn away from the sinful ways of the world.

Selena held on to her belief in the power of the occult. Although she didn't go to meetings of the cult, she hoped she could use the powers to gain control in her life. She read books, concocted potions, and studied rituals. The simple rituals promised success, happiness, love.

Michael thought that most of what Jenny was doing was nonsense. But maybe it was time they got out on their own. Maybe away from her family's influence he could make his wife see how she had to do right.

Michael began to make a subtle distinction that seemed to set his wife off from her family. Her mother and all her aunts, uncles, and cousins called her by her first name. Michael, in typical southern fashion, used her double name, Jenny Lynn. At times he called her simply Lynn, a name no one else used. In this way he gave her a kind of special identity as his wife.

After telling Jenny Lynn in the trailer that they were going to be moving, he walked over to the house to tell Gladys Faye. He had already made arrangements for a friend to use his truck to pull the trailer over to Michael's two acres in the country.

Gladys Faye nearly laughed at him. "You'll do no such thing."

"It's my trailer and my land."

"You're not moving my daughter out there."

Michael raised his voice. "We need to get out."

"Then y'all get out and stay out. I should never have let Jenny marry such trash."

Michael found a two-room house in Elkton to rent. He made Jenny pack up her things to move the next day. Gladys Faye gave the trailer Michael had made payments on for over a year to her son, Lloyd, and his wife.

Much older than Jenny, Lloyd played little part in her life.

He just seemed always to be there to be recipient of any of Gladys Faye's good graces.

About the same time that they moved to a house, Michael was forced to find a new job when he was laid off from the garment factory. He was lucky to get one at a small spinning mill. They told him it might be only temporary. Still, he had managed to establish his own home for his family.

For several months after they moved out on their own, Jenny Lynn seemed to fit herself exactly to Michael's ideas. Her dress and manner were subdued. There was no evidence of makeup or jewelry. She wore simple cotton dresses and kept her hair long. She was respectful to him — a good wife making a proper home for her husband. He had prayed over her so many times. At last, he thought, his prayers were finding answers.

CHAPTER 14

It must have been 102 degrees, with humidity almost to match, when he left work that day. The lint he tried to brush away clung to his sweaty arms and face.

"Jenny Lynn," he called as he walked into the sweltering little house. "What's for supper?" It was a full ten minutes before he heard the screen door slam and turned to see his wife hurry into the kitchen. Even with her face red from the heat and her hurrying, he could see the makeup, the bright red lips. Worse yet, she was wearing shorts.

"Get some clothes on and wash that junk off your face now. And may God forgive your sins."

"What in the hell has God got to do with it being so hot a body can't get a damn breath?"

"Don't cuss, and don't talk back to me." As his anger flared, he began to quote scripture. "Wives submit yourselves unto your own husbands . . ." (Ephesians 5:22).

Selena was caught off guard. Marcie had been hurrying home to fix supper, wearing the makeup and shorts Selena had put on that morning. Completely startled by Michael's being home already, Marcie ran, leaving Selena to deal with him.

Cornered, the only thing Selena could do was to stand up to him. Nina would never have defied him, Flisha would have just ignored him, and Marcie would have been reduced to tears. Selena didn't miss a beat. She matched fury with fury. In measured tones she made her position clear. "I've had it with your damn Holy Roller stupidity and your goody-goody shit," she flung at him. "I don't intend to take any more of it." She turned on her heel and was in the car and gone before he could get beyond open-mouthed staring.

Michael had never seen her behave like this. In the past, when they had argued, she had always given in to him. Even the time she was mad enough to scream and throw a pottery cat at him, she had calmed right down and apologized to him. It happened when she was sick with hepatitis. She claimed a neighbor told her she had seen Michael running around on her. Michael had no way of knowing that it was Hilda who had lashed out at him in fury when she believed him to be unfaithful. Michael just laughed it off and figured Jenny Lynn would forget about it. She must have. She never said another word to him about it.

He figured she would cool down this time, too, and come home in a few hours to say she was sorry. When she didn't show up by the next day, Michael was frantic. He found her at her friend Janice's house.

"Come on home with me now, Lynn."

"I'm not ever coming home to no Holy Roller mess. I'll leave for good first."

"Jenny Lynn, honey, I'm sorry. Y'all can do anything you want to from now on — just don't ever leave me." Michael meant it. He had come so close to losing everything. He took his wife home to the little rented house and went to work. He never spoke more about it. Gradually he just turned away from his church.

Michael and Jenny had a hard time staying settled. He changed jobs to driving trucks hauling asphalt and gravel. Jenny tried working at several different jobs in the mill. None of them suited her.

When it had to be done, Selena took care of working at jobs outside the home. Of all the personalities, she was best able to meet people and to tolerate the physical strain of work. The job in the dime store right after the marriage hadn't been so bad. It was harder in the mill.

In general, working was difficult. It put pressure on the whole system of personalities. Job pressure on Selena was compounded by the push of personalities reluctant to stay dormant and leave control to Selena. Hilda might force her way out and emerge on the job in a fit of temper, or Lisa might come out and leave Selena to cover for her childish behavior. Tensions fairly quickly took their toll, showing up in the form of physical problems with back pain or trouble with her arms and hands. Nervousness and depression were common, too, causing her to have to leave a job after a few days or weeks. She would try a different job in the mill, only to leave it for the same reasons.

They moved to a bigger, if somewhat more run-down house in the country. They painted it themselves, but with water only on the back porch and no heat except a fireplace, living there was rough. Jenny never seemed to like the place after one of their three beagle pups got run over on the road. Michael came home to find his wife sitting in the middle of the road crying and holding the already cold, stiff puppy. Tenderhearted Marcie had found the puppy and could not contain her tears to dispose of the dead animal. Marcie loved animals and children.

After four years of Nina and Michael's marriage, Marcie decided it was time to have children of her own. With his wife pregnant, Michael was eager to accept when Gladys Faye offered them their place again. She had moved down the road from Mamie's house, and Lloyd had moved in with her with his wife and children. The trailer was left empty. When Michael and Jenny moved back into the trailer parked next to the old rock house, Jenny's pregnancy was showing.

Michael was delighted at the prospect of having a baby, but Jenny Lynn seemed to be sick the whole time. Michael called her "Bubbles" and told her how cute she was, paying no attention to her telling him that she hated being sick and fat.

Though Selena would endure the labor that concluded Marcie's pregnancy, Marcie would be mother to the newborn. Marcie intended that any child of hers should never want for a mother's touch and protection from harm.

Michael was ecstatic about his beautiful daughter. Morgan was born on April 28, 1968, a tiny copy of her mother. The delivery was difficult. Jenny was depleted by blood loss and exertion.

Tension around the house increased after they brought Morgan home. Jenny Lynn claimed Gladys Faye was partial to Lloyd's kids, and wouldn't leave Morgan with her. Jenny Lynn didn't get on all that well with Lloyd's wife either, though Michael found her nice enough.

Michael tried to be patient with all of them. Jenny Lynn was moody. Gladys Faye's health was not good. Gladys Faye had had headaches and nosebleeds for a long time. Recently she had had a number of sinking spells. After the episodes of dizziness and weakness, she had trouble remembering things. Michael stayed out of her way and tried to get Jenny Lynn to do the same.

They had enough troubles of their own. During the winter a pipe had burst in the trailer while they were gone for a weekend. They tore up the carpet and dried it out and cleaned up as much of the mess as they could. They couldn't afford to have the pipes fixed. They used the bathroom and did laundry at the house. It wasn't easy with the baby, but they managed.

Nobody expected Gladys Faye to die. The doctor put her in the hospital because she was having headaches and dizzy spells and stomach pains. She didn't seem to be any sicker than she had been many times. But three days after she went in the hospital she had a stroke, a cerebral hemorrhage, and went into a coma. She never regained consciousness. Six days later she died.

Lloyd came over to the trailer to tell them at four o'clock in the morning. The night had been warm. A mist among the trees and by the creek added to a sense that the world was unreal. Michael sat silently and watched Jenny Lynn stare out at the mist, her cries soft in the predawn stillness. When she stopped crying, her eyes were vacant. For days she would not eat, would barely speak.

The trauma of her mother's death triggered reemergence of the alter, Penny, who slipped at once into a near-catatonic depression. Bridgette, who had remained dormant since her grandmother's death, reappeared to deal as best she could with the practical matters of helping to plan and attend the funeral. Selena, Flisha, and Marcie felt immobilized and abandoned as Jenny retreated to her most distant worlds.

Mamie, Jenny's aunt, made most of the funeral arrangements. She took Jenny with her to the funeral home to pick out a casket. Jenny was able only to nod agreement to her aunt's choices. Jenny seemed as a sleepwalker. She came awake only when Bridgette surfaced long enough to quietly insist that the satin pillow for the casket have a trim of yellow roses. Gladys Faye had always liked yellow.

Lloyd's wife had to help Michael get Jenny Lynn dressed for the funeral. Afterward Jenny Lynn was still in such a daze that Michael himself took her to Dr. Bradford. The doctor gave her some medicine, but she still was stunned, silent.

Eleven or twelve days later Michael came home from work to find Jenny Lynn her old self again, as if nothing had happened. Penny and Bridgette had receded, allowing Nina to resume her role as wife for Michael. Jenny's return to her crystal world allowed Selena, Flisha, and Marcie to resume their functions.

Later in the summer Flisha was determined that Jenny's mother have a gravestone. It was the proper thing to do. Flisha wouldn't let it rest until the stone, polished blue granite with roses cut into the sides, was in place. Engraved between the borders of roses was:

Gladys Faye Walters
Oct. 31, 1918
June 17, 1969

Lloyd and his family moved in with Mamie. The trailer was still a mess from the water damage, and Michael couldn't afford to have it moved. They left it where it sat. Michael and Jenny moved to a two-story house about two miles away. It was still in the country, but away from the woods and creek, so you could go in the yard without watching for cottonmouths and copperheads. The house had asbestos siding, a good tin roof, running water, and a decent heater. The house needed repairs, but was the nicest they had had.

CHAPTER 15

Billy Joe wasn't hard to find. The smell of whiskey hit Michael in the face as he stared through the ragged screen door at Billy Joe sprawled on the couch. "Might as well be a nigger," Michael muttered under his breath at the sight of the skin of the half Indian, dark against the gray-white of his sweat-stained undershirt. The slap of the screen door woke him.

"Hey, Mike, y'all catch any fish?"

"Come out here in the front yard." Michael didn't know if Rose or any of the kids were around. As far as he knew, the kids had all left as soon as they got old enough. Billy Joe followed him out unsteadily.

"Y'all been with my wife."

"I ain't done nothin' yain't done — nothin' she didn't ask for."

"She's my wife."

"Don't act like yain't had nobody else's."

The punch caught Billy Joe squarely in his gut. As he went down hard, his head hit the foot-packed earth with a thump, punctuating Michael's feeling of satisfaction. Michael left him in the dirt. "You're too triflin' to grow some grass in the yard," he spit at Billy Joe. "Coulda busted your head."

Michael had been sure he had to kick Billy Joe's butt. He wondered, though, if Jenny Lynn hadn't led him on. It was hot, so she was probably wearing little bitty shorts or cutoffs that showed her butt. She knew how to smile at a man, too, and what to say to turn a man on. Michael couldn't help but blame her as much as Billy Joe for what happened.

Michael drove around for a while. He wasn't ready to go back home yet. He played again in his mind the scene he had heard Jenny Lynn describe.

She was by herself, she said, in the house with Morgan, and baby-sitting Lloyd's two kids. The front door was open, with it being hot, and Billy Joe walked in on her. She didn't say much to him at first. She just said she had to put the kids to bed. She hoped he would take the hint and leave. She set her glass of iced tea down and took all three kids upstairs.

Billy Joe was still there when she came downstairs. She could tell he was high on something, so she tried to joke around with him. When she finished drinking her tea, she realized he had put something in it. She felt weak and dizzy. He was all over her. She couldn't fight him. He raped her on the floor.

This second rape by Billy Joe was as devastating as the first had been when he pulled her from the bathtub when she was nine years old. As before, Selena took the full brunt of the rape, the degradation and the sexual violation, without feeling the pain of the assault.

The Indian, Vera Ann Birchausen, the alter who came in response to the first rape, resurfaced. She was self-possessed, sullen, and chary of all men. She would see to it that Billy Joe would not catch her again off guard.

Michael's attacking Billy Joe did not relieve Vera of her perceived function. She had to avoid Billy Joe's advances. To do so, she was distant from all men, including Michael.

Michael did not contest her distancing behavior. After the time Jenny Lynn walked out on him, Michael pretty much let her do as she pleased as long as she had his supper ready and took care of his baby.

Michael had gotten on at Elks Mills working five and six days a week as a fixer. He felt lucky to have a steady job.

Jenny Lynn hadn't worked since Morgan was born. She took good care of Morgan, now a toddler, what Michael's grandma called a "knee baby." It pleased Michael that Jenny Lynn dressed her like a little doll, and would get right down on the floor and play with her. Sometimes, Michael thought, Jenny Lynn acted like a little kid herself. He did not know that it was Lisa, a personality who had first come to let the child Jenny play, or Lisa's playmate Becky, who came now to play with his daughter.

At night, many times, Michael woke up to find Becky with her thumb in her mouth, just like a baby. It aggravated him as much as seeing Jenny Lynn bite her fingernails. His response had become automatic to both offenses. "Get your hand outta your mouth, Lynn," he said, and pulled her hand away. It seemed he had to do it ten times a day.

She could be aggravating, too, worse than a kid not listening to you. Michael would tell her to fix him a bologna sandwich, and have to yell at her two or three times to bring it. Then she'd bring a cheese sandwich or banana sandwich, and swear up and down that's what he told her he wanted.

Nina struggled to keep Michael satisfied at home. Selena did not share her concern. When Selena realized she was pregnant, she told Michael immediately, making sure he knew that she believed the baby to be Billy Joe's. Michael responded with anger. He had been told that after the problems with Morgan's birth, Jenny Lynn should not have more children. Michael was furious that she would have a baby by that stinking Indian. While she was pregnant he would not touch her.

Selena struggled with the pregnancy. Marcie had chosen to have a child, but this unchosen one would be Selena's. As the pregnancy progressed, Selena got more and more scared of what might happen to the baby. She feared it would be dark like its father. Michael would hate it; maybe she would too. She forced herself to drink a mix of turpentine, and was convinced she had caused it when the unborn child died in her womb.

With the termination of the pregnancy, Michael resumed intimacy with his wife. Her moods, however, remained worrisome. She'd go for a few days just as happy as you could want, then withdraw into silence or cry for no reason. Michael couldn't see that she was upset by losing the baby. She got pregnant again right away. She assured Michael that this time it was his baby she carried. Michael hoped it would be a son.

Michael saw a settling of moods as Flisha pushed to complete her high school education. She had enrolled in courses at a junior college a year before, and enjoyed the intellectual stimulation. She found encouragement for poetry she wrote in a personal journal. She got two poems published in an anthology by answering an advertisement in a magazine. Although she had to pay nearly a hundred dollars for a copy of the book, it was worth it to see her favorite pieces in print. She saved the money over a period of time so Michael wouldn't know. Michael didn't seem to care about school and that she kept her nose in a book half the time, since it kept her happy.

Michael saw that along with her schoolbooks, Jenny Lynn read increasingly about magic and witchcraft. Michael couldn't see why she was so interested in that mess, but he left her alone about it. He let her order some things through the mail — books and candles and jewelry.

Sandy remained a serious student of the occult, and felt fortunate that Michael did not hassle her. She was content to solo, having never really liked the strictures of the organized cult. More serious than Selena, she collected the books, candles, herbs, and amulets to enhance occult powers. She carefully compiled a witching diary, hiding it in the closet so that Michael would not see her record of spells and rituals to conjure demons to serve her.

Michael did find the stack of books in the back of the closet. To him they looked like regular books and mail order catalogs. One book was like a school notebook. It had pages of handwriting and drawings of circles and stars and symbols he didn't recognize. The first page was printed in block letters: GRIMOIRE. The word made no more sense to Michael than did the rest of the writing. He left the books just as he found them.

While Flisha worked on requirements for a high school diploma, Sandy pursued study of the occult. She hoped someday to go to the School of Wicca in New Bern, North Carolina, to study witchcraft. She knew for now it was too far away and too expensive. It was hard enough for her to afford the prescription glasses she needed for reading. None of the other personalities used the glasses, as none had been able, because of allergies, to wear the wool robes used in the cult.

Jenny was eight months pregnant when she finished work for her diploma. Michael had to admit he was glad she was finished with school. His mother gave a family dinner in her honor. Michael was proud. Of all his mama's boys, he had the prettiest and the smartest wife.

In February Noel was born. He looked just like Michael. But the baby wasn't right. He didn't look at you when you talked to him. It was several months before they realized the baby was born deaf. Michael loved him fiercely.

As they had when she was younger, stressful events triggered new alters and the reemergence of existing ones, and Jenny retreated to her most distant worlds. For the most part, the periods of instability after stressful events were relatively short, and the strange behaviors others saw in Jenny could be accounted for by the circumstances. Michael saw his wife as nervous and moody, but did not see her as different from most women.

After Noel was born, the system of personalities became overwhelmed by physical and psychological stresses, as had happened when Jenny was fourteen. Jenny withdrew from her crystal world, and the switching of personalities escalated.

Nina tended to Michael. Marcie tried to keep meals cooked, and to keep the children dressed and fed and entertained. Flisha continued to try to keep up with business matters. She paid the bills, made appointments, saw to it that the children had checkups, and kept records of their health and growth.

Eventually Penny took over with depression, and Jenny lay in bed all day. Michael's grandma or one of Jenny's aunts took care of the children while Michael worked in the mill. Jenny had to go back in the hospital for treatment of a pelvic infection.

Since Michael had known her, Jenny had used drugs off and on when she could get hold of them. She had used bennies, acid, Everclear, illegal booze, whatever she could get. Michael knew about it, but he just ignored it. Now along with acid and alcohol, she was using heroin.

Selena had accepted the heroin offered by a neighbor. She knew the drug would make it easier for her to tolerate problems at home. Selena could take high doses without much effect. Nina, Marcie, and Flisha were all nonusers, but because of frequent switching, they were affected by what Selena took. The drugs and alcohol precipitated bouts of anxiety and depression and caused them to see hideous faces they feared.

Selena required increasing amounts of heroin, and because she lacked the money to pay for her supply, she agreed to make drug deliveries for the neighbor in return for drugs. She hid the drugs in mayonnaise jars under piles of leaves in the yard. She spent two or three hours a day several times a week making deliveries in two counties.

A couple of times Selena was sure the police were on to her. She managed not to panic the first time she noticed a police car following her on a deserted stretch of road. She slowed her car just slightly, hoping the policeman would notice Morgan and Noel on the seat beside her. Apparently he did. As the police car drove past, the policeman threw up his hand in greeting. Selena smiled and returned the gesture.

After that she was more confident she wouldn't be caught. She was the first to smile and wave whenever she saw a police car, whether she had the children with her or not. She realized she was not likely to be stopped. Thanks to Nina, Flisha, and Marcie, she could look like any housewife running errands.

Within months Jenny was again in the hospital, this time for a hysterectomy, made necessary by excessive bleeding. Out of the hospital, she cut her wrists, and was readmitted to treat her fatigue and depression.

After she cut her wrists a second time, Dr. Bradford asked that she be seen by a psychologist from the mental health clinic. Jenny had been seen at the clinic for nearly a year and a half, starting well before Noel was born. Michael had put a stop to her going to the clinic because it did not seem to help her depression or to slow her use of drugs.

The psychologist recommended readmission to the state facility. In the summary he prepared for the hospital, he noted problems of early childhood trauma, drug abuse, and marital conflict. He pointed out that Jenny had not had the chance to work out current conflicts, much less to get over her early experiences. He concluded his observations with: "It is our impression that unless she gains strength and is able to alter her environment, both present and future, she will either succeed in a suicide attempt or regress to a degree necessitating permanent hospitalization."

The situation became so urgent that they took Jenny out of the local hospital one night after midnight. Michael rode with the sheriff on the long drive through the mountains. Not much was said. Jenny dozed quietly in the backseat. Michael didn't know what to say. Except for a few observations about the hot summer weather, the sheriff kept his thoughts as much to himself as Michael did.

Michael was confused, scared, angry. He had had about all he could stand of Jenny's being sick. She had been in the hospital so much already. The hepatitis right after they got married had been followed by seven more times in the hospital, not counting the times Morgan and Noel were born. Michael worried about the bills, about papers to sign he didn't understand, about his children.

Michael sat in the admissions building and signed the papers for Jenny to stay in the huge brick hospital building with the barred windows. The ride home with the sheriff was as silent as the ride there had been.

In spite of the clinic psychologist's ominous prediction, admission to the state hospital had much the same effect it had had when she was younger. Away from the stressful environment, the system of personalities stabilized. Flisha, Marcie, and Selena were able to respond to the expectations of the doctors and staff, while minor personalities retreated.

On this admission at age twenty-one, no one recognized the dissociative nature of her illness as they had at age fourteen. This time in the hospital Jenny Harris was seen as a cooperative patient who recovered quickly from her depression.

Within three weeks Michael sat in the same building across from the doctor. "Jenny Lynn needs to be home taking care of her babies," Michael insisted. Michael had been surprised at the change in Jenny Lynn when he came to see her. She seemed happy. He didn't know what to make of the behavior he saw. Flisha gave him stuffed toys she had made in handcrafts for him to take home to Morgan and Noel. Marcie told him how much she missed the children. But Selena insisted she was not ready to go home. She would happily stay in the mountains. The weather was cool even in July. You could walk in the woods, ride horses, paint.

Michael could hardly believe that Jenny Lynn liked being in the hospital, liked it too much. He had to get her out of there.

The doctor agreed to release her. Her problem had been diagnosed this time as a depressive neurosis. The doctor recommended they seek help from their local doctor or mental health clinic if there was a need.

Michael had managed to get a house back in town to rent, a little mill house not far from downtown. He moved their things while Jenny Lynn was still in the hospital. He knew she would be all right once he got her away from the state hospital and away from the house in the country where she was getting drugs. She would be all right and be a good wife and mother again.

Jenny did not resist. She had managed in the seven years after her first stay in the state hospital to marry, have children, work at several jobs, and acquire a high school diploma. She would manage again. Jenny would stay in her crystal world and watch the surrogates, her system of personalities, live piecemeal her several lives.

Part VI

Cries from Safe Places

Dear Anybody, Everybody, Nobody:
You do not know how much I wish I could share with you what is inside of me. If we knew, could we share it with you, all the sober, awful truth of us, and our lives and deaths? Would knowing us help you to understand? Please let knowing help somebody. Please before I die.

Jenny's Journal

CHAPTER 16

As effortlessly as a snake uncoils, the double circle of black-robed figures unwound to columns flanking a path to the black-draped altar. Sandy walked with proud solemnity at the side of the high priest, not once looking into the faces of lesser members of the cult. She had earned her place and accepted it as right and natural.

On an unseen signal two figures stepped from the ranks to remove the robes of the high priest and his consort initiate, leaving the two to kneel naked before the altar. The ritual moved toward conclusion with the same precision it had begun.

Twenty-one-year-old Sandy had prepared herself for days according to rigorous specifications. She had fasted, then ended the fast with concoctions of herbal potions. She had bathed repeatedly in herbal mixtures. She had burned candles and incense, breathing in their fragrant smoke. As she readied her body, she readied her mind with chants and contemplations.

On the evening of the initiation, Sandy put on the white mask of makeup with special care, enclosing her eyes in circles of black to deny her identity and to symbolize her belonging to Satan. Once at the meeting place, attendants took up the task of preparation. They droned in focusing chants. They cleansed her again with herbal baths and laid out the ceremonial white robe. Before covering Sandy, they anointed her with the most precious of oils, rendered from human flesh.

To Sandy, the oil touching her fresh-scrubbed body felt as familiar to her skin as tears feel to the cheeks of children. Sandy welcomed the warmth of the robe on her soft, smooth skin. She stepped into place beside the high priest, and the brass bell sounded to begin the rite.

Sandy and the high priest moved among the people. Once they reached the altar, the high priest blessed the dagger and the cup, which symbolized the male and female principles. He immersed the objects in the chalice of blood-wine. After he drank first, he put the chalice to Sandy's lips for her to drink the still-warm outpouring of human sacrifice. After she drank, he placed the ring of a high priestess on her hand.

Sandy fondled the smooth silver of the band and the contour of the winged Satan carved on the ring. She thought back to the first time she had stood at the altar to drink blood from the silvery cup. She had replaced five-year-old Jenny when Jenny could not stand the horror of the blood drink. Soon after that Sandy had watched the women who stood in places of honor next to the high priest. She knew then she was to have a special place in the cult. Her training had proceeded in good order for nine years, anticipating her ascension to high priestess. Then suddenly it was all lost. When she was fourteen, after her stay in the state hospital, Gladys Faye stopped taking her to meetings. The training stopped. As far as Sandy knew, her place in the cult could never be regained. She resigned herself to seek the powers of the occult in solitary service.

Sandy's thoughts settled back to the moment when she felt the strength of the high priest's sinewy arms lifting her to the altar. The high priest was muscular, handsome, somewhere in his mid-thirties. He projected an air of knowing how to take what he wanted. He moved Sandy to the edge of the altar, extending her head backward over the end of the stone. Attendants held her arms at her sides. The high priest moved toward her mouth.

The stone altar had not lost its familiar feel to Selena over the seven years since she had lain there. Nor had she forgotten the need to feign pleasure as she struggled to satisfy the man who claimed her, and to arouse the men and women who watched.

The high priest was much aware of the audience. Once brought to full erection, he contrived his sensual play to display himself and make the altar a place of conquest. He stroked Selena's body, roughly pummeled her breasts, then curled his lips away from his teeth to bite at her nipples in a pulling, taunting frenzy.

In a smooth athletic leap he was with her on the altar. He entered her at once, driving, thrusting, making a show of possessing her. Selena moaned and matched his thrusts, making an accompanying show of being mindful of his satisfaction.

The scene of consummation on the altar signaled the conclusion of the formal ritual. No longer voyeurs, the cult members began their own sexual celebration. Taking more wine, more drugs, they reached to one another for stimulation and release.

Restoration to the cult was for Sandy as much out of her control as her removal had been. She simply found herself that day in the clinic waiting room, with a man stroking her long hair and saying, "The master will be so pleased with you." A second well-dressed man nodded his approval. The men seemed to know her, although she didn't recognize them. They talked in near whispers, telling her she must return to them, speaking of powers she had once shown. For several weeks there were telephone calls, the message always directing her to return, giving her the time and place of a gathering.

Sandy's sole purpose was in service to Satan. She had to go back. It was her place to belong, to be pleasing, to have power. It was ironic that she found her way back to the cult through the mental health clinic. As far as she knew, the members just chanced to find her there. She was at once reinstated, and her preparation to be high priestess resumed.

Sandy's return to the cult was the coincidental result of Flisha's attempt to find help for anxiety and despair which returned soon after her release from the state hospital. Flisha followed the doctor's advice to go for help to the mental health clinic.

Marcie came forward to cooperate with the therapists at the clinic. She reiterated the problems that had caused the most recent hospitalization — drug use, fears that Michael was unfaithful, problems with the children. She told them no more than had been told before, that her childhood had been difficult and she had been raped by a relative.

Afraid to disclose too much, Marcie was relieved that the therapists did not probe the past. On the contrary, they focused on her day-to-day life and insisted she look to the future. Flisha was indignant when the therapists chastened her for missing appointments and questioned her desire to get better. She didn't dare admit that she missed appointments because she was not always out at the time of appointments. She was afraid the lost time meant she was crazy. She would not risk telling about it and being locked up in the hospital again.

Selena kept the clinic appointments sometimes. Her behavior seemed paradoxical. She fretted about gaining weight and, in the next breath, bragged about getting high on hundred-proof alcohol. She showed little concern with Michael and the children beyond occasional annoyance. She didn't say so to the doctors, but she would never have married Michael, and those kids were Marcie's concern, not hers. If the therapists found her flippant and reacted to her cavalier attitude, Selena just left Marcie or Flisha to deal with them.

Flisha was placater, peacemaker. She wanted things to go smoothly. She delighted in the children and was happy to be at home with them, although she wished she could show them the world. Morgan was a beautiful little girl, and Noel, after having his hearing restored by surgery, was developing into a happy, robust toddler.

Marcie didn't care that they couldn't afford fancy toys or movies or vacations. She could make do. She could make a holiday of taking the children to the park and a feast of hush puppies and Cokes, or cheese crackers and orange drinks. She played with the children on the swings and the slide and grinned to see their delight in clambering over the smooth rocks of the creek that ran along the border of the park.

Marcie didn't understand the nervousness and depression caused by the internal pressures arising in the system of personalities. While Marcie was happy at home, Selena needed the freedom of an adolescent to get out and have fun. Flisha longed to escape the low-class life of a hick mill town; she loved books and music and fine art. Justin liked a chance to smoke his pipe or to fiddle around with cars. Sandy studied the occult rituals and sneaked off to the meetings. Lisa and Becky wanted their own toys and time to play. All these and others answered to the name Jenny Harris, and all vied for the time and energy of a single body.

Anger and fear, unresolved from years of abuse and kept in abeyance by the system of personalities, took their toll in anxiety and depression and in expressions of self-hate. The concomitant bodily tension led to repeated headaches, back pain, and arm pain. She had examinations, X rays, consultants called in, but few physical causes for her problems could be found.

"Lynn, I'm just tired of it — y'all sick all the time. We'll never pay all the bills. We can't even feed these kids half the time. Why don't y'all just stay away from doctors?" The longer Michael talked, the louder he got.

Flisha avoided confrontation with Michael. Marcie usually cried and trembled at his angry outbursts or felt guilty at his ridicule. He made no secret that he thought most of the time she wasn't really sick.

Selena listened to his latest tirade. "You ought to feel one time how it is to be sick," she flung at him, and walked out of the room. As soon as he left for work, she pulled out the spell books. She'd let him see how it felt.

The spell called for burning personal objects over a special candle and repeating an incantation for a series of nights. Selena cut up a picture and used strands of his hair and scraps from one of his old shirts. For good measure she added an additional spell and buried broken glass in the yard, where he would walk over it every day.

Nina was frightened enough to run when Michael doubled over with pain one evening after work. Selena had to drive him to the hospital. The doctor said it was kidney stones, said they were about the most painful thing a man could have. Nina sat with him during visiting hours the whole two weeks he was in the hospital.

Selena's satisfaction in the secret lesson she taught Michael was cut short by the realization that there were more bills and Michael was missing work. She went back to the spell books.

Selena took some pills for her nerves and had a few drinks of Everclear and tried her hand at using Sandy's black and white makeup before she began to deal with the bill problem. Selena was alone in the house. The children were at Mamie's, and Michael was still in the hospital.

Selena prepared a circle and set up the candles according to directions. She had trouble keeping the directions straight, and after taking a hit of acid, sat on the floor and began to feed the offending bills into the candle flames. She didn't notice the rug start to burn.

Somebody got the fire out before it did much damage. Somebody called a preacher and left the phone off the hook. Selena figured Marcie made the call. Marcie was always keeping contact with preachers.

Reverend Tom Carnes, the preacher from First Holiness Church, and his wife arrived and made no effort to conceal their alarm at finding Jenny Harris sitting dazed in her house with trappings of witchcraft around her. By this time Selena was hallucinating badly. Her descriptions of what she saw and heard further upset the preacher's wife. Still, Brother and Sister Carnes managed to sit with her through the night.

The next evening the preacher and his wife came back to

check on her. In near panic they dragged her out of the house. They told her that as they drove up they could see legions of demons encircling the house and lining the driveway.

They drove her to the safety of their church, where a hurriedly assembled group waited. Pouring oil on her head and down her throat, Brother Carnes began the exorcism. The group clasped hands and began to pray and sway and speak in tongues, pleading for Jenny's deliverance from the threatening demons.

Selena had taken more acid and continued to hallucinate. She made no effort to resist the Christians who had come, unasked by her, to give her help she didn't need. She saw angry faces snarl and spit at the exorcists. She saw sad faces cry for help. She could not tell if they were faces she had seen before or if she imagined them. Maybe there were demons.

"We bind you, Satan, and all your legions in the name of Jesus! Praise Jesus. Beguum, haurris, hoolden."

For Selena the words moved from nonsense to nonsense as the night wore on. It was morning before the preacher and his wife drove her home, apparently satisfied they had wrested her from Satan's grasp.

Sandy was not drawn away from the cult by the church. Rather, she was pushed away by the cult's practices. Sandy's triumph in returning to the cult deteriorated to disappointment when she realized she had not gained power by becoming high priestess, but had, in fact, given over more of her own power.

The high priest treated her more as concubine than consort. He demanded she be available to him whenever he wanted her. Making concessions only for the hours her husband was home, he showed up at her house anytime he pleased, sometimes rewarding her with money or piddling gifts.

In formal matters of the cult, Sandy was pushed to participate more and more in ritual torture and sacrifice. The seven years on her own had made a difference. She had used her own blood in solo rituals, even in summoning demons. She could not turn back to sacrifice. Also, she had become too independent to tolerate the subservient place the cult made for women.

But the cult was not easy to resist. Sandy agreed to doing some cutting under the influence of drugs and after the high priest tortured her, to concentrate her powers, he said. As the months went by, she knew it was inevitable she would be expected to use the knife at the high black mass of Halloween.

She began to have disturbing thoughts. She kept seeing in her mind an infant on the stone altar. As the mind picture blurred in a swirl of blood-red, she heard the plaintive, piercing cries of the infant. The cries echoed in her head. She thought of Morgan and Noel. She stopped going to the meetings.

Jenny and Michael were living for a while with Mamie again. After the incident of the fire, the house had smelled of smoke. Michael was behind on the rent anyway.

Michael was at a buddy's house working on cars, the children were in bed, and Mamie was in the kitchen when the knock came at the door. Selena answered the door, but Sandy came out at the sight of the two men.

"Come back to us — where you belong."

"I won't be back."

One man grabbed her while the other cut a chunk of her hair. Sandy ran, leaving Selena standing at the still-open door clutching her head to hide the missing hair.

Selena went in the bathroom and finished cutting her hair to a medium bob. Mamie was satisfied with her answer that the knock had been people looking for someone else. She never mentioned the haircut. The family was used to Jenny's changing her hair the way she changed her clothes.

Because none of the personalities felt entirely comfortable in anyone else's things, when there was switching, the emergent alter would, as soon as possible, take a bath, shampoo, and change clothes. It was common for Jenny to have four or five baths a day. Some of the personalities were aware of the others' bathing, some were not. None of them cared much, except little Lisa. She was almost twelve, and she hated to have her hair washed so many times.

Jenny's closet was crammed with everything from Nina's plain cottons to Flisha's silk dresses and nice slacks. Selena had some sweaters and jeans and some flashy outfits Marcie was embarrassed to get caught wearing. Justin's robe and smoking jacket were pushed to the back.

There were shampoos and cosmetics enough to stock a drugstore, and included Justin's Prell and Old Spice. Selena used musk fragrances. Marcie liked Avon's Here Is My Heart, and Flisha used Cinnabar or White Shoulders. Nina used whatever shampoo happened to be handy. She never used makeup or perfume.

Bookshelves were filled with items from comics to classics. There was a whole row of Bibles. Barbara, the alter who had helped Jenny deal with her mother's misuse of the Bible, saw to it that each one had a suitable copy. There was a children's Bible for Lisa, a King James Version for Marcie, the New English Bible for Flisha, and the Living Bible for herself.

Closets and drawers overflowed to cardboard boxes. More things were stashed under the bed. No one dared discard anything, though there were items no one seemed to recognize.

The family reacted as little to Jenny's changing moods as they did to her changing clothes. They took little notice when she slipped again into depression.

Selena knew that the feeling she called a deep lostness was brought on by the death ritual that had been done on Sandy. That had to be the reason the men had come and cut her hair. Sandy was down, too, but she would not give in to the feeling. She would not let the cult win.

Driving home that October morning after dropping Michael at work, Selena heard the whistle of the train in the distance. She resolved to stop her deep bad feeling and drove toward the crossing, intent on putting herself in the path of the train. A moment of lost time, and Selena realized the car was parked away from the crossing. Again she pulled onto the tracks. More lost time, and the car was again clear of danger. With the train nearly at the crossing, Selena slammed the car into low gear and headed forward. She lost consciousness as the car crashed into the side of the braking engine. The car was badly damaged. Sandy's glasses lay unbroken on the front seat.

The emergency room doctor described Jenny Harris as uncommunicative, noting that she denied knowing her name and could remember nothing of the accident or events leading up to it. No physical injuries were found. The diagnosis was acute brain syndrome, confusion caused by the stress of the accident, with a schizophrenic basis. She was admitted to the hospital. During the three days there, Marcie made contact with her preacher. She had seen him only a few times, but Bruce Kerr, a Methodist minister, let the doctor know he was Jenny Harris's pastoral counselor. The doctor discharged Jenny to her family's care and referred her to the mental health clinic for immediate treatment.

CHAPTER 17

Sandy was methodical in her preparations—the bath in jasmine, the makeup, a linen robe. She cleared a space in the upstairs bedroom and chalked a circle on the floor. She enclosed the first circle within a second, and in the band between them wrote alternately: ALGA, AGLA.

Above the door and each window she inscribed a pentagram. She walked the perimeter of her area backward as she wrote: MIHOLE, HAVOHEJ, IANODA, completing her protection with the act of widdershins.

Within her circle she placed candles, seven white, two red, a single black. Her candles weren't the best. They weren't made of human fat, but they were good enough, with the color solid all the way through.

Satisfied with the preparations, she lit the candles. In a voice even with confidence and determination, she began: "Come peacefully, visibly, and without delay . . ."

The howling, rushing wind belied the evening calm. The tightly closed windows may as well have been gaping vents. Sandy heard snarls, saw hands reach for her, felt herself snatched from her safe circle.

She came to lying on the floor. She was sore and bruised, not sure how much time had passed. She looked around the room at the signs of struggle, and saw too late that she had failed to put a shielding star over one of the dormer windows. She believed she had failed to control the demons. She had let one come back on her.

Determined to avenge the cult's death ritual, Sandy added the missing pentagram and repeated the ritual, beginning again with a jasmine bath. Once done, she could forget about the people in the cult. She neither needed nor feared them now.

After Jenny and Michael and the children had lived several months again with Mamie, a house to rent in town came available. Michael had worked at the mill for only five years. He was lucky to get a three-bedroom mill house.

The white clapboard house was bigger than some but much like the others that lined the streets of the mill town. It had been modernized. Gas heaters had replaced the coal stoves which once replaced the wood stoves in the kitchen and bedroom and the fireplace in the living room. The ceilings had been lowered to ten feet, and some insulation had been added a few years back. The eighty-year-old house was large. The children could have their own rooms. Michael got them moved in the winter before Morgan started school.

Marcie and Flisha stayed busy fixing up the house and keeping up with the children. Flisha was good with her hands at crafts and needlework. She bought kits for making pillows and wall hangings to make the house attractive. It took extra money to decorate. When she had the chance, Marcie earned what she could selling Avon products.

By the time both children were in school, Selena could hardly stand to stay cooped up in the house. Often as soon as Michael left for work and the children were gone, she changed out of the housedress Nina or Marcie had put on, and headed downtown.

She'd have a Coke at the drugstore and walk around the stores. She'd chat with the clerks and flirt with the men. She didn't have to try hard to get attention. Men were always making passes at her.

It felt good to be wanted. What the hell, she needed the

money. With a little booze or dope she could handle anything they wanted her to do. All her life men had taken what they wanted from her. Now they would pay for it. Yes, it felt good.

Even before she met Ezra, she had acquired a number of regulars. They parked down the street or walked to the house from downtown. If she didn't have anybody coming over, she'd head downtown herself. Something usually developed. She had to be finished by two, two-thirty at the latest. Marcie never failed to be home to have Michael's supper ready.

Ezra was a friendly old man. He ran a little pantry market Selena stopped in sometimes. He kidded around with her, halfway flirted. When she went to pay, he dropped an extra pack of bubble gum or a candy bar in her sack of groceries. One day he waved away her money. "Y'all just come back to see me."

Ezra was one of her regulars for a while before he got her to work for him. Selena needed drugs to be able to handle the men, needed men to be able to buy the drugs. Ezra supplied both and took half of what she made.

With Evan, it was altogether different. Selena met him about a year after she ran into Ezra. Evan was good-looking, blond, and slender. He had a good job in the mill with men working under him.

Selena had heard a lot of men tell her things: they loved her, she was pretty, they couldn't do without her. She knew they didn't mean those things. But when Evan said them, she almost believed him.

Evan was tender with her. With him Selena felt something she had never felt before, a warmth, a time of being safe. He wanted to be with her, not just for sex. Sex meant nothing to Selena. She didn't know what love was. But if she could love or could be loved, she thought, that's what it would be with Evan.

Evan talked of marriage. Selena laughed it off. "I'm too young to get married," she'd say. He followed her lead and made no reference to the husband he knew she had.

"I'll just have to wait, then." Lying with her in the sweet

clover at the park, Evan stroked her hair. She sang softly to him, a low, sweet, country love song.

When he gave her money, he always made a point of saying, "This is just for you, nobody else." Selena supposed he knew about the others, even learned about Ezra, though Evan never brought it up to her.

He called her several times a week. For holidays and birthdays he gave her something extra. He took her shopping to be sure she and the children had a good Christmas. The children knew where the gifts came from, but they knew better than to say anything to their daddy.

If Michael knew something was going on, he didn't dig into it. He had left paying the bills to Jenny since they got married. He gave her the money after he took out his own from his paycheck. If he noticed she had extra money to spend, that there were new clothes and things for the children, he didn't talk about it. He just let it go.

When some of his buddies told him they saw Jenny downtown, he asked her about it when he got home from work. "I've been here all day," Marcie answered in all truthfulness.

"You're lying. Mason saw y'all in town."

"I sold Avon yesterday, but I didn't go nowhere today."

Marcie got upset and began to cry at Michael's refusal to believe her. She held on to her truth. Michael relented. After all, she was always home when he got there.

The next time Michael questioned her whereabouts, Selena responded. She didn't figure it was any of his damn business where she went, and she told him so. Michael never got beyond Marcie's tears or Selena's indignation. He wasn't sure what went on with Jenny Lynn during the day, but he let it go.

Constantly searching for love and constantly doubting love created an emotional roller coaster. One personality or another was always caught in the timeless instant between the climb and the descent. And always there was fear, as much of going up as coming down.

For Selena the ride was impelled by childhood's

absolutes. A word, a flower, a phone call meant Evan loved her and no one else forever. She laughed, joked, felt terrific, and filled a journal with writings about love.

A slight, real or imagined, meant Evan had someone else. He never loved her, never would. Words of sorrow and pain at his betrayal poured into the journal.

A week passed, and Evan hadn't called. She and the children were staying at Mamie's while Michael went hunting. Selena went upstairs by herself and started drinking straight vodka. The depression only deepened. She used the vodka to wash down pills.

The house became full of faces, threatening, accusing, ridiculing. Afraid that demons had surrounded the house the way the preacher said they did that time before the exorcism, Selena climbed out the dormer window onto the roof.

The tiny gravel of the composition shingles scooted under her feet, then dug into her hands as she caught her backward fall to stop her slide. She settled in to stay. The warm grit of the roof was reassuring to her hands. She felt safe, sat silent, didn't look up at the sound of the police siren.

The policemen scared her. She must have done something wrong, but she couldn't let them lock her up. She scooted farther up the roof when they demanded she come down to them.

His voice was soft, reaching, not demanding. "Jenny, could I just talk to you? My name is Tim. I want to help."

The policemen pulled back to give Tim a chance. Tim was pastor at the Community Christian Church, and had had experience working with people on drugs. Patiently he talked her down from the drugs and coaxed her down from the roof.

It took several weeks of counseling with her before she agreed to go to the drug program. Once she agreed to go, Selena stuck with the program, but could not bring her drug use under control.

The drugs, physical complaints, anxiety, and depression all still were problems. Dr. Bradford hospitalized Jenny for a vaginal infection, and called in Dr. Stanger, a psychiatrist with the mental health clinic, to deal with the emotional problems. Jenny was moved from the medical ward to the ward reserved for mentally ill patients.

In interviews with Dr. Stanger, the same information was revealed as had been before, her abusive mother, rape by a relative, using and dealing drugs, the stress of her husband's demands and caring for the children. The childhood commands to keep her mouth shut still held her, though the hold was not as tight as it once had been.

Selena dared not tell of the things that had been done to her in the cult. She did risk telling of her own dabbling in satanism. She admitted casting a spell on Michael that made him sick. Flisha wanted to tell the doctor about Selena, about how she did wild things the others weren't responsible for doing. Afraid to tell of the lost time, Flisha just said she flipped out sometimes and did things she couldn't understand.

As had happened with other therapists, Dr. Stanger did not probe the past. He gave her a series of psychiatric tests and diagnosed a schizophrenic reaction, paranoid type. The truths disclosed by her at great risk were treated by him as delusions.

Selena sat on the edge of the bed, trying to clear her thoughts. She remembered a nurse giving her a shot. She remembered seeing Dr. Stanger's face and hearing his voice as her arms and legs were bound with straps.

Dr. Stanger was an imposing man. He wasn't tall, but his large features among bushy eyebrows and a full beard made him seem so. As much as anything, his heavy European accent gave him authority, the authority readily afforded the unfamiliar.

Most of the time Selena was left to the doctor; the others were afraid of him. Marcie came out some and cried. Lisa and the other children were there only late at night to play. Hilda was intimidated and held back her anger.

The electric shock treatments caused so much confusion. It was a struggle, but Selena managed to change out of the cotton hospital gown into her favorite nylon nightie with all lace at the top. She waited for Dr. Stanger to make his evening rounds.

Selena knew her way around men, knew what Dr. Stanger meant when he touched her leg and said he'd see her later. He talked about the shock treatments and how the injection kept her from feeling the electricity. The way he said "I keep from you the pain" scared her. He controlled how much electricity would be put through her brain. She was relieved when he'd left her room.

"Do just as I say to do."

Half asleep, she knew his accent. The night light cast a circle of light on the floor and a faint glow in the room, not enough to see a face. Selena didn't resist. She began to do just as he instructed.

Dr. Stanger kept her in the hospital for two weeks after the series of six shock treatments was completed. She had time to recover from the phase of most debilitating confusion. After that she went once a week to his office for outpatient treatment and took the drugs he prescribed.

No one could remember much of what went on at the office visits. Flisha made herself walk up the steps in back of the old brick building behind the hospital, but left Selena in the room that was dark with wood paneling and the browns and deep reds of a heavy wool rug. On high shelves around the room there were masks and small statues. Souvenirs of his trips to Africa, Dr. Stanger said. Selena ventured glances at the small figures and faces that surrounded her, so like charms and voodoo dolls she had seen in other dark rooms.

Six months later hospitalization was again required for discomforts and depression. Selena remembered the ward. Not so subdued this time by shock treatments, she spent less time in her room and interacted more with the other patients. She got friendly with Rosanna, at eighteen, just a year older than Selena. (Jenny was twenty-five, not Selena. The personalities first appeared with different ages and aged at different rates. Some were older, some were younger than Jenny.)

"I've got something going with ol' Stanger," Rosanna confided to Selena. "He comes to my room at night after the others are asleep."

Selena's assurance that the doctor really cared about her was gone. She didn't mind that he used her. She cared only that there were others. It meant she was nothing special to him.

CHAPTER 18

Jenny had ever-present, pressing needs to feel better, to be special to someone. In one guise or another she reached in every direction, to doctors, drugs, sex, religion, witchcraft. When they failed her, when she failed to be special, she tried again, a new doctor, a different church, and so on.

Selena, Marcie, Flisha, Sandy, and many of the others were opportunists. They looked to every situation to find what they needed or to help another personality in the situation. They all defined the need and prescribed the help according to their various perspectives.

Evan was a good friend, a sugar daddy really, for six or seven years. Selena had fun and sex with him. Flisha went to concerts or listened to classical records with him. Sandy got involved when she felt Evan wasn't being faithful to Selena.

Evan was pulling back from the relationship, and Sandy suspected there was someone else before Selena did. Sandy didn't want Selena hurt, and decided to deal with Evan in her own way.

It took a little while for Sandy to collect what she needed. Then she waited for the new moon. She recited the ritual words exactly and burned the items in a teacup: Evan's picture, a piece of toenail, some of his hair, and a tuft of cat hair. She collected the ashes carefully, wrapped them in aluminum foil, and put them well back in the freezer. If Evan didn't love Selena, he wouldn't love anyone else either. To Sandy's satisfaction, he settled down and started paying more attention to Selena.

Selena related to all men in much the same way, the way she had learned from Jenny's mother years before. Unaware of her easy, natural manner, Selena seduced men whether she tried or not. Many times she tried.

She tried with Tim Rafer. Tim was the pastor of the Community Christian Church who helped her when she overdosed and climbed out on the roof. He stayed with her, got her help, and spent hours counseling her. He encouraged her to come to Sunday services and Wednesday night prayer meetings. When she was sick, he visited her in the hospital. Tim's wife liked her and began to invite her to stay for supper after Tim's counseling sessions.

Sometimes Marcie went, sometimes Selena. If Tim noticed a difference, he didn't comment at Marcie's modest dresses, or at Selena's miniskirts and tight sweaters. Nor did he pull away when Marcie's demure manner was replaced by Selena's deliberately brushing his shoulder or laying a hand on his leg.

The sexual relationship developed slowly. They found times to meet while Tim's wife was at work. Tim was minister, friend, counselor, lover for five years, until he moved away to answer a call to another church.

It was a time of heartbreak for Selena. She vowed never to trust anyone again. But she still had her sugar daddy, Evan, and soon there was another friend, another lover, another preacher.

There were so many preachers. In the heart of the South's Bible Belt there were so many churches. The ministers served a parish or congregation for a while, then moved on to another church, to be replaced at the first by another minister. Those looking for religious belonging could select from among long-established churches, storefront newcomers, traveling evangelists, and media ministries. At one time or another, in one way or another, Jenny Harris tried them all.

Barbara, the personality who as a child dealt with the black book, kept trying to solve the mysteries of religion. As an adult, she continued to question and, as much as she could, to understand theology. After trying several churches, she settled, to the chagrin of other personalities, on Presbyterian.

Marcie went from one fundamentalist church to another, always trying to muster the faith the brethren said would cause her to be healed. She accepted the encompassing welcome of the Pentecostals, even experienced herself speaking in tongues. She sat on the folding chairs at tent meetings, fanning herself with a funeral home cardboard picture of Jesus the Good Shepherd, hoping that surely this evangelist was the one who could give her God's peace that passeth understanding.

Flisha loved the church for its beauty, the stained glass, the liturgy, and the music. Even in this hick town, at some churches people dressed properly. For several years Flisha sang soprano in the choir at First Baptist, the biggest church in town.

For Sandy, church meant distress, real physical pain. She had been taught she must not look upon the cross or listen to words blaspheming her master. Baptism or communion would mean certain death. She stayed as far from churches as she could. But she found herself there at times when the one who went ran for some reason and left Sandy to respond to the religious symbols.

Countless preachers found themselves unsure, trying to minister to a woman who was humble and pious (Marcie) at one encounter, and indignant, almost hostile (Sandy) at the next. Many of them responded to Selena's seductions; many resisted. Some quickly despaired at dealing with her. A few persisted in their caring, offering what they could of prayer and counseling to lessen her general distress or to help her through a crisis. The preachers could be sure of one thing — when she had a crisis, Jenny Harris would call one of them.

With all the crises, Jenny managed to maintain her home and rear her children. Marcie was good with the children when they were small. She was the room mother, joined the P.T.A., and helped to chaperon the picnics and the swimming parties.

As the children got older, Flisha took a bigger part with them. She instigated school field trips to museums, wangled discount ballet tickets. She made sure the children were exposed to good literature and to fine music.

Morgan and Noel outgrew Lisa. Lisa, who stopped getting older at age twelve, still played with dolls and coloring books. At least, as they got older, Morgan and Noel would still watch cartoons with her.

Selena got along better with the children as they got into their teens. She horsed around with them, and sneaked them beer for parties.

Discipline became an issue. Softhearted Marcie wouldn't set any limits. The children wouldn't listen to Selena when she acted more like a child than they did. When, as Justin put it, the girls lost control of the situation, he came out to put the children in line.

Morgan was quite tractable. Noel tended to be the rowdy. He was hyperactive as a little boy, but settled down a lot as he got older. He didn't help around the house and expected his mother to wait on him and pick up after him, not unlike his father.

Justin dealt with the children with firm authority. When he came down on them, Noel did his share around the house without being told twice.

Keeping the house in any kind of reasonable order was no small feat. There was so much stuff. There were so many opinions of how things should be done. There were so many ideas of what looked good. Marcie had a fit when Selena painted the bedroom black and replaced her pictures of clowns with psychedelic posters.

Everyone had favorites. In the mornings, three or four personalities would have coffee, or tea, or cocoa, and the sink would be filled with dishes. Marcie did the best she could to keep the place tidied. On her occasional appearances, Hilda usually did the dishes, and sometimes took on a big cleaning chore. Hilda, who could feel and express anger, went about the chores with a frenetic energy.

On one of Hilda's appearances, she bustled about cleaning out the refrigerator and defrosting the freezer. She muttered under her breath about how nobody did anything around there. She came across a little foil-wrapped packet. She opened the packet, and, still muttering, threw away the foil and the useless pile of ashes it contained.

A week later Evan told Selena that he was getting married. He and his wife moved out of the area. Depression triggered by Evan's leaving set Selena again to abusing drugs and sent Flisha again to the mental health clinic.

Jenny was known by the clinics in two counties and had been treated at this one for the last three years. The therapist noted in the progress summary that at twenty-seven, Jenny showed "old behavior patterns of calling pastors and faking overdose and periods of depression." Treatment strategy was to continue to hold her responsible for her behavior and to accept no excuses.

Jenny continued sporadic attendance at the clinic, presenting problems of hallucinations and suicidal thoughts along with drug abuse. The six-month progress report noted the difficulty of telling if the hallucinations and suicidal thoughts were serious or "part of her character disorder pattern, in where [sic] manipulation and 'gaming' is the main motivational factor." Therapy aimed at improving her self-concept was added to the treatment strategy.

Jenny began counseling with Ron Davis, a Lutheran pastor, in addition to her attendance at the clinic. The clinic recommended she see just one counselor. She chose to continue with Reverend Davis. The clinic therapist noted the suggestions to Reverend Davis that he "stick mainly with goal oriented therapy and minimize insight therapy." The therapist further suggested that Reverend Davis deal with the "immediate present and future . . . while minimizing past history."

As much as Jenny needed to tell about her childhood, as much as she needed to remember, she could not. The admonitions of her counselors confirmed what her abusers had required, what some inner child had crayoned on a wall over fifteen years before: *I must keep my mouth shut because if I don't I will get in trouble.*

Flisha was elated at the prospect of getting a piano of her own. Mrs. Thomas at Marcie's new church said her son had a piano for sale, and invited Marcie to come to supper and have a look at it. Flisha pushed her to go. With Michael gone fishing, Marcie gathered the children and drove over to the Thomases' house.

Marcie had seen Beau Thomas at church with his mother. He seemed nice enough. He was a small man with bushy brown hair, and a small mustache above thin lips. He lived alone with his mother. His father had died a few years before in a fire.

"Come up here. I want to show y'all something."

Marcie herded the children up the stairs, expecting to see the piano as promised. What she saw frightened her. Selena came in her stead.

Beau led them into a bedroom. The walls were covered with pictures and flags. The flags were American and Russian. The pictures were of nude women and men and children. On the doily of a cluttered dresser a smiling portrait of a pretty young woman was draped with a heart locket over a black veil.

Through the bedroom door Selena saw another door marked at its base with a semicircle of black-red drops of dried blood. A rough wooden sign above the door had SHOP printed in the same black-red. Selena thought she could see guns among piles of papers in the "shop." She was sure she saw guns in the bedroom. She tried to take the children back downstairs.

"How good to bring my little ones to me," Beau said in a voice that sounded strained. His grin showed gaps in tobacco-stained teeth.

The more Selena tried to leave with a casual "We gotta be getting home. Michael should be back soon," the more insistent Beau became. He grabbed Noel roughly by the arm and held him still while he poured oil over the child's head.

"Y'all might take him away from me, but he'll come back."

Morgan made a dash for the stairs from the corner where she had hidden from the crazy-acting man. Beau started after her, but changed his mind and slammed the bedroom door, trapping Noel and Selena with him.

Mrs. Thomas, crying as hard as the terrified Morgan, banged on the door and tried to reason with her son. "Come on, Beau, honey. Let these good people go on home now."

"Get away from me, old woman."

Near midnight Mrs. Thomas called the police and stood silently by as they took Beau off to jail.

As soon as Beau was out on bail, he began making harassing phone calls, threatening to take the boy. Flisha had the telephone number changed to stop the calls. Still she, Marcie, and Selena were frightened. Even Sandy was afraid Beau Thomas would drag her back to the cult. She did not know the man, but he was surely a Satan worshipper.

Flisha went back to the mental health clinic. She was seen by a woman counselor. Selena told about being held hostage, gave details of the whole incident, and hinted at other run-ins with the cult.

Encouraged by the counselor's believing her and helping her plan precautions to protect herself and the children, Marcie began to disclose more. She reiterated that her mother had been hard on her, didn't want her, locked her in closets. She couldn't bring herself to tell of the potato box.

Selena told about beatings, about being sold by her mother for sex, about the rapes. She told of being able to turn herself and her feelings off when she was beaten.

Flisha admitted being in the state hospital when she was fourteen, and told the counselor that there were two years before that of which there was no memory. "Even now," Flisha explained, "there are periods of lost time, sometimes hours, sometimes days." She talked about finding items she couldn't remember buying or starting to go one place and winding up somewhere else. (Much of the time, Flisha, Marcie, and Selena were aware when another personality was in control. At times of increased stress, awareness was lost, resulting in the confusion and distress Flisha described.)

James Mooreland, the social worker who had first seen her in the clinic when she was fourteen, and who had recommended her stay in the state hospital, came back on the case to replace the woman counselor. He made note of Jenny's revelations of abuse and dissociation, while also making note of his opinion that Jenny "is full of endless tales of horror." He noted plans to confirm details by checking medical records, and further noted: "It absolutely strains one's credulity to listen to the stories this girl tells." Jenny was thirty years old.

Mr. Mooreland's stance in treatment was to help Jenny to improve her self-concept and to deal more appropriately with life situations. He planned focusing on positives rather than dwelling on her emotional distress. He saw Jenny regularly for about three months. During the same period, she entered the partial hospitalization program.

Selena continued to tell of much distress, of being upset by a movie's reference to Judgment Day. She told about more periods of memory loss as well as chronic headaches and episodes of numbness in her arms and hands. She fretted about gaining weight and confessed that a year before when she was eating too much she ate rat poison to keep from getting fat. Mr. Mooreland noted: "It is hard to tell how much of distress is real and how much is put on." He suggested a diagnosis of inadequate personality.

The report of the Minnesota Multiphasic Personality Inventory, a standard psychological test given to Jenny, confirmed Mr. Mooreland's opinion that his client was "probably exaggerating her clinical problems to a rather marked degree."

Although Jenny was seen as making some improvement with supportive therapy, she left the clinic for about six months. When she returned again for help, her reports of being pursued by the cult were seen by Mr. Mooreland as "clearly psychotic." He again noted: "I continue to feel that she is disturbed but tends to exaggerate this in keeping with her self-image." He recommended she return to partial hospitalization, and entered a diagnosis of chronic undifferentiated schizophrenia.

Michael had been unhappy before when she spent so much time at partial hospitalization. Neither Flisha nor Marcie would buck him, nor would Selena. Again therapy was interrupted.

Less than a year later Jenny showed up at the clinic again, brought in by a minister friend because she was making suicide threats. This time borderline personality was added to the long list of diagnoses. After two appointments Jenny declined further treatment at the mental health clinic.

During the time she was looking for help from counselors and ministers, she was also seeing medical doctors about an array of physical problems. She had workups for headaches; no physical cause was found. She had a workup for convulsions, seeking explanation for her periods of memory loss; no physical cause was found. She had a myelogram for back pain; no distinct physical cause was found. She had examinations and X rays for a variety of pains; physical causes found were insufficient to account for the extent of her discomfort. She made regular visits to Dr. McCracken, a chiropractor, but found only temporary relief from her pain. She had surgery for pelvic relaxation. Scar tissue was removed from her vagina. There was no record that anyone considered the possibility that the scars were caused by abuse.

Surrogates for Jenny displayed her scars, emotional and physical, again and again. She was hospitalized twenty-seven times in twenty years. The doctors, counselors, and ministers saw her distress, but none saw that she was multiple. Twenty years after the diagnosis of dissociative reaction at age fourteen, she had a string of diagnoses, but none that explained why her life was in pieces or why Jenny stayed trapped in worlds of her own.

In spite of all the problems, the system of personalities was faring relatively well. Flisha and Marcie were happy enough at home. Selena was working in the mill. The mill was on short time, so she could take off with Michael for motorcycle trips.

Selena trusted Michael on the Harley. She loved the feeling of freedom riding behind him. She loved the little parties they got into with their riding buddies.

"The only danger," she giggled to Dr. McCracken, "is to your eyes when you ride behind somebody that chews tobacco." Selena liked the chiropractor. She liked to talk and kid around with him.

Flisha had come to him because of back and leg pain. The tensions of working had forced Selena to apply for sick leave from the mill. The treatments gave the personalities some relief, but the pain kept recurring.

Selena lay on the table enjoying the banter with the doctor. Dr. McCracken kept talking to her while he rummaged in the top drawer of his desk. His voice turned serious. "You don't seem to be getting much better. You have so much tension in your muscles, it puts tremendous pressure on your back. These people may be able to help you." Selena didn't say anything.

"Ah." He found the card he remembered saving two years before when he had received the announcement in the mail that a local psychologist, Dr. Alexander, was offering therapies for pain control and training in relaxation techniques.

Part VII

Telling Secrets

Help me.
I'm still a child.
I'm inside a grown-up body.
Trapped, trapped in a grown-up world.

Trapped in a world of closed time
That everyone has forgotten.
I'm still a child,
Trapped and lost in a grown-up body.

Jenny's Journal

CHAPTER 19

Flisha pulled the card Dr. McCracken had given Selena from her purse and dialed the number on the card. She wasn't sure what this Dr. Alexander was supposed to be able to do, but Flisha was ready to try anything.

It wasn't just the back pain, although the pain was bad enough. Things were falling apart again. Flisha could hardly keep things under control. Selena had gotten out of the job in the mill. She was on sick leave, and was spending her time with friends and with men, drinking and using drugs.

Nobody could think straight. The drugs hardly affected Selena, but they made the others feel terrible. There was so much confusion. Jenny was pulled way back, and no one could sense her at all. Flisha wasn't sure what had caused Jenny to pull so far into her own worlds. There didn't seem to be one specific thing. There were the usual problems with Michael and the children. With Selena not working, the bills were piling up faster than usual. Michael was coming down hard on her about it.

Nobody was getting sleep. Marcie would go to bed early, but within a few minutes Selena would be up, awakened by a bad dream. Back to bed, Lisa would get up to play, then be too frightened to go back to sleep. If Flisha got control and went to bed, as soon as she fell asleep someone else took over. Everybody had bad dreams.

Selena seemed bent on being hurtful. She left some sexy pictures where Marcie would find them. Marcie got upset and ashamed and worried that the children might see the pictures.

Marcie was torn up enough already by the way Mama and Papa Payne were acting. Papa Payne was the preacher at her new church. He and his wife insisted that Marcie come to church and prayer meetings, acting as if she were their daughter. Marcie went, although their talk of demons and exorcism frightened her. Maybe the Paynes were right. Marcie told them about the faces and voices troubling her. The Paynes said they wanted to help, but they questioned her faith, and that hurt.

There was trouble, jealousy, between Flisha and Selena over David Alman, the minister whom they had been seeing for counseling for about a year. He seemed to be honestly caring. Flisha appreciated his intelligence and his smooth manner. She believed she loved him. Selena was puzzled by his not responding to her seduction. He talked about how he cared for her, but insisted that their relationship have limits. Selena hoped to stretch those limits. She saw in David her first chance for real love since losing her sugar daddy, Evan.

The results of the pressures, external and internal, were anxiety, restlessness, and hallucinations, emphasized by the ingestion of alcohol and drugs. The frequent switching of personalities, characteristic of times of stress, created more confusion and despair, and led to deepening depression. In the switching, the personalities lost touch with Jenny and with one another, leaving each alone in the despair.

Michael and the children weren't much help. Michael had no more patience with her emotional problems than with her physical ones. He stayed away from the house most of the time. He worked a lot of overtime. After work and a hurried supper, he was off to his friend Mason's garage to work on cars. At home he flopped exhausted on the sofa to watch television until time for bed. When he had time off, he went hunting or fishing with his friends.

He did not respond much to Jenny's depression or to her using drugs. He didn't want things to get out of hand, but he had not seen her helped by doctors or counselors, and he didn't want her wasting time and money on any of them. He couldn't keep up with the bills now. As long as she didn't go overboard with the drugs, he wasn't too concerned. He was accustomed to her moodiness.

The children were more affected than Michael by Jenny's depression, Morgan more than Noel. Morgan was busy with high school and a job, but she helped around the house and made sure her mother had supper ready so her daddy wouldn't get upset. She bought her mother gifts and talked her into shopping excursions at the mall.

Noel was busy too. It was his first year in junior high school, and he had practice every day for football. He didn't like to see his mother sad and crying. He joked around with her when he was home, being more patient than his father with his mother's moods. But as his father did, Noel just waited for the moods to change.

Through her personalities Jenny met the family's expectations. For them she was the average housewife and mother. Only when the anxiety and depression were severe enough to pervade the whole system of personalities did the family become aware of the difficulty.

Flisha dressed carefully in cream-colored slacks and a sweater of mingled pastels. She smoothed hair she saw as auburn, and which she wished were longer, into a soft, pretty style. She was relieved that she had gotten out in time to keep the appointment. She put on her favorite jewelry, including her baby ring, and drove to the office. Her relief increased at the warmth with which Dr. Alexander greeted her. "Come in. I'm glad you've come. I'm Rachel."

Rachel Alexander looked relaxed. Her brown hair, just beginning to be flecked with gray, was cut short in an easy-to-care-for curly style above a pretty face. She wore little makeup except for lipstick, and was dressed in a tailored skirt and sweater. She was a small woman, without pretense in dress or manner. Her speech was crisp for a southerner. At first Flisha couldn't think of a word to describe her. Honest, uncomplicated, natural — that was it, natural.

Flisha talked with Rachel for some time. She told the psychologist about going to college to get her high school credits, and about writing poems. She would have told more, but Flisha could not maintain control in the interview. Selena pushed out to add her perspective about childhood things, the bad things. Marcie came out when Rachel asked about her present family. Marcie had to talk about the children, and about how she felt she missed her own childhood. Sandy talked about the witchcraft and gave some information about things that happened in the cult.

The personalities used their expert skills of deception, honed by years of practice, to conceal their separate identities. Each responded unerringly to the name Jenny, and each made the transition to a new topic smoothly enough to give the impression of continuity.

The appearance in the interview of the several personalities was prompted by both internal and external cues. Flisha would have maintained control, but Marcie had to respond to questions about the children. Selena responded to her own need to tell her story. Once Selena made reference to involvement in the cult, Sandy moved forward to address the issues.

The result was a story told in a calm, matter-of-fact manner, apparently by a single individual. With little prompting, this "individual" moved from the reason she had come — to deal with her back problems, which started eight or ten years earlier when she pulled her car in front of a train — to a discussion of her husband and children, and finally to a history of abuse, cult involvement, and mental illness. She spoke dispassionately, as if the events had happened very long before or to someone else.

Only after the others had their say was Flisha able to regain control. The transitions from personality to personality were accomplished easily because Flisha, Selena, and Marcie were co-conscious, that is, each could choose to be aware of the others' thoughts and actions. Each had the ability to tune out the others and not be aware of the one in control at a given time. But in the calm atmosphere of the psychologist's office, awareness was maintained.

The relationship with Sandy was somewhat different. Selena could know with co-consciousness of Sandy's behavior, but chose most of the time to ignore it. Marcie and Flisha knew of Sandy's existence, but were not co-conscious with her. However, both of them could tap Sandy's memories for information after an event. For now Flisha knew Sandy had intruded into the interview because she had put on her glasses. None of the other personalities used glasses. Flisha did not have time to review the event through memories. She knew it was safe to assume that Sandy had spoken of cult matters. Flisha removed the glasses and turned her full attention to Dr. Alexander.

Flisha was pleased to see that Dr. Alexander, Rachel, was just as accepting at the end of the interview as she was at the beginning. Rachel gave no advice, made no judgments, just offered an invitation to return.

After the interview Rachel had time to think about the young woman who had sat across from her. Rachel had no way of knowing she had seen a person with multiple personality disorder. For the better part of an hour, the woman had related details of her life. The details were startling, not the kind of information usually disclosed in an intake interview, but rather more often discovered in prolonged therapeutic interactions. Rachel had jotted down brief notes without letting the writing interrupt the attention she focused on her client.

For Rachel, Jenny Harris was an enigma, not seeming to fit into the ugly picture she had drawn of her life. Jenny was pretty. Her softly curling red-blond hair framed features enhanced by makeup expertly applied. Her hands were small and well manicured. Of the several rings she wore, Rachel noticed especially a dainty gold baby ring on her little finger. Her speech, proper and controlled, matched her manner of dress, although at times her soft drawl slipped into the colloquialisms of a southern mill town.

Rachel was struck by how young Jenny appeared to be. She surely didn't look old enough to have lived through all she claimed to have happened. She could easily pass for twenty, maybe less, although from the birthdate she gave, she would be thirty-four years old in less than two weeks. While she looked young, sadness and distrust in her eyes confessed to longstanding psychic pain, which Rachel thought she could do little to ease except to be there for her if Jenny chose to deal with it.

Rachel was more optimistic about helping with her physical pain. Jenny had described an ability to dissociate when she said that she could "go into" pictures and that she had gone into her own worlds when she was little. Her exceptional imagination and ability to visualize could, Rachel reasoned, be used to help Jenny separate herself from her pain.

Rachel had reached for something positive on which to base the next appointment. In an otherwise bleak interview, Jenny had seemed animated and spoke with pride of having had some poems published. Rachel suggested she bring her poems and any other writings she chose to the next session. Rachel also got her agreement that she would be comfortable working with a male therapist. Rachel was eager to share her impressions with Karl, her husband and co-worker, and to plan with him how to help Jenny Harris with pain relief.

The practice Rachel had begun seven years before, when she completed work on her doctorate, was a varied one. Psychological testing and work with schoolchildren occupied much of Rachel's time. After Karl joined her in the practice, they were able to offer more counseling as well as hypnotherapy. Karl began working in the office as he was finishing up a master's degree in counseling, fulfilling a desire to work more directly with people, after years of a successful business career.

Their working relationship reflected the open communication and mutual respect developed in twenty-two years of
marriage. They had been high school sweethearts, had
married while in college, and were proud of their two
children, now in college.

At this point in their lives both Rachel and Karl focused
much attention on their work. Their working styles were
quite different. Rachel was more pragmatic and logical;
Karl, more intuitive, more openly sensitive. It was Rachel's
practical nature that prompted her to suggest that Jenny
Harris see Karl for help with her back pain. Karl simply had
more time right now.

Karl met Jenny by telephone before she came for her first
appointment with him. Selena found the telephone number
on the appointment card. She called the office saying that
she was coming down from drugs and that she wanted to
die. Using Jenny's name, Selena gave a rambling account of
problems with bills and the house and children, and her
feelings of confusion and despair. Karl offered reassurance
and urged her to just get through the day until her appointment the following day. Selena indicated she had not taken
an overdose of drugs. She said that her husband and
children were at home with her. She said she would keep her
appointment.

Even with as much experience as he had had working on
suicide prevention networks, Karl still felt the sense of
helplessness, sadness, and anger such calls aroused. There
was no way to be sure he had read the situation correctly. He
hoped Jenny Harris would be all right.

The co-consciousness of personalities, possible during the
meeting with Rachel, was abandoned in the stressful environment at home. Flisha was unaware of Selena's phone
call. When she went for the second appointment, she was
surprised to find the same warmth in Karl she had found in
Rachel. He seemed a man comfortable with himself, not
smug or self-satisfied. Comfortable was the word. He was
casually but neatly dressed in jeans and a knit shirt. A

beard, gray mingled with brown, met graying temples and underscored hazel eyes. The tint of his glasses complimented his eyes and did not obscure their responsiveness. There was a slight hesitation in his speech, not the result of his being unsure, but the remnant of a childhood speech impediment almost completely overcome. He was not strikingly handsome, but he was a good-looking man.

Flisha was surprised that Karl seemed to believe them, all of them, and accept them, as had Rachel. As they had in the interview with Rachel, Selena, Marcie, and Sandy surfaced. Karl made no distinctions among them. Even Selena's blurting out about working the streets brought no words or looks of disapproval.

To Karl, Jenny seemed in remarkably better spirits than she had on the phone. She brought a stack of papers and some notebooks, her poems and diaries, she said. Her distress became apparent when she reiterated much of what she had told Rachel.

Karl experienced the same kind of puzzled response as did Rachel. He saw that Jenny was undeniably pretty. An unblemished complexion and soft, shiny hair gave her face a childlike innocence. Whether by the mystery she presented or the hurt in her eyes she could not conceal, Karl felt himself drawn to this client. He responded to her immediate expression of confusion and despair, and deferred dealing with her back pain for the time being, offering the support and reassurance of his and Rachel's concern for her. He asked Jenny to leave the writings with him until her next appointment.

Karl talked again briefly with Rachel about her impressions of Jenny Harris, then reviewed the intake notes to get a better sense of the woman who had just left his office. The encounter had been unsettling. He knew there was more of concern than seeking relief from back pain, much more.

The intake notes, in sketchy phrases, covered a great deal. Karl sorted through them and found information about:

Her problems with pain
— Pulled in front of train 8 or 10 years ago
— Rehab. pain clinic over a year ago
— TENS unit (Transcutaneous Electrical Nerve Stimulator, a device to control pain)
— Pain 5th lumbar goes down left leg
— Quite a bit of headaches
— Muscles in neck like knots

Her current family situation
— Married since 15 to same man
— Kids 16 and 12
— Son birth defects, lot of surgery, hyperactive
— Worked in mill last two years
— Problem to keep bills going
— Wants to go back to work
— Can't handle work
— Preacher is David Alman
— Uses drugs to get up
— Can come off drugs when I want to

Her childhood
— No father
— Lived with grandmother till 2
— Hated school
— Mother never touched me
— Locked in cellar
— Potato box — locked up
— Mother and boyfriend did something bad, doctors thought would never have children
— Had some blackouts when little
— Mother sold me out in sex when little
— Cousin put me on drugs at 9
— Cousin raped me at 9 and 21
— Had cousin's baby at 21, carried dead three months

Her accomplishments
— High school diploma
— Published poems
— Taught arts and crafts at senior citizens' center

Her mental illnesses
— In state hospital age 12 for mental breakdown
  [was actually at age 14] and age 21 for mental
  breakdown and drugs
— Saw Dr. Stanger 5 years, schizophrenia
— Dr. Stanger did ECT
— Has been on Thorazine

A background in the occult
— Mother in occult, raised in that
— Exorcism at local church, poured oil down throat
— Called up several demons on Friday night before
  took acid
— Cult sacrifices people, bring from out of state
— Saw them split man from here to here
— Witches and warlocks shoot their drugs and rape
  me
— Not involved now in occult

Her distress
— Don't remember from 12 to 14
— Something back there making me miss growing up
— A child in a grown-up body
— I talk to flowers, they talk back
— Hear voices, soothing
— See things other people don't see
— I stay confused, can't control feelings
— I don't fit in no matter how hard I try
— I wish someone would hold me

The notes were puzzling. Did they describe all actual
events? Was some of the material delusional? Clearly Jenny

Harris was in distress. And clearly she wanted to be heard and believed.

As soon as they could, Karl and Rachel looked over the writings Jenny had brought to them. There were a number of poems and many diary entries in prose. Many were typed, some were handwritten, dating as far back as five years. The writings were about love, nature, religion, death, love lost, pain, confusion. There were clear plaintive pleas for help. A typed entry of 1978 asked:

> Isn't there someone who will hold me and touch me? Someone who is not afraid of me, who will make me feel human? Someone who will make me feel as if I am in this world and not somewhere else?

As disturbing as the content of the writings were the marked variations in handwriting, from printing to careful cursive to messy scrawls. The most telling of the writings were in a small spiral notebook dated just one month before. Following a diary entry in a clear and careful hand about seeing her son's teacher and visiting her mother-in-law in the hospital was an entry in tight, pinched script:

> *It is so easy for me to remember when she can't. I know everything. Bad, bad girl. We won't let her be. I'll write some more because she can't. She won't ever know us. But we know her.*

An entry of a week later, again in the careful hand, included:

> *There is something driving me deep inside. I can feel it. There is something horrible inside of me.*

This was followed, in still different handwriting, by:

> *I'm not horrible, she is.*

The carefully entered date of three days later was followed by what appeared to be a child's awkward printing:

I can't write well but I don't like her making me sick.

Included among writings about confusion and depression was the question: *Who am I anyway?* And entwined with feelings about seeing a vision with no eyes to see was the rest of the question: *Who are they?*

CHAPTER 20

Rachel had no mind-set to suspect multiple personality in any client. Her formal schooling on the subject had consisted of her Abnormal Psychology 401 professor's making reference to the scant paragraph in the text, saying, "That's hogwash, Hollywood stuff. You'll never see it."

Karl had no mind-set not to suspect multiple personality. The subject hadn't been covered in any of his classes. He asked Jenny's permission to share her writings with his colleagues. On Friday he took Jenny's diaries to one of his major professors. After studying the diaries and asking about a history of abuse, the professor validated Karl's hunch. The client could well be multiple.

Karl spoke to several professors who had clinical practices. All declined to accept Jenny as a client. He checked with local colleagues and contacts in different parts of the state, asking if they knew of anyone who treated multiple personality disorder. No one did.

Although his colleagues were polite, their refusals carried a hint of disapproval, or maybe it was disbelief. Not one asked for information beyond what Karl first offered. Karl explained only that he had initial contact with a thirty-four-year-old female client who quite possibly suffered from multiple personality disorder. He mentioned that she had no means for payment beyond some limited insurance coverage.

Karl could not be sure how much the refusals were based on the probable diagnosis and how much on the inability to pay. In either case, the responses were frustrating and isolating. His colleagues offered no alternatives for care for his client nor any suggestion of consultative support for him. He turned to his mentor in the counseling program. "What do I do if I can't refer her for treatment?"

"Treat her yourself," his mentor responded.

Karl had no illusions of being qualified to treat such a client. His diagnosis had been based more on intuition than on knowledge. As a student, his experience was limited, and Rachel had not encountered this sort of complex client in her practice.

Jenny Harris presented an interesting challenge and expressed a desperate need for help. The Alexanders could offer her their concern, their time, and a willingness to learn. Perhaps these would be enough until they could find someone qualified and willing to treat her.

Already Jenny was making frequent phone calls to Karl, several a day. Karl was sure he detected changes in voice tone and quality during the somewhat lengthy conversations. In one such conversation Karl was listening to a childlike voice saying she had been sitting outside in the rain. Gently Karl asked, "Who am I talking to?"

"Are you sure you want to know?"

"Yes, I'm sure."

"My name is Lisa."

"Are there others with you?"

Lisa admitted there were others, but wouldn't name them. Karl asked to speak with one of the others. After a brief pause an adult voice said, "Hello."

"Have you been sitting outside in the rain?"

Again a pause, then she answered, "I must have, because I'm all wet."

"Who is this?"

"Jenny," she answered with surprise that Karl didn't know registering in her voice.

During the weekend Karl and Rachel went over the diaries again. Unable to access the professional literature before Monday, they both reread *Sybil*. It had been ten years since either of them had read the best-selling book, which described the eleven-year treatment of a woman with sixteen personalities.

Karl talked again to Lisa on the phone. Asked to describe Jenny, Lisa said, "She's a nobody, just somebody we have to stay with." Lisa seemed to be afraid of someone and wouldn't give that someone's name. She just told Karl that there were two others there with her, and one of them did bad things.

Karl soon met the "bad one" on the phone. This time Selena used her own name. She made no bones about herself and told him a few things about Flisha, Lisa, and Jenny as well. Selena said she was seventeen and worked the streets to help pay bills. "Everybody wants to screw me up," she said, "but they can't run over me."

Selena described Lisa as a little bitty twelve-year-old girl, a bore. She called Flisha a modern-day bitch, but described her as a classy person. About Jenny she said, "I don't think she knows about us. She can't work things out."

Karl asked if Selena would come to the office for the next day's appointment. "No," she said. "I don't need you! Only crazy people see people like you."

The Jenny Harris who showed up for the appointment was dressed in a miniskirt and a tight sweater, which contrasted with her conservative appearance of the week before. She seemed cocky somehow, but chewed nervously on bubble gum. Karl chatted with her for a time, then asked, "What is your name?"

"Selena," she said with a look of relief.

"How old are you?"

"Seventeen."

"Have you ever heard of multiple personality?"

Karl had chosen to share his suspicions at the earliest opportunity. His candor was rewarded with Selena's immediate, albeit unintentional validation. She readily admitted that she experienced having periods of lost time, finding herself places without knowing how she got there, being accused of actions she did not commit, being called by different names, having items such as clothing come into or be lost from her possession without her knowledge. Selena did not know that all these phenomena are common to persons with multiple personality disorder.

The variable nature of co-consciousness meant that Selena had intermittent awareness of some personalities, such as Flisha and Marcie, and no awareness of some other personalities. She did not understand the phenomenon of sometimes knowing what another was doing and sometimes not. She did not realize that those she knew about were alter personalities. She saw them as separate individuals, perhaps related to her in some way. She knew only snatches of their existence, and knew her own existence to be discontinuous and confusing.

Much as a traveler in a strange country who chances upon one who speaks her language, Selena responded to Karl's understanding. She nodded agreement as he accurately described occurrences commonplace to her but bizarre by most standards. She admitted knowing Flisha and Lisa and Jenny as separate individuals. But in no way would she give credence to his suggestion that each of them was part of the same person, a person who in spite of these parts was a single individual, and who because of these parts was a very special one.

Karl talked about two factors he believed necessary to the formation of multiple personality: being born with the ability to split or dissociate, and being exposed to early traumas or severe abuse. (These factors are affirmed by Braun, 1986.) Considerable abuse had been disclosed at the first interview with Rachel and again in the session with Karl. From what he had seen and heard so far, he suspected that Jenny, with a sensitive and creative mind, had used an ability to dissociate.

Selena was willing to listen to Karl talk about the formation of personalities in abstract terms. She conceded that

Jenny was sensitive and creative. She was even willing to consider that "they" might be multiple, but would not see herself as any part of it.

When Karl went on to say that creating the personalities could be seen as a form of trance or self-hypnosis, Selena became indignant, closed her eyes, and was gone. Karl was not sure at all how much Selena had understood or accepted, but it was a start. (The term autohypnosis is used by some as more descriptive of the unconscious nature of the phenomenon.)

Selena was replaced by Lisa, who acted shy and frightened. Despite the fact she inhabited a thirty-four-year-old body, Lisa was clearly and openly a child. Her face seemed softer. Her movements showed the subtle clumsiness of a youngster not quite at ease.

Rachel, who had remained silent while Karl spoke with Selena, began relating to Lisa as she would to any child, speaking in a quiet tone and staying seated to be at the child's level. Rachel asked a few questions about Lisa's purpose and place with Jenny. Her responses were the short and direct ones of a child. "I just stay with her. I like to play." Lisa said she was twelve, but seemed younger as she fidgeted in her chair.

In her work with schoolchildren, Rachel often helped them to express themselves through art or play. She offered Lisa drawing pens and Play-Doh. Lisa eagerly reached for the synthetic clay, chose blue from among the selection of colors, and quickly fashioned a little man. When asked to tell about her creation, she would only say it was a little man she saw sometimes.

Lisa receded, and Selena appeared again to talk briefly about Flisha. Concomitant body changes made Selena appear the flippant, flouncing teenager. The differences in the personalities were becoming obvious, as if they were allowing themselves to be seen clearly.

Selena said Flisha was beautiful, but was always buying expensive clothes and jewelry and expecting Selena to help pay for them. She said that Flisha was strong and protected Jenny, but that Jenny had become very confused around age twelve. "Everything fell apart then. It was a hard time for everyone."

Karl asked to speak with Jenny. When Jenny came out in the session, she was embarrassed to have been playing with Play-Doh, especially blue Play-Doh. Blue, she said, was a sad color, and she wondered why she had picked it. She appeared older. The expression in her eyes was quieter, and her body movements were more settled. Reticence replaced Selena's seductive posturing. She seemed upset with the flashy clothing and with having on too much makeup. She closed her eyes and was gone.

Selena came back to warn the therapists that Jenny couldn't handle knowing about "them." Jenny would hurt herself if she knew.

CHAPTER 21

The clangor of the telephone pulled Karl from his contemplation. The voice on the phone was that of a woman, mature, polite, and insistent. She wanted to discuss the session he had had with "them" this morning. Karl had hardly had time to put his thoughts together after his and Rachel's early morning encounter with Selena, Lisa, and Jenny. The caller identified herself as Flisha, saying, "I don't come out much. Most of the time I'm trying to hold the others together and taking care of Jenny."

"What do you mean?"

"Well, I have the most trouble with Selena." She told about letting Selena take over the bedroom a few years back. "What a mess — black lights and awful colors. I had to just take it back from her and get some decent pictures and candles."

"How do you take care of Jenny?"

"Like when she tried to kill herself by cutting her wrists, I stopped her after the first light cut, and then made up a story to tell people about what happened." She went on to say that she had come when Jenny was very small, she thought about two years old. She was a good little girl, so her mother did not hurt her so much. She said that Jenny might have some concept now of what was going on, but no real understanding of the situation.

When Karl spoke about multiple personality disorder, Flisha grasped the idea without showing the defensiveness he had seen in Selena. Flisha was willing to accept her own part in being multiple. Not that she believed completely what Karl was suggesting, but at least she was willing to consider the possibilities. Flisha cautioned Karl that Jenny could not handle being told about the other personalities. "What Jenny really needs is someone to like her. Nobody does because she acts so weird."

Karl ventured that perhaps Jenny seemed weird because of what the other personalities were doing. When Flisha agreed that could be so, Karl hoped he had found a strong ally in Flisha. To be accurate, she had found him. At any rate, he was rapidly realizing he was going to need all the help he could get for Jenny Harris.

Flisha began to fill him in about Selena. She was ashamed of what Selena did with men, ruining Jenny's name all over town. She was aggravated, too, with the hurtful things Selena did, like eating onions and junk food. If Flisha or one of the others came out after Selena did that, the alter who emerged would be sick from allergies or worried about gaining weight, although Selena would be unaffected. (Differences in physiologic responses among alter personalities have been recorded by Putnam, 1984.)

As disgusted as Flisha was with Selena, she was touched by Selena's concern that Jenny could not deal with knowing about the personalities. Flisha echoed Selena's fear that things would fall apart again as they had at age twelve, "when no one could hold things together."

A dog barked in the background, and Flisha's strong voice was replaced by a tentative one. "Hello."

"Who is this?"

"It's Jenny. Who are you?"

Jenny excused herself from the phone to keep an appointment, leaving Karl again with his thoughts. Karl was surprised at the apparent eagerness of the personalities to reveal themselves. He resolved not to discourage the telephone calls. They seemed to be a way for the personalities to feel safe in their disclosure.

Within a few hours Jenny called back, upset that Mama and Papa Payne, the preacher and his wife from her church, had fussed at her for going to see the Alexanders. The Paynes told her she didn't need to be seeing doctors of any kind. If she had enough faith, the people of God could heal her. Jenny told Karl she had heard that said and seen it fail too many times. She didn't want to deal with the Paynes, but she didn't want to hurt their feelings either. "I'm just a bad person," she told Karl, "always hurting everybody."

Karl tried to reassure Jenny that he and Rachel found her to be a good person, but a harsh voice interrupted with "No, she's not. No, she's not." Selena had come out.

"Shit," Selena muttered. She asked Karl to hold on. The soft music that was playing in the background switched to hard rock. Karl had to strain to hear above the music as Selena talked about Flisha. She said Flisha had been to college and could read well, not like Selena, who had only gotten through the fifth grade. Flisha dressed well, drank spiced tea, and did needlepoint. At times Karl could not tell, without seeing Selena's face, if she was expressing contempt or grudging admiration for Flisha.

There was a pause, and Flisha spoke to him. She excused herself, and the background music changed to soft classical. Flisha was sympathetic with Jenny about the Paynes, and criticized Selena as someone who came down on Christian ideals.

As if on cue, the music blared hard rock, and Selena came back on the line. After she talked a bit, Jenny returned, confused that so much time had passed, eager to end the conversation.

Karl had barely hung up the phone when Lisa called, sounding frightened. She was afraid that Flisha and Selena were going to be mean to her because she had been first to tell Karl about them. She described Flisha as strict and Selena as vengeful. Karl tried to reassure Lisa by explaining that she was, as were Flisha and Selena, a part of Jenny, that to hurt her would hurt Jenny and themselves. As Karl listened to himself talk, he thought that what he was saying sounded crazy. But the words apparently made sense to Lisa. She seemed pleased to have a chance to talk and to be accepted as herself, even if she was a part of Jenny.

A voice Karl hadn't heard before interrupted to say that Jenny had cut her arm. The voice sounded mature, and reported the injury as something that happened often, finally describing the cut as just a scratch. Not identifying itself, the voice said another personality named Kathy would soon make herself known. Then the telephone connection was broken.

Karl discussed the conversations with Rachel. It was already quite a week, and it was only Monday. They would see Jenny together the next day and ask her permission to tape-record the session.

Flisha appeared for the session and agreed to the recording. Karl and Rachel were surprised at the candor and compassion with which she talked about what caused the problems for Jenny. Flisha spoke of abuse by the mother, of Jenny's being tied up and beaten, of her being left alone at night. "The worst," Flisha said, "was being put in the potato box. There could be spiders or rats. It was dark and cold, and you never knew how long it would be."

Karl did not press for details, but let Flisha talk freely. Flisha said Jenny had been raped by a cousin when she was nine. A Cherokee Indian, mean and rough, he had pulled her out of the bathtub and threatened to kill her or cut out her tongue. "After that he messed with me when I played the piano, but I could just ignore him. Jenny couldn't handle it. Mother sold her out to men even before the rape. For a long time nobody knew what happened."

Flisha's compassionate tone edged toward anger when she spoke of Selena. "She uses sex to get what she wants from men. She's just out for herself and doesn't care how she hurts Jenny when she acts like a tramp. I can't stand it when she uses drugs or gets drunk with her friends. Still, I have to admit" — compassion returned, and Flisha smiled — "she can find fun in anything."

Flisha admitted she saw men, too, but for conversation and companionship, not for money. She worried that Jenny had no friends at all. "Jenny doesn't know about us. We used to talk a long time ago. Now we get angry and push in and out. She hides everything too. There's no one to care about her." Flisha said that over the years she had taken Jenny to doctors for help. But the therapists would see her a few times, or for a few months, and that was all. No one would stick with her.

Karl voiced the reassurance for both of them. "Rachel and I care about Jenny and all of you as part of Jenny. We think we know what is happening. We'll be around for a long time and will go as slowly as needed to help, for as long as Jenny wants our help."

Flisha looked down, hardly more than a blink, and Jenny appeared. "How did I get here?" She seemed, as she had before, shy and confused, although not so fragile as Flisha and Selena portrayed her.

Rachel and Karl, reacting to the Jenny they believed to be the original personality, explained that another personality, Flisha, had come for the appointment, while Jenny experienced amnesia. Rachel and Karl explained that the amnesia could be brought on by stressful situations, as a defense against traumatic experiences. Rachel ventured, "You might have learned to do this in the potato box."

Jenny sidestepped the reference to the potato box. "I do the things people tell me, huh? I feel strange. Do I act strange?"

"Not strange at all. You can listen to a tape recording of the session whenever you are ready."

Jenny showed no interest in the tape. She was concerned that Mama Payne had called that morning to say "I'm not talking to you." Jenny was genuinely baffled.

"I don't know what the shit she meant." The last Jenny could remember was fixing Michael's lunch and putting the dog outside. "I must be going crazy or I'm just a bad person."

* * *

The next session Selena was miffed. "Why don't you just leave her alone? She can't handle it. She can't figure it out. She keeps me at home curled up in a corner."

Karl and Rachel suggested Selena help Jenny understand multiple personality, and help her regain her knowledge and memories. "When you all come together, something called integration, then she can figure things out and handle things."

"You mean she'll find out the things I've done? She'll stop me from going out with guys and getting drunk." Every inch the independent and determined teenager, Selena gave Karl a look that suggested he couldn't possibly be serious. She closed her eyes. Jenny appeared, unsure how she got there.

Karl began to explain. "When things are rough for you, you sort of hide out."

"Huh-uh," a child's voice interrupted. "I ain't been out since yesterday." Lisa grinned impishly at the chance for some attention. She had been staying away, she told Karl, because Selena and Flisha were fighting. "When I finally came out, Michael fussed at me for rocking. I don't want to grow up if I have to fight and fuss." She made a pouty face.

"What has it been like?" Rachel asked.

"When I'm not out," Lisa said, "it's like someone shuts me up. I can hear their fussing, but I can't see the sun and the rain." Lisa told them she liked to roll in the grass, to watch cartoons on television, and to play with her friends. "Becky's seven. She came to play when her mother was mean to her on her birthday." While Karl wondered if Becky was a separate child or another personality, Lisa moved on to lament that Jenny had no friends and was very confused.

After talking a bit more with Lisa, Karl asked, "Is Flisha here?" He nearly winced at Lisa's sad response.

"Do I have to go?"

Flisha looked around the room and at her hands and body as if to orient herself, and at once regained her composure. She spoke again of childhood, describing Jenny as living a nightmare. She was left alone so much, and still her mother laid into her, not once or twice, but every day. From the time she was small, she was taught she was the devil's child, and she was used in rituals for everything from the time she was four or five. She was afraid, afraid to move. She tried to die. "Sometimes the feelings were so bad, they scared me and made me want to . . ." Her words trailed off.

"Are the feelings bad now?"

"I've felt like some other people or force is there so strong." Flisha expressed fear of a time of confusion, a time of numbness returning, of being called crazy and being sent again to the state hospital. She had little memory of the first time in the hospital at age fourteen. It was like feeling dead for her. She recalled events before the second time at twenty-one. There was a pregnancy and feeling bad and taking poison. She remembered that in the hospital she made a teddy bear for Morgan and a stuffed dog for the baby, Noel. Perhaps Selena could remember more.

Before asking for Selena, Karl offered Flisha reassurance that she was not crazy. Although there is a tendency to confuse multiple personality with split personality, a term applied to schizophrenia, multiple personality is not a psychosis, nor is it a thought disorder.

Schizophrenia encompasses the craziness Flisha feared, with its characteristics of delusions, disturbances in thought, and loss of touch with reality. Multiple personality is a dissociative disorder in which the individual fragments to alter personalities who maintain touch with reality, and who, except at times when overwhelmed by stressors, keep the individual functional in life situations. (The protective and adaptive functions of dissociation in multiple personality are discussed by Young, 1988a. See also Crabtree, 1987.)

Karl acknowledged that there could have been diagnoses of schizophrenia made for her by therapists unaware of multiple personality disorder. He and Rachel would review her medical and mental health records to help with their understanding of her experiences of being labeled "crazy" in the past.

Selena wanted to talk about the present, not the past. She was upset that "Flisha dragged us off to the mall last night." Karl and Rachel noticed her use of the plural pronoun as well as her resentment of Flisha's having control. Selena said they had run into the Paynes at the mall, and she had told them to butt out of her life. "I couldn't stand to see the way they were upsetting Mar . . . er, Jenny."

Karl noticed her stumbling over the name, but did not interrupt her. He knew now why Jenny didn't understand Mama Payne's rejection. Selena continued. "I would have told them more if Flisha had left me out. They get close, and they think they're so goody-goody with that Christian shit. Give all your money to the church and they'll cure your demons all right."

Selena shifted her emphasis, but remained adamant. "I don't let nobody get close. I can't stand it when guys tell me they love me. The word is sickening. Jenny's mama would beat her and then say 'I love you.' It's just funny when a guy tells Jenny he loves her, and she doesn't even know what's going on, that I was with the guy the night before."

"What if we say we love you?" Rachel asked.

"Nobody ever will. I don't know what love is. I work the streets." She cracked her bubble gum sharply, as if defying the therapists to care.

"I wouldn't relate to that," Karl said. "I respect you too much. We don't like the numbers you do on Jenny, but we see you have many fine qualities. You are a part of Jenny."

"I don't see how — so boring, so dumb. I am Selena, and I'm not like nobody else."

Karl smiled. He couldn't argue that.

Karl and Rachel had a great deal to think about and talk about after the session. A pattern for the treatment was evolving. All the personalities they had seen or who had spoken on the phone related more easily to Karl. Given the abuse by the mother the therapists had heard about so far, they could understand "their" reluctance to work with a woman therapist alone. Too, the sessions were stretching long. Karl had available time, and the standard therapeutic hour could not be effective if divided among so many personalities. More time was needed. Karl would take the primary role in conducting the therapy. Rachel would attend as many sessions as she could, taking the role of observer, contributing when it seemed appropriate. Between sessions Rachel and Karl would talk about their observations, feelings, and ideas.

The personalities had revealed themselves so quickly that the Alexanders had to question if they were being put on by a malingerer or a clever actress. In just a little over a week and a half they had encountered four personalities, one of whom they presumed to be the birth personality.

In spite of their doubts, there was a genuineness to the distress and a distinctiveness among the personalities that could not be ignored. The changes in voice tone, appearance, and ways of moving were more than role changes. It was as if the therapists were encountering entirely separate people. It would take an extremely clever impersonator to accomplish such convincing changes.

Rachel was more skeptical than Karl, not so much about Jenny's being multiple as about the horrendous abuse being revealed and about the references to involvement in the occult. Rachel was aware of many instances of child abuse, but Jenny's experiences were described as almost too extreme to be real.

The cult references must contain at least some elements of fiction in their suggestion of strange tortures and human sacrifice. Cult belief presumed the existence of Satan as an entity, and further presumed human depravity in his name nearly beyond the imaginable. Rachel was Christian; however, her beliefs did not include the concept of a literal devil as the embodiment of evil.

Karl, with much the same background in the Christian faith, allowed himself to consider the existence of God and Satan in dichotomy in the universe. He did not like to think that people involved themselves in the kinds of evil the personalities suggested, but he was more open to the possibility of such experiences.

The Alexanders reviewed briefly what they knew so far. In the sessions they had seen Flisha as confident and mature, dealing with business matters and accepting the idea of multiple personality. She showed compassion for Jenny and was ready to consider ways to help. Selena seemed the rebellious, streetwise teenager who used men to earn money. She showed resentment for Jenny and rejected any part of being multiple. Lisa was a charming child who seemed young for twelve, but was disarming in her bids for attention. She regarded Jenny as a given, just someone she had to live with. Jenny, who identified herself as the original person, seemed shy and confused. She wanted to be compliant, but was upset by the suggestion that there were other personalities.

From the phone calls Karl knew there were still others, either by hearing voices new to him or through reports by known personalities. He had spoken to an old woman and had heard about a man, another young woman, and a child who cried. He and Rachel wondered what more was to come. They would not press, but would let things evolve at their own pace.

The information obtained from the various personalities was surprisingly consistent, with one exception. Flisha, Selena, and Lisa all described Jenny as very withdrawn and friendless. Yet the Jenny they had met was shy, not extremely withdrawn, and was interacting at least with the Paynes. Selena's stumbling over Jenny's name when she was talking about the Paynes was also curious.

In their review of the literature, both popular and scientific, concerning multiple personality disorder, they had found the original, or birth personality, described as withdrawn, frightened, and depleted, often having been in a sleeplike state since childhood. Perhaps they had not met the real Jenny Harris.

The Alexanders were correct in their deductions that they had not seen the birth personality. At the start all the personalities used Jenny's name with the therapists. As Lisa, then Selena and Flisha revealed themselves, Marcie continued to use Jenny's name. The Alexanders assumed she was the original personality, and Marcie continued the masquerade. The personalities had protected Jenny with their presence since early childhood. They would be very cautious about giving up that protection.

But the personalities were impressed with what Karl was saying about multiple personality. He knew about lost time, about finding yourself someplace you hadn't gone. He even had some idea of the terrible confusion. He recognized they were different, and it was all right.

Karl's recognition made it possible for each of the personalities to recognize and openly acknowledge the others. A long time ago, when they were children, Flisha, Selena, and Marcie had played together and watched each other and Jenny. As time passed, they vanished to each other one by one. There were times over the years that they were in contact, but often they were alone. Now it seemed safe for them to acknowledge each other and to reveal Jenny.

They held a meeting to talk about being open with the Alexanders. Flisha took the lead. Justin came. Lisa came but kept quiet. Flisha and Marcie spoke in favor of letting Jenny out, of pushing or pulling her from her own worlds. They felt that the Alexanders could be trusted, and that Jenny desperately needed their help. Something was wrong inside her, very wrong. (Internal communication among personalities and its use in therapy is described by Caul, 1984.)

Justin hadn't actually met the Alexanders, but he was aware of what was happening. He supported Jenny's coming out, but cautioned: "We have to be careful because she is so fragile."

"If she's so damn fragile, let her stay where she is." For a long time Jenny had not been part of Selena's awareness. Wasn't it enough now to admit that there were others? She could hardly bear being forced to admit Jenny continued to exist. Selena was afraid of her and hated her. She feared the power that made Jenny able to escape from pain, and she hated Jenny for leaving her alone with the pain. Let Jenny stay in her own worlds forever.

In spite of Selena's protest, Flisha and Marcie agreed to push Jenny into the real world. From Selena's perspective, Flisha and Marcie always got to run things as they wanted. Marcie would end her masquerade at the next session with the Alexanders. She and Flisha had been patient to be sure they could trust the Alexanders, although they were desperate to find help to keep things from getting so bad that anxiety and depression would overwhelm all of them again.

At the same time the personalities were deciding to reveal the real Jenny, the Alexanders were planning a technique to encourage the emergence of the birth personality. Perhaps the one who claimed to be Jenny was the original personality; however, her demeanor just did not fit with what the Alexanders expected. They realized, based on their reading, that it could take months, even years, to uncover the birth personality. Still, they had to make an effort to reach her.

They would provide a place specifically for Jenny. They would designate the recliner in the room adjacent to where they regularly held the sessions as the place. When there was an appropriate opportunity, they would ask that Jenny come out in that chair.

The next session began much as the others had, with Flisha talking of early childhood. She had brought some old photographs. As she showed the therapists the pictures, she talked about how Jenny always wanted to be dark like her father. She said that was the reason Selena sunbathed all the time.

Marcie appeared, still calling herself Jenny, and asked, "I've been that way again, huh?" Karl assured her that things were all right and asked that she go with him and Rachel to the recliner in the adjacent room. The recliner, he said, would be Jenny's chair, a safe place where she alone could be. No other personality could use the chair.

Marcie went with them without hesitation. She sat in the chair and allowed her eyes to close. Then, as Rachel and Karl watched, she seemed to shrink, to pull into herself. When her eyes opened, a florid rash appeared across her upper chest. Her hands clenched into tight fists, and generalized muscle tension gripped her whole body. She stared at the floor. After some time, she dared a brief glance at Karl as he spoke. "Hello."

"Hey," she barely whispered.

"What is your name?"

"Jenny, Jenny Lynn Walters." Her voice trembled with fear.

In that safe place Jenny did not resist so much her return to the real world. It was two weeks after Flisha first went to see the Alexanders, three days past her thirty-fourth birthday, and twenty-seven years after she made her escape into her own worlds that *Jenny reappeared.*

Briefly Karl introduced himself and Rachel and told Jenny they would be there to help her. Her eyes closed. Selena appeared. Gently but firmly Karl took Selena's arm and led her from the chair. It was Jenny's chair. They had met the real Jenny Harris.

CHAPTER 22

None of the personalities let Michael know about seeing the Alexanders for counseling. Marcie, Flisha, and Selena all remembered a time he dragged "them" out of the mental health clinic because he felt things were getting worse not better. Flisha believed that Michael had no real concept of what life was truly like. If he knew about the Alexanders, he might put his foot down against any treatment for mental problems.

The Alexanders were aware that Jenny could not pay for the extensive psychotherapy she required, and agreed to provide the care without pay. Michael could not complain that she was running up bills again. Selena told Michael that the Alexanders were friends of hers and that she "hung out" at their office sometimes. Michael was used to her spending time during the day with friends. None of the personalities raised his suspicions by interfering with Marcie's being home on time to fix his supper every day.

The Alexanders encouraged Flisha to see a medical doctor to rule out physical problems and to prescribe medications if necessary. The emotional depletion and extreme physical tension they observed in Jenny emphasized for them the stresses put on the body by the system of personalities.

Coping with the additional external stresses of her family, the bills, and so forth could lead to physical and emotional exhaustion, they feared. Too, the therapists wanted to determine if there were any organic components to the back pain that originally brought her to them, her mental disorder, or the headaches experienced by Jenny, Marcie, and Flisha.

All the problems could be accounted for on the basis of multiple personality disorder. For instance, headaches commonly accompany the switching of personalities and are often intense if the switching is frequent or rapid. The muscle tension manifested by Jenny could cause the back pain, or the pain could represent "body memories" of past hurts. Karl was able to help her control the pain somewhat with relaxation techniques; however, it was important that physical causes of her problems not be overlooked.

Flisha made arrangements to see Dr. Bakker. She had been to him once before for a minor illness. At this new visit he seemed caring, if somewhat hurried. After a brief examination Dr. Bakker recommended she go into the local hospital for a few days for her to get some rest and to give him the opportunity for a more thorough examination.

Flisha and Marcie made the decision to go into the hospital. Selena was resistant at first, but finally agreed to cooperate. Selena did not feel the headaches and back pain or experience the fatigue that made Flisha and Marcie feel unable to cope. Once Selena decided to cooperate, she helped Flisha convince Michael to agree to the hospitalization. Selena told him that if she went to the hospital she could probably get disability payments for her back problems for at least a year. Michael offered to drive her there.

At home Flisha unpacked Selena's skimpy nightgown and Lisa's doll and coloring book at least a dozen times. But when she opened the suitcase to unpack at the hospital, she found Selena's *Seventeen* magazine and the coloring book under her own *Cosmopolitan*. The gown and doll were there too. Flisha tucked them under her things and hoped the nurses wouldn't notice them.

With Flisha's approval, the Alexanders shared with Dr.

Bakker their impression that his patient, Jenny Harris, suffered from multiple personality disorder. Dr. Bakker could see that she was much disturbed. He asked the psychiatry fellow from the university medical center who provided consultation at the community hospital to see Jenny. Dr. Louise Samuels, the psychiatrist, agreed to see her at the regularly scheduled consultation visit.

Dr. Samuels's immediate impression was classic multiple personality disorder. She agreed to follow up in a few weeks and to see Jenny again after a chance to research the disorder. She would make recommendations, particularly about medications, but she declined to see Jenny for long-term treatment.

During Jenny's six days in the hospital, no definite cause for her back pain was found except for chronic lumbar strain; however, some evidence of a peptic ulcer was noted, and medicine was prescribed. The medicine helped, and she gained strength and profited from the respite from the stresses at home.

The Alexanders saw her daily for brief visits during her hospital stay. They felt it important to be available for support, given Jenny's so recent return from her inner worlds.

Flisha was able to maintain control most of the time in the hospital, but Selena popped out when a doctor or nurse came into the room, or if the phone rang. She embarrassed Flisha by acting flippant and by going in the halls in her revealing gown. Selena resented Flisha's uppity attitude and argued with her despite Karl's suggestion that they cooperate for Jenny's sake.

During one of Karl's visits he watched as Flisha fell silent, and the characteristic rash began on her chest even before the clenched fists let him know Jenny had emerged. She was as withdrawn as before and very confused by seeing Karl in this unfamiliar place. "Are you real?" she whispered.

Karl explained about her being in the hospital. He gently extended his hand toward hers. "You can touch things that are real. I am real and here with you." He sat as silent and still as one would with a frightened animal.

Long minutes passed. Then slowly her fingers uncurled from her palms, and she reached the few inches to touch his hand. Relief relaxed the tension in her body. Just for a moment Karl could see the soft, vulnerable beauty held within her, then her hand pulled away. Flisha regained her proper distance and chatted with Karl until it was time for the visit to end.

The telephone calls continued between the Alexanders' hospital visits, and between office sessions once Jenny was out of the hospital. Still Karl did not discourage the calls because they continued to be essential to the revealing. Within the space of a month the Alexanders talked to or heard about some thirty personalities. Once the initial contact was made, the personalities gradually revealed themselves "in person."

Being a student gave Karl sufficient time to accommodate the calls, although they were frequent. After one of his morning classes, Karl was discussing Jenny's progress with his major professor. Karl explained how the telephone seemed to allow the personalities to introduce themselves or to speak their needs from a safe distance. "Though," he said, "it is a bit like having thirty hysterical women know your phone number."

That afternoon the voice on the phone sounded much lower than that of any of the personalities Karl had heard. Karl smiled as he remembered the offhand remark about hysterical women. That would teach him to slip into male chauvinism. The voice was distinctly male, polite, and direct. "My name is Justin. I don't usually come out, but I need to talk to you."

Karl assured Justin that the call was welcome and asked him to tell more about himself. Justin explained he had been with Jenny a very long time, since she was six and needed to feel she had a father. With a good-natured chuckle Justin admitted that at fifty-seven, his hair was beginning to gray, and he was getting a little paunchy. He said he smoked a pipe, cherry-blend tobacco. In the past he had had frequent opportunities to relax in his own clothes at home. Even then, cutting his hair had caused somewhat of an uproar.

With so many women around now, he was hardly out at all. He had come out for a special reason. "Jenny is reaching out to you, and that's what she did with me."

"Why is she reaching out?"

"She's trusting you a lot. More than we thought she could. She likes you. Sometimes she doesn't think you're real. In the hospital, her taking your hand was one of the good things. It let me know she was trusting you."

"I will try very hard to deserve her trust."

"She's very fragile, like a satin rose, because of the creativity she has. Her mind is beautiful. Not the others, but hers alone. You're working with someone who is very fragile and very beautiful."

Karl was touched by the sincere caring Justin expressed. Karl saw it as an expression of self-love. He heard the mix of sadness and relief in Justin's relinquishing to the therapist his long-held role in Jenny's life.

"She thinks her daddy hated her because he never came to see her, not even on weekends, not once a month, not once a year."

"So you have been the dad she needed?"

"Yes, but not like you. I'm on the inside. She needs someone like you."

"From your perspective, how can I help her?"

"There's lots of things. Whether you want to do them or not, that's another thing. She thinks of you now as a doctor or a counselor. But take care of her. Call her and talk to her when nothing else is happening. Take her to concerts. If she was a boy, I'd say play ball with her, all the things a daddy would do."

Justin was very convincing in his open bid for Karl to provide friendship, even parenting, for Jenny. He was flattering with his description of her trust, and compelling with his description of her need. Karl had never encountered a client so hurt and so deprived of childhood. Justin made her seem so vulnerable that it was easy to forget for a time the strengths and skills she used to survive her past. Too, it was easy to take on at least some of the responsibility Justin posed as necessary.

"What should I never do?"

"Never lie to her. She herself is very honest. If she gives her word, it is good."

"I wouldn't lie to any of you."

"She knows that about you, or she would never have reached out."

Karl thanked Justin for the information. He acknowledged Justin's discomfort at being in a woman's body and suggested that Justin could watch what was happening with Jenny and supply information to Karl by telephone. If someday Justin could feel comfortable doing so, perhaps he would meet with Karl at the office.

Karl was pleased to have Justin's advocacy added to that of Flisha and Marcie. Karl and Rachel met Marcie soon after they met the real Jenny. Marcie admitted it was she who posed as Jenny after Lisa made the blue Play-Doh man. Marcie disliked blue, but it was Jenny's favorite color. It was also Marcie who was involved with the Paynes and who hoped to patch things up with them. She genuinely cared about people who cared about her.

Marcie remained protective after giving up her ruse. If in the therapy sessions Marcie felt that Jenny was taxed too much, or that Karl was in error, she popped out to chastise him. Her interventions were good-natured but firm.

Jenny's hope for recovery resided in the personalities who not only lived her life for her, but also held the memories and emotions that would be the keys to making her whole. Jenny herself was like a frightened child suddenly thrust into a world about which she knew little. For her, the therapists' office was a safe place, although she had to ask again and again if it was okay to smile or to cry there. Even there, the telephone, the typewriter, the copier, and the recording equipment all were threats, accepted tentatively by her only after much explanation from Karl and Rachel.

At every session Karl made contact with Jenny if he could, to help her feel safe and to help her learn. Often he took her hand to ground her in the real world. She had so much catching up to do. The external world was a mystery to her. For her, her mother still lived, and she herself had no children, no husband. She did not even recognize the clothes she wore as hers. She could not drive a car, would not look in mirrors, and could not dial a phone. The task of teaching her seemed staggering, but Karl began.

First he helped her learn her way around the office. He noticed she was attracted to pretty things, soft music, flowers. He coaxed her to venture with him and Rachel to a nearby park. She would walk among the flowers and shrubs as long as there were no other people in the park. The therapists introduced her to foods she had never tasted, or had forgotten. Her first taste was a fresh orange. Next she tried chocolate ice cream, Lisa's favorite. For Karl and Rachel there was pleasure in the teaching, in watching Jenny's joy in discovery. But she could not learn all she had missed. She would have to recover the knowledge and experiences of her other selves.

For now she had to recognize the alter personalities. Someday she would realize that they were of her own creation. Karl used the recordings of sessions with the personalities to help Jenny know them.

As they met each personality, Karl and Rachel obtained permission first to audiotape, and later to videotape, the sessions. The tapes could be used to convince any personality, but especially Jenny, of the existence of others.

It took several sessions with Jenny before she could agree to listen to the first audiotape. She sat silently and listened to the voices of Flisha, Selena, and Marcie. As the tape ended, Karl spoke, and Jenny closed her eyes. Marcie responded. "It was too much for her." Karl didn't press. It was enough that Jenny had listened.

At the next session Jenny was able to talk about the tape and to admit that she had seen people here in the office who looked like her, but not like her. "They are a part of you," Karl told her.

"Then I must be crazy, or very bad to make them do what they do."

"It happened when you were very young. It was necessary for you at that time, to cope with things you could not otherwise have handled." Jenny looked at the floor, incredulous, ashamed. With his index finger Karl lifted her chin so that she faced him. "Look at me. You have no reason to be afraid or ashamed."

"You have a wonderful creative mind that helped you to survive. That same mind will help you to get better," Rachel interposed. Jenny listened, then she was gone.

Jenny's reemergence from her worlds put a strain on the tenuous stability the personalities maintained at home. Karl sought their cooperation to help Jenny be less confused in the real world. He asked that they refrain from moving the furniture around in the house, so when Jenny came out, she could get used to her home. Karl knew that most of them continued to make entries in a daily journal. Their sharing the journal with him helped him to keep the various events of their lives sorted in his mind. The journal kept him abreast of the feelings of known personalities and told of still more to be met.

He encouraged Jenny to read the journal, and to make entries when she could. He asked Flisha to write notes for Jenny so she could understand what was happening. Flisha made notes of family events for her. Other personalities wrote their own thoughts and feelings, often not bothering to sign the entries.

Jenny was upset by seeing the many different writings. They were undeniable evidence of the others. Still, they helped her understanding. She began to write feelings and perceptions of her own. Juxtaposed to the writings of the others, she wrote:

I'm so afraid. I'm even afraid to remember, for the things are too bad, too unbelievable. I'm really so bad, so mixed up with all the other persons. So many people say I am. Oh, God, what am I, who am I? Will I ever know? Will I ever be sure?

Flisha's messages were to the point:

> Jenny, you took Noel to get his glasses at 4:00, Flisha.

> Jenny, you went to see Michael's mom. You were sick, so Michael didn't keep you up long. Selena took some pills that made us sick. Also Hilda broke all the things in the house today. So you will know what happened, Flisha.

Flisha's matter-of-fact approach let Karl know how common the small upheavals were in the home. With many entries unsigned, Karl wasn't sure which personalities wrote about one another. He was sure, however, that others were upset by Hilda.

Someone wrote: *Hilda is hell. Don't mess with her.*

Karl asked Selena what she knew about Hilda. Selena said Hilda had a violent temper, was hell on wheels if you messed with her. Just recently she had been on somewhat of a rampage, breaking things in the house and then turning on the gas. Selena wasn't sure what had provoked her. Karl didn't have long to wonder.

During the same session Karl was talking with Jenny, telling her that it was natural to get angry, when a coarse voice interrupted. "You're wasting your time. She ain't gonna get mad. She just takes all that shit off Michael, him yellin' at her, and she won't say nothin'."

Well, now he knew that Michael had provoked her. "You must be Hilda."

"Yeah. What the hell do you want?"

"Tell me about yourself."

Hilda told him she was thirty-four and had always been with Jenny, because Jenny would not show her anger. She told him about the time she threw a porcelain cat at Michael for running around on Jenny. Her speech was punctuated with many impatient or disgusted sighs, as if Karl must be stupid not to know what she was saying.

"Jenny was lucky to have you. Everyone needs to get angry sometimes, and she has much to be angry about."

"Yeah, but she won't ever show those feelings. She just takes it. It would be best to end it."

"Would you want to help Jenny?"

"She'll never get better."

"You are a part of Jenny."

"I ain't either."

Karl spoke of his hopes that he and Rachel might become friends with her as a part of Jenny. Hilda's look let him know she hardly expected such acceptance. "I don't know how to be a friend."

"You can talk to us, let your emotions out. Come see us or call when you feel rage. Don't tear the house up or try to hurt everybody."

"She'd be better off dead, but she hasn't got the guts to do it." Hilda told how Jenny was beaten, had sex things done to her, how she was told her tongue would be cut out, and how her mother put wax on her tongue. "So she never talked to nobody."

Karl understood how Jenny as a child held in her anger. Even as an adult the anger was held in check until it built to a rage and Hilda emerged, almost mad enough to kill. Hilda was strong and suspicious, but she hadn't run when Karl spoke of caring. She had some concern for Jenny.

Jenny was having trouble just recognizing what was real. She could not always differentiate internal happenings from the external world. She expressed fears of being crazy. Many of the alter personalities were having trouble too. As their awareness of one another fluctuated, they sometimes saw or heard the others and sometimes not. Hallucinations were superimposed on these already shaky perceptions.

Karl could explain that the hearing of voices common to victims of multiple personality disorder is different from the auditory hallucinations of psychosis. In multiple personality the voices are generally heard inside the head, not perceived as coming from an external source as occurs in schizophrenia. The voices of multiple personality are either those of alters in conversation among themselves and overheard by the personality in control, or those of alters in direct communication with the personality in control. (See Ross and Norton, 1988.)

Karl could not so readily explain the visual hallucinations. They could be bits of memories partially surfaced. They could be the result of current drug use, or flashbacks from previous drug use. He chose not to share with Jenny his concern that psychosis might have to be considered secondary to the dissociative disorder. It could be that schizophrenia existed in one or more of the alters and would therefore have to be faced as an aspect of Jenny's problem. For now Karl assured her that he would help her and the others as much as he could to differentiate hallucinations from events in the external world.

Karl was out of the office when Selena came the next afternoon. She was agitated, jumping up from the chair periodically to claw at the wood paneling. She admitted to Rachel that she had taken acid, but grew more agitated when Rachel suggested she go to the hospital detoxification unit.

As Rachel sat with her, Selena was able to realize that she was in the therapists' office and not back in the potato box. She stopped trying to claw her way out, although she picked at her arms, removing invisible objects which she placed on the table. Finally she raked them into her hand and dumped them into the wastebasket. Rachel thought perhaps there was some key in the behavior to understanding Selena's past. "What is it, Selena?" she asked in a calm, very professional voice.

"Bugs."

"Where do you suppose the bugs came from?" Rachel was quite serious in her approach.

"Other bugs." The reply was as serious as the query.

Rachel grinned. Selena relaxed and grinned, too, for a time, no longer tormented by her visions.

At the next session Karl asked Selena about the hallucinations. Selena talked about seeing scary faces and snakes. She also said she often saw a little man, a short guy with brown hair and eyes, who wore a red shirt and baggy blue pants. "Lisa made a sculpture of him."

Karl realized it was the Play-Doh figure Lisa made the first time he saw her. He wondered how many of the personalities saw the same visions. He asked Selena, "Is he real?"

"Yeah. He talks to me and touches me."

"Is he here now?"

"Sure." Selena pointed to the corner of the table. "He's standin' there lookin' and smilin'."

"I can't see him."

"He just lets himself be known to me." Selena glanced toward the corner of the table. Karl reached where Selena's eyes led him. Her face registered surprise as she gasped, "Your hand went through." She moved her hand toward the little man to reassure herself by touching him. When Karl reached toward the corner of the table again, Selena was gone.

Marcie and Flisha in turn admitted they saw things, but they didn't talk to them. Marcie explained that the mother threatened to lock her away for seeing things, so she could not speak to them. Flisha said that when things appeared, Selena would come out to deal with them.

Karl thought he had come full circle, when Hilda appeared, angry and questioning what he was doing. He told her Selena had seen a little man on the table, and asked her about the visions.

"Yeah, hell, I see them, talk to them."

"Is the little man still here?"

"Yeah, he's over there." Hilda pointed at the floor behind Karl's chair. Karl reached toward the spot. "Ha, he runs from you."

"Can you catch him?"

"I reckon." Hilda walked about the room, reaching toward the floor, then scooped up her invisible quarry and sat it on the table. Karl passed his hand over the table. The same incredulous look that Selena had had let Karl know that Hilda saw his hand go through the little man too. Here was a chance, Karl thought, to begin to help the personalities understand the hallucinations. "Why," he asked Hilda, "do you think I can't see him?"

"Maybe" — Hilda shrugged, not hiding her disgust with his stupidity — "there's something wrong with you."

So much for lessons in the real world.

CHAPTER 23

Therapy with Jenny Harris was unlike any Karl or Rachel had encountered. With the appearance of so many personalities, it was as if they were suddenly working with that number of clients. When one personality became tired or unable to cope with issues, another surfaced. The personalities seemed, as they surfaced, to be rested, as if they had been in the deep relaxation of a trance state. The overall effect was the presentation of a tireless client who needed unlimited attention. The need was urgent. In childhood needs had never been met. Now each personality required expression and acceptance.

Karl found himself spending lengthy sessions with Jenny nearly every day. The days stretched to weeks. Karl did not feel fatigued by the long sessions. The phenomenon was fascinating, and for some reason he could not explain, Karl felt energized by his interactions with the personalities. He remained alert, interested, and challenged for hours. Rachel found time to sit in on a portion of Jenny's sessions and to maintain ongoing dialogue with Karl to sort out the incredible information being presented to them.

Therapy moved forward on many fronts at once. As the

personalities became known to them, Karl and Rachel began to build, and then to sustain trust with each of them. Trust was no small issue. Karl's and Rachel's caring was constantly tested by Jenny and the alters. Time spent or words of acceptance could be instantly negated by a perceived slight prompted by something no more significant than a delay in returning a phone call. For Karl and Rachel it was difficult always to have their intentions questioned. However, they could understand the reluctance to trust. They started over building trust as often as was necessary, Karl with more patience than Rachel. With trust established, even tentatively, the therapists could discover the life histories of personalities, their experiences and memories, the original reasons they had come into being, and the purposes they served.

Karl and Rachel were careful in early encounters with personalities. They knew they were laying groundwork for possible eventual integration, that is, bringing together the separate personalities and sustaining function as a unified individual. They were aware that integration is not an event, but rather a process. The process would involve Jenny's recalling a past almost impossible to acknowledge, recovering memories and emotions dispersed among many personalities, learning new ways to cope in her environment, as well as causing her alters to arrive at a new level of cooperative functioning. (Different terms — fusion, merger, and unification — are applied to various aspects of recombining personalities into one being. See Kluft, 1988a.)

The Alexanders saw integration as encompassing intermediate unions of separate groups of personalities and the overall process in which all would be joined. They needed to know how each personality felt about and related to Jenny. They needed to know the meaning of integration for each personality, what unpleasantness could be escaped or what reward could be gained by giving up a separate existence.

They learned, for instance, that Lisa wanted not to be fussed at and to grow up without fighting. Justin could hardly tolerate the woman's body he inhabited, especially when he knew Jenny had someone else to care for her. Flisha and Marcie looked forward to the end of their confusion and were willing to do most anything to help Jenny. Only Selena felt she had nothing to escape and nothing to gain by integrating with Jenny.

For Jenny to gain control of her life, she had to recover knowledge and emotions, develop strength to overcome her depleted state, and learn to cope in the real world. From the start, Karl insisted that whatever changes were made through recall of memories and through the process of integration, they could never settle for less for Jenny than what she now had. She had functioned for over thirty years with her personalities. She would have to be able to function at least as well without them.

Both Karl and Rachel were trained in the techniques of hypnotherapy. Karl was more comfortable in their use. With Jenny they had not used any formal hypnotherapy in the sessions. She had expressed fear of hypnosis. Selena explained that they were afraid of being hypnotized ever since Dr. Stanger, the psychiatrist with the mental health clinic, had used hypnosis and then electric shock treatments to make them do what he wanted.

While Karl scrupulously avoided the use of hypnosis, he noticed that much of Jenny's behavior suggested self-induced trance. Changes in muscle tension, pupil size, and hand temperature, apparent with personality switching, were indicative of physiologic responses to trance states. Usually switching was preceded by eye closure and a momentary relaxation, then the emerging personality took on the facial expression and posture characteristic of that personality.

Karl was accustomed to Jenny's running, that is switching to an alter, when she became frightened or otherwise upset in a session. Often Marcie came out, but sometimes a new personality surfaced. Whenever Jenny closed her eyes, Karl waited to see whom he would encounter. He was able to recognize on sight most of the personalities he had met. If he did not recognize the alter who emerged when her eyes opened, he simply asked, "What is your name?"

Karl had been talking with Jenny about her grandmother.

The topic had come up in a rather strange way. Jenny, without any apparent reason, began moving her lips and tongue as if in response to an unpleasant taste. She told Karl she could taste snuff. Karl asked her to relax and think of a time she had tasted it in the past. She smiled as she recalled her grandmother's sitting in the upstairs bedroom sewing a little dress for her, blue, like the color of Karl's shirt. Seeing the color had triggered this very early memory. Jenny remembered tasting the snuff accidentally, and the hugs Mamaw gave her to comfort her.

The pleasant memory was short-lived. Jenny spoke of her grandmother's death, and the hint of a smile was replaced by lips drawn into a tight line. Jenny looked briefly dazed, then closed her eyes. Her shoulders slumped, her hands released their fists, and her head tilted forward.

Karl waited for her eyes to open, signaling the presence of an alter personality. Jenny slipped more deeply into a state of relaxation. After several minutes her eyes remained closed. Karl asked, "What is your name?"

"Mind." The response was barely audible. This personality state remained with eyes closed, deeply relaxed, apparently in trance. Karl moved closer to hear the responses to his questions.

As far as he could ascertain, Mind had no personal history. She had the memories of and awareness of the experiences of all the personalities and of Jenny. Mind described herself as delicate, having white skin, blue eyes, fragile fingers, and silky hair reaching past her waist. Karl pictured the ethereal being, Mind, as more energy than substance, as beautiful and benevolent.

Mind said she had been with Jenny always, that Jenny had escaped into her own mind even before she developed speech. Mind was the reservoir of Jenny's collective awareness, of wordless knowing and unspoken remembering. Mind could control, she said, the return of memories and emotions to Jenny and thus protect her from becoming overwhelmed during the process of integration. Mind came, it seemed, from the very center of Jenny's existence.

With the surfacing of Mind as the primary inner-self-helper, or center, remembering was facilitated. Mind permitted the deliberate use of hypnosis and directed Jenny and the alters to allow it. All were such excellent hypnotic subjects that trance could be achieved with little more than a three count and instruction to relax. Karl was able to deepen or lighten trance as necessary to allow recall of memories without producing intolerable distress. (Easy hypnotizability in multiples is thought to be indicative of an inborn ability to dissociate. See Ross and Fraser, 1987.)

Remembering had begun gently enough with Jenny's recall of her grandmother, but other memories stimulated more violent responses. At Rachel's mentioning the potato box to her, for instance, Jenny became visibly upset and shivered as if very cold. She scurried from her chair to the corner of the room and cowered, looking very small. Karl called her name, "Jenny."

"Let me out." She cried silently and clawed at the wood paneling. Her voice was that of a child.

"What's your name?"

"Becky." The playmate Lisa had told them about weeks before was not a separate child.

"Who put you here?"

"Mama. It's dark and cold." She clawed harder at the walls.

"How old are you?"

"Little."

"Can you scream?"

"I'm afraid to scream. If I scream, Mama'll come back."

"What's Mama doing?"

"She went away, a long time." Becky got still, her eyes closed, and Selena appeared.

"Why did y'all do that? She can't handle it."

Karl explained that it was situations in the past that Jenny couldn't handle. Now the personalities could bring the memories of past experiences out, talk about them, and let them be gone.

"What you mean is we'll disappear." Selena was angry. She left Marcie to deal with Karl. Karl asked to speak with Jenny.

Jenny was still visibly upset. "I feel like I'm coming apart."

"Actually, you are beginning to come back together," Karl told her. "I can explain what happened, but that won't explain how you are feeling."

Jenny didn't remember anything in particular about the potato boxes, although she said she got upset just seeing them in the basement at her aunt's house. She sort of remembered a red rocking chair, but thinking about it made her feel sick. She accepted Karl's telling her that her mother put her in a potato box. They would consider the rocking chair at another time.

The warm, comforting memories of the grandmother's love had been replaced very quickly by the cold realization of the mother's abuse. Jenny knew her grandmother for only two years, but her warmth persisted in the personality, Aunt Sue. It was Aunt Sue who had told Karl on the phone about Jenny's cutting herself.

It was easy to accept Aunt Sue's stated age of eighty-four. When she came out in the office, she gingerly removed Selena's bubble gum from her mouth. "It hurts my teeth," she said. "I've not got many left." Her head moved constantly with the rhythmic twitch of palsy, and her hands shook with a fine tremor as she smoothed her hair back and held it temporarily in an "old lady" bun. Even her voice had the tremulous quality of advanced age.

She said she had been with Jenny since she was two, looking out for her. When Jenny was little, Aunt Sue got things from the house for her when her mother locked her out—dry clothes, something to eat, a toy. As Jenny got older, Aunt Sue could see how much the bad things hurt her. So Aunt Sue told her the bad things were dreams, not really happening to Aunt Sue's smart and pretty girl.

All Jenny wanted, Aunt Sue explained, was for her mother to love her, like any child. She even tried to be like her mother, but she couldn't do it. "Wahnola did it, with the mental problems and the abuse," Aunt Sue said. "She did things to Jenny, burned her and cut her. But people thought Jenny did it to herself."

Aunt Sue warned that Wahnola must be kept in check. If she were allowed to get out, no one could control her. Karl wondered when or if Wahnola would surface.

He explained to Aunt Sue as well as he could his understanding of the reason for an internal abuser. Aunt Sue's perception that Wahnola was created in an effort to please the mother had much validity. Every child internalizes aspects of a parent, imitating both attitudes and behaviors. If these happen to be abusive, that is what the child tries. Often these behaviors are turned on the abused child's own children when he or she is grown.

In Jenny's case, other factors could account for self-abuse. In instances of repeated abuse, there is often a period of respite after an abusive episode, or the abuser is contrite or atoning. The child anticipating abuse experiences relief when it finally comes, knowing that there will be safety for a time, or even a time of caring attention. Too, often a child comes to believe that he or she deserves the abuse, and causes self-hurt if there is no one else to do the harm.

Understanding, even explaining the dynamics did little to help Karl deal with his feelings about the self-abuse. He could feel anger creep into his voice as he talked with Aunt Sue about it. He could accept that Jenny had been many times a victim. He could not countenance her victimizing herself.

In recent years Aunt Sue had become an observer, getting too old to intervene, but still watching over Jenny. She was as relieved as Justin to have someone else look out for Jenny. Aunt Sue was old and tired. She thought she might die soon.

It was an overcast day, and Karl didn't think about Jenny's aversion to the light in his office. He flipped on the switch while talking with her. "The buzzing," she said, before giving way to Kathy.

Kathy was the same age as Jenny. She had come when Jenny was small and could not bear to look in mirrors because she felt so ugly. Kathy wasn't ugly. She could look in mirrors. Jenny could not because she wanted to see only pretty things.

Kathy remembered how the pretty things made trouble for Jenny. When her teacher told about her pretty things, her mother had held her down and put an electric drill to her eye. The drill made a buzzing sound, Kathy said, like the sound the lights made. Until Kathy mentioned it, Karl had paid no attention to the buzzing of the fluorescent fixture.

He talked more with Kathy, learning that she had a good awareness of the world. She got dressed in the morning if no other personality was around. She knew how to cook and drive a car, and had some memories of childhood. Karl asked her if she would share the memory of the drill with Jenny. Kathy agreed. Karl gave them a few minutes to communicate, then asked to speak with Jenny.

Jenny looked as if she would cry, but held back the tears. She told how her mother had hurt her eye and screamed at her about her pretty things. Karl reassured her that the event was real, but in the past. The light fixture continued its buzzing, but Jenny seemed not to notice.

Jenny was incredibly sensitive to her inner feelings and to the things around her. Every sense was especially acute and responded to internal and external stimuli. For Jenny, the responses often meant pain and fear.

"Blood." Jenny spoke, then slumped in her chair.

Karl asked, "Mind, are you there?"

"I am here." At Karl's urging, Mind explained what was happening. Jenny had seen writing with red marking pen that Selena had done on the art board, and had begun to remember other writing in red. She reacted to the color, not to the content of the writing.

Karl thanked Mind for the information about Jenny's reaction. He asked to speak again with Jenny. He drew Jenny's attention to the writing.

"Red," she said. "I dreamed of signing my name in a book in red. Mother did it."

Karl urged her to go on. "She hurt me below so I would bleed. Then I wrote my name and drank the blood. Sealed forever as bad and evil." Her breathing quickened, then Barbara appeared. Barbara was calm, her breathing regular.

She spoke with a heavy accent. Karl noted her use of *ja* and *nein,* and was not surprised when she said her people had come from Germany.

Barbara's purpose had been to protect Jenny from the black book. As a child, Barbara knew how the preacher at church and the high priest in the cult used the Bible. Jenny got very confused about and afraid of the black book, but Barbara understood that the book was good. She held on to that for Jenny.

Barbara detailed the incident of Jenny's writing her name in blood, from the mother putting her on the kitchen table to her putting Jenny in the red rocking chair to hold the book. When Karl spoke to Jenny, she hyperventilated. He helped her to calm her breathing, then let her know what she had experienced was a memory, not a dream. "But you were not then, and are not now, bad or evil."

As if to contradict Karl surreptitiously, writings in the journal began to make reference to evil. In a stylized block printing, a warning appeared. *Save her, for hell is all there is for her.*

A few days later an entry in the same printing stated: *I'm not telling you; I'm warning you. There's something bad, Sandy.*

Not far from that entry was one in a childish hand. *I'm afraid of Sandy. She's so deep in losing her mind.*

The journal messages seemed urgent. Karl did not wait for Sandy to appear. While working with Selena, he asked to speak to Sandy.

Acting indignant at being summoned, Sandy came nonetheless. She was restless and walked about the room, with her shoulders back, in a determined stride. While she maintained a studied distance, she talked freely with Karl, and with Rachel, who joined them in the session.

Asked to describe herself, Sandy said she had dark hair, long, and that she wore glasses because of eyestrain. She said she had been to the office before and had talked with Rachel about cult things. She talked casually about her involvement in witchcraft. "When I was twenty-one, I was made a high priestess. But I left the cult. I do my own thing. I practice, you know, a soloist, not really full-fledged into it. I have my own rituals, my own people."

"How did you get into it?"

"Years ago we were sold to the devil. We lost our souls. You are sacrificed, condemned for life. All the children of the cult are sacrificed, then tortured. Her mother pushed her, and the rest of us followed."

"Was the mother a witch?"

"Oh, she had no kind of power, just mean. The torture was a thing she had to do; she was commanded. After a while she'd do it anyway."

"Does Jenny know about the cult?"

"I don't know for sure. Jenny hates the mountains — a lot of rituals there. And the house she lived in with her mother — horrible things happened, things we did." Sandy spoke of much sexual abuse, still unsure of how much Jenny knew.

Finally Sandy sat down, and became less guarded than when she first appeared. As they had at the meeting of each personality, Karl and Rachel acknowledged Sandy's importance and their caring for her as a part of Jenny. They asked if she would be willing to help Jenny.

Sandy was indifferent to Jenny. Her own fate was unchangeably determined. Her only hope was in reincarnation. She would help Jenny if there was no cost to her, or better yet, if there was something in it for her.

Sandy's appearance and identification of herself as a witch caused the Alexanders to have to give credence to the references to cult involvement they had heretofore thought might be delusional. There must be something to the idea of Satan worship if an alter existed to deal with it.

The nature of the activities and beliefs Sandy presented to the therapists was consistent with what they were ready to accept. Sandy spoke of doing solitary rituals and spells for herself, and suggested that the mother had done the same. The group activities she made reference to apparently consisted of secret sexual excesses and drug use. In the group, children were frightened, even terrorized, to make sure they kept the secrets.

Karl and Rachel surmised that Gladys Faye expanded on the cult's practice of frightening children and actually caused physical harm to her daughter. In the hands of this very disturbed mother, relatively harmless quasi-religious beliefs could have become dangerous justification for child abuse.

Neither Karl nor Rachel asked Sandy to explain what she meant by saying that children were sacrificed to the devil and were tortured. Neither therapist remembered the reference to human sacrifice made during the first meeting with Jenny Harris, when it was said that she "saw a man cut from here to here," nor did they question Sandy about what happened in the rituals. Their oversight could be readily explained by the flood of information they had been required to process in the revelations of thirty-four personalities in a period of just over a month. Later they would realize that had they asked the questions, they would not have been ready to deal with the answers.

CHAPTER 24

Prolonged daily sessions accelerated the early therapy for Jenny. What would normally be accomplished in months or years of once- or twice-a-week conventional sessions was compressed to weeks. The intense therapy was demanding, but seemed to be justified by the gains. In just over a month the therapists uncovered a complex system of personalities.

At this early stage therapy was almost more demanding for the therapists than for the client. In addition to time spent in sessions, the therapists had hours of information, recorded in notes and on tape from thirty-four sources, to sort through and discuss. They explored the literature looking for clues to direct their care of Jenny. They found little written on the subject in professional journals.

While waiting for a computer search to be completed at the local library, Rachel thumbed through the *Social Issues Resource Series: Mental Health Volume II*. Article Number 38, printed with permission from the *Palm Beach Post*, West Palm Beach, Florida, November 12, 1980, quoted Dr. Bennett G. Braun, a Chicago psychiatrist, recognized as one of the few specialists in the nation treating multiples. Dr. Braun's words, "Dealing with such patients is no simple one hour a week or five-minute phone call. A session can last as long as eight hours," were emphasized with the article's referring to the need for twenty-four-hour attention at times to bring personalities together.

The ideas presented in the article were consistent with how the Alexanders saw Jenny's needs and their involvement in response to those needs. Lengthy phone calls and hours of talking over impressions of Jenny's situation brought their work with her into their home. Their schedules of therapy and their habit of separating work and home life were changed remarkably when they began to care for Jenny Harris.

For Jenny, the early therapy had little effect on life at home. In a completely compartmentalized life, the events of therapy were kept separate from functioning at home. The various alters maintained their roles of responding to Michael and the children, so that Jenny's family did not see her as any different from usual.

Although the family did not show concern, Flisha asked the Alexanders to talk with the children. She wanted the therapists to help the children understand what was going on with their mother. With the children informed, the personalities could decide whether to disclose their own identities to them.

At the same time she asked that the children be told, Flisha asked that Michael not be. She felt he could not, or would not, understand, and feared that he might make "them" leave therapy. For now he was not interfering. Karl would wait until Jenny herself, or through one of her alters, let him know she was ready for Michael to be brought into the picture. He and Rachel would deal first with the children.

In the therapists' office, Morgan was remarkably at ease for a sixteen-year-old girl. She was as small as her mother, though somewhat thinner, and her hair was slightly more blond. Their physical resemblance and Jenny's youthful appearance gave the impression they were sisters. Too, their interaction was more like that of sisters than mother and daughter. "Quit your smackin'," Morgan told her when Selena surfaced and began to chew bubble gum. The criticism of her mother's gum chewing was accompanied by a smile.

Twelve-year-old Noel was less at ease. He covered his discomfiture with casualness. He slouched in his chair and feigned disinterest, answering the therapists' initial questions with "yeah" or "naw." He was a husky boy, not tall but muscular. His main interest, he finally disclosed, was the military. That explained the fatigue hat covering neatly trimmed brown hair.

After giving the young people some time to get to know them, Rachel and Karl broached the subject of multiple personality. Both Morgan and Noel accepted the discussion with equanimity. Yes, they knew their mother was different. She could be moody, strict one minute, and like one of their friends the next. Morgan said there were a lot of times when her mother acted like two completely different people.

The Alexanders' description of multiple personality seemed to explain a great deal for the children. The therapists spoke in generalities. They explained that the personalities had evolved as an understandable response to bad experiences Jenny had had as a child. The personalities had helped Jenny through the experiences and protected her from very bad effects. But now the personalities were no longer needed to protect her, and they created confusion in her life, accounting for the mental problems of which Morgan and Noel were aware.

Still in generalities, Karl said he had met personalities who had helped take care of Morgan and Noel when they were small, and others who were still children themselves. Noel acknowledged his understanding, saying, "I just wish she'd keep her little friends out of my stuff." Showing less of the essential self-interest of children than her brother, Morgan admitted she often wondered why sometimes her mother sucked her thumb.

The explanations about multiple personality elicited neither judgment nor indulgence from the children. Karl sensed their relationship with their mother would change little. They both expressed warmth toward her, and both accepted her behavior as they had in the past. Now they had a name for the behavior and a way to understand it.

At first blush, the children's responses to their mother were surprising. To the Alexanders, the overall effect of Jenny's behavior was so bizarre and the differences in individual personalities so obvious that it was difficult to understand Morgan's and Noel's acceptance, even protectiveness, of their mother. The therapists looked for some resentment in the children, some anger with the disruptions their mother caused.

The children seemed genuine in their reactions. They responded to the only mother they had ever known— moody, often sick, sometimes aloof, sometimes loving, but always their mother. They showed the same allegiance to their mother that most children would. Children are loyal to parents, loving or abusing. Whatever their situation, they adapt to it.

Karl and Rachel had concerns that given the profound abuse in Jenny's background, she had abused her children. Often persons abused as children later abuse their own children. At the very least, her parenting of Morgan and Noel had to be markedly inconsistent. However, it was unlikely that either Morgan or Noel could disclose such information to the Alexanders, whom they knew to be their mother's therapists and friends.

Given enough time and interaction, the therapists might establish relationships with the children that would enable accurate evaluation of the effects of their mother's illness on them. However, the Alexanders had neither the time nor the expertise to pursue therapy with the children at this point. Nor could they expect any more success in referring the children for treatment than they had had for Jenny. Both Morgan and Noel were doing adequately well in school. They both had friends and seemed content. It would be irresponsible to uncover problems for which they could offer no solutions. The therapists gave to Jenny's children what they had to offer — help in understanding her behavior, its meaning, and its causes.

At the same time the Alexanders were trying to help Jenny's children understand her condition, they reached for better understanding for themselves. One article in the scant number in the professional literature was most helpful, actually building on the information they had gleaned from the newspaper article and the book *Sybil*. In *The Journal of Nervous and Mental Disease,* October 1980, an article by George B. Greaves, Ph.D., addressed issues of frequency of occurrence, origins, mechanisms, and treatment. (See references.)

The description of diagnostic features coincided with the Alexanders' observations of Jenny. The description of alter personalities arising in response to trauma, the number reflecting the extent of trauma, also seemed to fit. A new personality could be required to deal with a single traumatic episode or could arise as the result of repeated trauma or to express thwarted needs or emotions. Seen in this light, each personality does not directly correspond to a specific trauma, but rather represents a new attempt to defend against physical or emotional pain. Dr. Greaves proposed that in treatment the alter personalities be freed from the memories and emotions that once necessitated their existence, then be involved in a process of integration.

The information was reassuring and gave some guidelines for treatment. However, there was so little in the literature regarding diagnosis and treatment that Karl and Rachel had to depend, for the most part, on their own knowledge of human behavior and their own intuitive responses to their client.

While looking toward full integration for Jenny in the future, to see her function as a single whole individual, the therapists had also to look for ways to help her function in the present. They considered what changes could be made in her environment and what changes could be made in her personality system to help her cope in the here and now.

Getting the personalities to cooperate by communicating

with each other and Jenny through the journal, and having them stop changing things in the house helped make the real world more stable for Jenny. Letting the children know about her being multiple made less pressure on her.

Still, there was confusion as well as anxiety. The sheer number of personalities vying for time created discontinuity and frustration. Their functions ran the gamut from Aunt Sue's loving protection to Wahnola's devastating self-abuse, from Barbara's holding to the Christian faith to Sandy's continuing practices of the cult.

Of the more than thirty personalities known to them, Karl and Rachel were aware that some were full personalities with significant histories of life experiences and a variety of behavioral and emotional responses. Others were personality fragments, having limited experiences and responses, and surfacing to deal with specific situations.

It was not always easy to differentiate between personalities and fragments. Some personalities had more depth, were more fully formed than others; some fragments were more complex than others. In some ways there was not a need to differentiate. All of them, personalities and fragments, were important to Jenny, collectively containing her experiences and ways to respond. All of them would have to be united with others to bring about Jenny's recovery. The personalities would require more attention in therapy than the fragments to work through various problems and needs, and to ready them for integration.

The uniting of two or more personalities or fragments to form a new functional being would be steps in the integration process, augmenting Jenny's recalling past experiences and learning new ways of coping. Personalities, including Selena, Flisha, and Marcie, as well as fragments such as Aunt Sue, Kathy, and Hilda, would each be asked at some time to give up a separate existence. (Having made the distinction between personalities and fragments, hereafter all the alters will generally be called personalities, recognizing that they have different features of longevity and influence.)

For a variety of reasons it was important to begin the

integration of alter personalities as soon as possible. Not only would confusion be diminished by reducing the number of elements operating in the personality system, but the system could be enhanced by strengthening positive features and attenuating negative ones.

To prepare for the integrations, Karl learned as much as he could about the personalities — when they had come, what purposes they served, and the experiences they remembered. He conferred frequently with Mind, seeking her insight into the backgrounds and motives of the personalities. Mind's knowledge of the system gave her some accuracy in predicting the risks and benefits to be expected from the integrations.

Karl was able to gain access to Mind through any of the personalities just by asking. The personality whom he asked relaxed into trance, and Karl asked simply, "Mind, are you there?"

"I am here," Mind invariably responded, remaining in deep trance. Together Mind and Karl decided they should begin with the integration of minor personalities, such as the four male personalities whose only function was to help discipline the children, with the more complex Justin.

Justin had maintained his function as observer for Karl, often speaking with him by phone. Finally overcoming reluctance at being seen in women's clothing, he came out in the office one day when Selena was dressed in jeans and a plaid shirt. He expressed embarrassment at being seen wearing earrings, then removed them, relaxed to a comfortable cross-legged posture, and extended his hand to Karl. He spoke at some length, man to man.

Karl approached Justin on the issue of integration. As he expected, Justin was cooperative. The other men surfaced so rarely that Justin was hardly aware of them. The few times they did surface, they were no more comfortable being dressed in women's clothing than was Justin.

Karl spoke to each of the male alters in turn — Jeff, Bob, Phil, and Terry. Karl found they had come into being fairly late in Jenny's life in response to her frustration with dealing with her young children. Since the children were older, there seemed to be no issues to resolve with these alters before integration.

Karl returned his attention to Justin, who suggested that the men first talk among themselves. Karl waited quietly and watched his client, a small, pretty woman, close her eyes in apparent repose while a five-way conversation took place inside her head. When the internal conversation ended, Karl would again be speaking to an individual who perceived herself/himself a man.

Although it was difficult to understand, Karl did not disbelieve the assertion that the personalities could converse. He respected the reality of their experiences. It was not so hard to see how one personality or consciousness could inhabit the body serially with others, one consciousness in control at a time. It was more difficult to grasp co-consciousness — one personality concurrently aware of the thoughts and actions of another. Internal conversation seemed to require still another level of existence. To talk together, personalities would have to inhabit the body concurrently, many minds coexisting.

When the personalities ended their conversation, Justin spoke for all of them. They agreed for the integration to take place at once.

Karl used imagery techniques to facilitate the process. He helped Justin to relax and to visualize himself standing on a top step, calm and peaceful, watching the other men walk up the steps. "As you remain deeply relaxed, I will count from one to five. When I reach five, Jeff, Bob, Phil, and Terry will enter you one by one, the integration will be complete, and you will open your eyes."

Karl was not sure what to expect. If integration occurred, it would be Jenny's doing. The mind capable of fragmenting into alter personalities was said to be capable of reuniting these personalities. Karl merely provided the environment and an attitude of expectation for change.

Justin opened his eyes and smiled. He appeared no different to Karl, although he behaved as if he felt different. The experience had been pleasant, he said. He had watched the others walk up to him, and then just sort of melt into him. He felt no ill effects except for a mild sensation of fullness and heaviness. Karl asked that he again relax, but not so deeply, and at the count of five to let the heaviness, a common result of deep relaxation, be gone. The process seemed to work well.

Karl did not test the integration. He behaved as if a change had occurred. He honestly did not expect to encounter the four minor male personalities again. The process seemed deceptively simple, perhaps because it involved personality fragments. Too, the act of integration was not a complicated maneuver by the psychotherapist, but rather an act of will by the client, an act which demonstrated motivation to achieve wholeness.

For this first integration, little time was needed for adjustment, apparently because of the compatibility among those involved. Karl realized, however, that integration could create stress for the personalities and tried to prepare them for a period of adjustment to new thoughts and feelings as the result of joining with others. He encouraged them to talk among themselves, to become as comfortable as possible about the process before entering into it.

Barbara agreed readily to Karl's suggestion that she accept Sandy in integration, confident in God's protection and her own piety. Sandy was the one to resist. She was convinced that no one would want her. She was too evil. Even if another personality would accept her, Sandy would not risk giving Satan hold on someone else. Only she should be damned.

Karl hoped not only to salvage the positive remnants of faith for Jenny, but also to end at once allegiance to the cult and the possibility of renewed contact with the Satan worshippers. He remembered Sandy's speaking of her belief in reincarnation. What if she were reincarnated to Barbara? Because an entirely new entity would be created, each could let go of any bad qualities and combine good qualities, such as knowledge of the Scriptures and the strength to stand against adversity.

At the time of integration, Barbara saw herself standing near the enclosing black curtain, and felt the cold hardness of the stone altar, so well had Sandy described it to her. The warmth of a bonfire touched her cheeks as Sandy joined with her.

As Justin had done, Barbara behaved as if the joining changed her. She spoke of a deeper understanding of the Scriptures and expressed gratitude for the knowledge instantly obtained. Although Sandy had seen the religious words perverted to justify a place in satanism, her goal to help Jenny understand the Bible was not that different from Barbara's. With Sandy as part of her, Barbara could use her knowledge and influence to assure Jenny of the Book's inherent good. The integration had the effect Karl hoped for. The focusing of the once-divergent endeavors of these two alter personalities helped to calm some of Jenny's confusion about religion.

Lisa telephoned Karl. Flisha and Selena were fighting again. This time it was over the preacher, David Alman. After three years he was pulling back from the relationship, and each blamed the other. Karl told Lisa he would talk with Flisha and Selena about David.

Before Karl got a chance to see them in the office, a crisis occurred. David accepted a call to a church out of state and left the area abruptly.

When Karl saw them, Flisha seemed able to take the circumstances in stride, but Selena was thrown into a deep depression. She broke into tears in the office. "He reached out to me once, but not anymore."

Karl made every effort to help her see that as a minister and a married man, David had to set limits on the relationship. Perhaps he needed to pull back to deal with his own feelings. In a way, David could be showing his true concern for her by ending a relationship that could never develop further. Selena was not convinced.

"I wanted him to love me." She was almost pleading. "I mean without sex. I want to make someone's heart sing. I want someone to laugh, to cry with me. I want someone good, not off the street. I'm a foolish little girl. I opened up. I don't like always getting hurt."

As if embarrassed at being caught with her guard down, Selena became remote. She had walls, she said, where it was like pretend, and nobody could touch her. She began to joke with Karl. She told him about the time she threw Kool-Aid on the preacher at vacation Bible school because he was fussing at Jenny. Karl wondered if there could be more to the incident, something to help explain her apparent need to connect with, and then to put down, ministers.

He asked her to relax, and Selena slipped easily into trance. He asked her to go back in her mind to any other time with the preacher that had a special meaning. She began to frown. "He's touching me — down there," she said in a small voice, "after he made Flisha run away."

"How old are you?"

"Little." She finished the story for Karl in a child's voice. Karl realized that the child who spoke was not a new alter personality, but a regressed Selena. She told him that Jenny had a part in the Christmas pageant, and Flisha was there to help with the singing. The preacher took Flisha by the hand and led her downstairs to the room where the choir robes were kept. He molested Selena there. It was the summer after the incident when Selena got her revenge, although she had already forgotten the reason why.

Perhaps with the incident remembered, Selena could begin to feel somewhat better about herself. Karl encouraged her to express her feelings about David's leaving. She hardly knew how; she wasn't used to having feelings.

Although things were easier with the number of alters decreased and with Selena settled down, Jenny was still quite fragile. She was able to stay out for such short periods that she could not learn much from her experiences. Karl was ready to see if Jenny could gain strength by having an alter integrate directly with her.

Mind agreed that Kathy was the logical choice. Kathy was the personality who had made it possible for a school-age Jenny to see only pretty things. Jenny could not look into mirrors because she saw herself as ugly, so Kathy used mirrors for her. Kathy had good feelings about herself, had a reasonable knowledge of the world at present, and had limited memories of childhood traumas. Jenny had earlier been able to accept Kathy's memory of her mother hurting her eye with a drill. Mind would pace the input of all Kathy's memories to Jenny so it would not be too much of a shock to her. Karl asked that Mind let Jenny remember as much as possible in the office, so he could be there to help.

This time Karl dealt only with the personality whose separateness would be eliminated. He explained to Kathy that at the end of his counting, she would exist only in Jenny, giving Jenny all of her good qualities and knowledge of the world. At the end of the count she opened her eyes.

"Hey Jenny, how are you?"

"Okay. Why's the Dictaphone here?"

As far as Karl knew, Jenny had not known what the Dictaphone was. She looked at him squarely. It was hard to explain, but it was as if she had gained substance. The characteristic rash appeared on her chest, but her fists were not clenched. "What is your name?" He had to check.

"Jenny. My head felt funny, like it busted."

"But you feel okay?"

"I feel funny, different, like I know things. Like when my head busted, mixed up stuff flew out, and something opened up."

"You look great, bright and aware. Come look in the mirror." Jenny stared at herself, backed up, moved closer, touched the glass, much as a child would play with the reflection. She had not seen herself clearly in a mirror since she was small. Kathy had given her back her image.

Rachel was not in the office, and Karl wanted very much for her to share this moment. He had not expected so great a change. He asked Jenny if she would call Rachel at home, just to talk with her. But first he wanted to ask Jenny a question. "What do you know about multiple personalities?"

"They are different, but all in one."

"Are you multiple?"

"Yes."

"Can you tell me the others' names?"

"Flisha, Selena, Marcie, Lisa. There are lots of them."

"Are you married?"

"Yes, to Michael, and we live in Elkton."

"You have learned a lot today."

Jenny picked up the phone and dialed. She had not known how to use the telephone. Now she even knew the number. The line was busy, so she and Karl talked a little more about how the personalities helped her to cope. As Jenny reached for the phone to dial again, it rang. She jumped nearly out of her skin and was gone. She had gained a great deal, but she was still very fragile.

CHAPTER 25

Selena's strength and dominance in the personality system became increasingly apparent. First identified to the Alexanders as "the bad one," she presented herself as a carefree teenager who was streetwise and self-absorbed. She denied any sense of responsibility for anything or anyone other than herself. Her behavior, however, belied her self-perception. She actually showed much responsibility in her concern for her home, her sensitivity to Jenny's children, and her struggle to earn enough money to keep the bills paid.

Without contradicting Selena's affirmation of independence, Karl suggested that she might have some trouble with having to pay bills and deal with things at home. He wondered aloud if she liked working the streets, really wanted to do that.

"It don't matter none to me," Selena responded. "I make good money."

"Do you know you could get hurt or catch a disease?"

Selena was genuinely naive about the risk of venereal disease. She was unconcerned with the risk of being hurt. She felt no pain related to sex. She said she didn't mind some of the guys; they were nice to her. With some it was a hassle.

Karl could see her begin to bristle as if she expected him to pass moral judgment on her. He assured her that what she did made no difference to him, except that he did not want to see her be hurt or become sick or be arrested because of prostitution. "Rachel and I want to help you, all of you, and Jenny. We can't do that if you are laid up in some hospital or in a jail somewhere." Karl asked if she would consider staying off the streets for two months as a kind of trial period.

"I reckon, if Ezra will leave me alone." She explained that Ezra sent men to her for a cut of the money. He could be very insistent, but she thought she could put him off for a couple of months. "Only thing is, what am I gonna do for money?"

"Maybe you could get a job."

Selena shrugged. "Yeah, I reckon. I worked in the mill before. I guess I can find somethin' to do."

It didn't take long for her to find work. Selena knew a woman who managed a small jewelry store. She hired Selena for the Christmas season, and said she could work five or six days a week through December.

Selena drove blocks out of the way to avoid passing the little market Ezra owned. He called a few times in the evening to say he had tried to reach her during the day. Selena told him she was working, leaving the hint that she might be available later. She didn't want to offend Ezra. She might need him sometime.

For the time being, Selena focused her attention on selling jewelry. "Any woman would love a bracelet like this." Selena grinned and held her arm to display the jewelry for the paunchy little man. He bought the bracelet and a ring to match, laughing along with Selena that "It's only money," as he paid the sizable bill. A lot of men bought jewelry at Christmastime. By the third week on the job Selena was making more sales than the regular clerks.

One Friday, Selena stepped outside to feel the cool air after walking a customer to the door. When she returned to the counter, she panicked. The two-hundred-dollar watch she had been showing the man was gone. The manager was in the back room, where she had been all morning. No one else was in the store.

Selena didn't dare say anything to the manager. She had to think, but it was difficult. Her head hurt. She was not used to feeling pain. She remembered seeing a gray-haired woman in the store. The woman had spoken to the customer before Selena walked him to the door. Could the woman have stolen the watch? There was no way Selena could pay for the lost merchandise. She would just have to hope nobody missed it.

She started back outside, to clear her head, and turned to glance at the window display. There in the front window was the watch. Selena didn't know how it had gotten there. She must have lost time.

It had always been hard for Selena to work for any period of time. Now she could feel the headaches caused by switching or by having to hold back another personality. The job increased pressure on all the personalities. It was hard for the others not to be able to come out all day while Selena was at work. They all felt frustrated. Selena was afraid she might not keep control. She worried that Hilda would come out and smash the display cases or something. She managed to keep Hilda in check, but could not keep complete control.

Once she was sure she saw Jenny's mother walk into the store, then walk out into the street. Jenny tried to come out to follow her, but Selena was able to get back in control.

No one in the store noticed a problem, and Selena didn't mention seeing the mother or the gray-haired woman to anyone. The people she worked with might think she was crazy. Even Karl might think she was becoming like Jenny.

Karl continued to encourage integrations to reduce the number of personalities vying for time and attention. Lisa agreed that she was ready. "I'll go with Marcie so I can grow up, and anyway, she doesn't do bad things like Selena." Lisa was nervous about her decision, but resolved.

"Selena's not a bad person. She needs to think better of herself."

"How can you think you're good when you're not?"

Karl tried to explain that Selena's behavior was her way to cope, but Lisa was buying none of it. She changed the subject. "I want to ask you something. Will you always love us?"

"Sure I will. Why do you ask?"

"I get kinda afraid — you know, when we're gone."

"I'll always know who's there, through Jenny."

"You have to love Selena too. She needs it more than the rest of us. She carries all the pain." Lisa did understand.

Karl had observed that the integrations produced some sense of loss and feelings of loneliness in the personalities. Still, he was not quite prepared for Marcie's response, or for his own.

When the integration with Lisa was completed, Marcie's eyes filled with tears. She had felt light and playful while Lisa was coming into her, but as soon as it was done, she realized that the child was gone. Karl's own eyes were moist. He was surprised to realize that he, too, would miss the charm and warmth of Lisa.

Karl's response did not surprise him as much as did Selena's. Selena was openly touched. "You and Marcie ain't the only ones feel like cryin'," she said. "I don't have to hear the cryin' and fussin' anymore, or pick crayons and dolls off the floor, but I'll miss it." Selena had never spoken well of Lisa, or of Jenny's children, for that matter. It was new for her to admit the soft feelings.

The changes in the system of personalities caused even Hilda to soften somewhat. She lamented to Karl how she hated washing dishes. "Can you imagine the dirty dishes around there? Everybody has a dish and a cup every morning, just like they have their own clothes."

"Can't each one clean up his or her own dishes?"

"That's my chore. One does the beds, one does the dusting, one mops, others do this and that. I just get the raw end. I get everybody's dishes."

Karl smiled and offered, "The one who does the furniture

gets everybody's dust." Hilda gave Karl one of her looks questioning his intelligence, but she smiled and conceded that things were better since the numbers were down.

Flisha decided it was time to reduce the numbers even more. She was ready for integration with Jenny. She felt she could help more by giving her strength to Jenny than by being separate. She wanted just one more day to take Morgan and Noel one last time to her favorite museum before the integration.

The next Saturday, Flisha walked with her arm around Morgan's shoulders and explained the fossils and some of the art. Noel wandered through the exhibits on his own, occasionally catching up with Flisha and Morgan to share a find. Flisha took her time, as if absorbing all she could and sharing all she could as her legacy for Jenny's children.

The integration of Flisha with Jenny went smoothly. Jenny became aware of knowing how to play the piano and of being able to sing. She felt the usual fullness and some confusion, but experienced no unpleasant memories or emotions from Flisha.

Other integrations were accomplished, with the personalities, sometimes singly, sometimes in groups, giving up separateness. The new Justin and the new Barbara integrated with others, as did Hilda. Aunt Sue died, as she had predicted. Wahnola was getting very weak, according to Mind. Wahnola had never surfaced in Karl's presence, and was apparently losing strength as Jenny gained it.

Selena continued to resist integration. She could believe the others were part of Jenny, but not herself. She admitted to sometimes dreaming she was Jenny's twin. Even that was not a very comfortable situation to consider, more a nightmare than a dream.

Selena had her walls, knew she did some bad things, but she didn't go zapping off to other worlds the way Jenny did. Because of the things she did with drugs and men, Selena believed no other personality would join with her, and she would not be put together with Jenny. She insisted she was different. "I know a lot of things Jenny doesn't know, except for those couple of years." She referred to the years from age twelve to age fourteen. "Maybe somebody knows about those years. For sure Jenny doesn't."

Selena balked at the whole process of integration. "All the people we were raised with, always been there, are gone. It scares me. Like people die and you're losin' somethin', yet gainin' a whole different stranger to live with. Like a stranger and not a stranger. Like when Justin was here, if the car broke, he fixed it. The others have all changed, not doin' their own thing like they used to. I don't know them anymore. And I've never been alone."

Mind acknowledged the inevitability of Selena's position, telling Karl that in the end it would come down to Jenny and Selena. "And," Mind said, "it will be a fight. Selena and Jenny will not integrate willingly. There is so much hate. They will fight for their own identities. It will be very painful for the one who finally stands alone."

For now Karl was concerned with improving Jenny's grasp of the real world. In particular, he wanted her to understand that her mother was dead and could no longer hurt her. He had tried telling her, but she could not believe him. Jenny believed she saw her mother and talked to her. Karl thought she may be less afraid, less distressed, once she knew of her mother's death.

Karl asked Selena what she knew about the mother's death. Selena let him know she never considered Gladys Faye, Chunk, to be her mother. She had taken little part in the funeral, but she did know the details of the sudden brain hemorrhage when Jenny was nineteen years old. She knew that Gladys Faye died in the hospital and was buried at New Hope Church.

"How did you feel about Chunk's dying?"

"I was mad at Jenny's mother for dying," Selena answered with bitter conviction. "I hoped to destroy her someday."

Marcie had clear memories of Gladys Faye's illness and death, but did not express anger at her being gone. She would share her memories with Jenny as she integrated with her.

Marcie was ready to relinquish her role in the system of personalities. She had nearly despaired of reconciliation with the Paynes. They claimed to love her, but said she was rejecting them. At least they had stopped the talk about demons after Marcie talked to them about multiple personality. Maybe they were trying to understand. But Marcie was tired of the struggle. She could no longer deal with the problems at church and at home. The children were nearly grown and didn't need her anymore. She was ready to join with Jenny.

Karl discussed the process with Mind and reviewed the qualities Marcie would take to the integration, her easygoing nature, her love and care of the children, her ability to laugh and cry.

Karl facilitated the integration in his usual manner. When he finished counting, Jenny opened her eyes and laughed lightly. As she had in the integration with Kathy, she seemed to gain substance. She held her shoulders more squarely, and her hands were not in fists. Karl asked her to relax and to think of Marcie's memories. She looked quizzical for a moment, then stated as a simple fact, "Morgan and Noel are really mine."

Karl affirmed her knowledge, then asked, "Are there memories of your mother?"

Jenny appeared almost to crumble as she cried out, "My mother is dead." Her shoulders slumped and shook with her sobs. "She left before we could ever make her love us."

"Your mother loved you in her own way. She was very sick. She can no longer hurt you." In a soothing voice Karl reviewed the details of Gladys Faye's death.

Jenny's expression changed. She spoke to Karl as if to her mother. "You hated me. You hurt me. I needed you to do things. I was so lonely, so afraid. All the other bad things don't hurt as bad as you not holding me, not wanting me."

Karl steadied her heaving shoulders and let her sob and sob. She got quieter, then whispered her desperation, "What am I gonna do? You're gone and you can't love me now."

Part VIII

Being Heard

There's this thing within that we are so afraid of.
How strong is it?
Is it stronger than all of us and Jenny too?
Is that why no one knows all the missing pieces?
Will we ever know?

                                        Jenny's Journal

CHAPTER 26

Once the pattern of integrations took shape, the process moved rapidly. By mid-January, three months after the beginning of therapy, the system of thirty-four personalities was reduced to three — Jenny, Selena, and Mind. Karl assured them that this number could be maintained for as long as was needed. They would continue in therapy to resolve issues and work on new ways to cope. When and if Jenny chose full integration, that could happen for her.

For the time being, the three of them should be able to handle anything. Mind had knowledge of the past, kept the ability to regulate Jenny's recall at a pace she could tolerate, and could prevent Jenny from harming herself. Selena could handle things at home, Michael and the children. She could even work if necessary. She could deal with people and have fun. Jenny, although still very depleted, was gaining strength as she reached for closeness and experiences in the real world.

Jenny had access to the knowledge and skills of all the personalities, who were, after all, her creations. In the integrative process, parts of the knowledge and skills returned to her. Jenny could look in mirrors, laugh, sing, play the piano, know her children. But there were limits. Jenny could sing, but she could not reach Flisha's high notes. She could laugh, but not with Marcie's abandon. She knew Morgan and Noel were hers, but lacked motherly feelings toward them.

The partial return of abilities once dispersed among many personalities was like a promise. The abilities could return when Jenny became able to handle them. A sudden return of abilities would overwhelm her by giving her tools she did not know how to use. Her renewal could not be instant, but had to evolve in its own time. Karl could not predict when Jenny would reclaim her abilities. He could only show her the logic that made him expect that one day it would happen.

Jenny came out more and more in the safety of the office and began to venture glimpses at other places. She came out at home just long enough to write in her journal or to listen to a song on the radio. She still needed the safety of the Alexanders' office or the reassurance of their presence to stay out for very long.

Selena felt that she was left to do everything, clean the house and cook, handle Michael and the kids, do the laundry. Mind could tell her how to do things, how Marcie had cooked beans for example. Still, Selena had to do the work. She had to pay for her new freedom and control with added responsibilities.

With all the personalities gone, Selena didn't know what to do with all their things. She began to experiment with wearing some of the clothing, but nothing felt exactly right to her. Lisa's jeans were too short, and Flisha's dresses were too fancy. About the only things she could use were some of Marcie's sweaters and blouses. She moved the other things to the back of the closet.

She packed the cosmetics that were not her brands in a cardboard box and shoved the box far back under the bathroom sink. Maybe she or Jenny would use them someday. The bottles of shampoo were too large to fit in the box. Selena used them to do the laundry. They made too much suds in the washing machine, but it saved buying laundry detergent, and the clothes never smelled nicer.

At first Selena thought she had mislaid her necklace. But when her earrings were missing, too, she decided Jenny must have put them someplace and wouldn't tell her. When she got to the office, she told Karl she thought Jenny was playing tricks on her.

When questioned by Karl, Jenny denied knowing anything about the jewelry. Selena was getting upset. "I'm not just losin' things," she admitted, "I'm losin' time and havin' headaches."

Karl knew that headaches often signaled the presence of an alter personality trying to surface. Could it be that there were other personalities as yet unmet? Could it be they had instituted the integrations too quickly? Perhaps therapeutic support was not adequate for Jenny, and she had to revert to dissociative defenses to cope with her daily life.

With Selena in trance, Karl asked to speak to whoever was there. His direct approach elicited the first of a series of alter personalities who had no awareness of Jenny, but functioned in the service of Selena. All were female and had come first when Selena was young. Several helped her deal with men without anxiety and guilt; a child allowed her to play, and a protector kept her from pushing the mother too far. It was this protector who had put Selena's jewelry safely away and had put the watch in the jewelry store window, not meaning to make them lost to Selena.

Mind was just as surprised as Karl to discover more personalities, who apparently were offshoots of Selena. Mind surmised that creating the personalities was Jenny's way of caring for Selena, since Jenny could not stay herself to help.

"Do you think there are others?"

"I didn't know about these." With the slightest hint of inflection in her voice, Mind continued philosophically. "In time we will know."

Selena resisted seeing any relationship with the personalities. She feared it meant she was like Jenny, and she thought Jenny was crazy.

Karl showed Selena his notes of sessions with "her" personalities. She shrugged. "They must be Jenny's. They're not mine." Karl filled in details of her lost time with information the personalities had given him, things Jenny didn't know. He showed her videotapes of the personalities' explaining how they helped her. "That means I'm sick like Jenny," she acceded.

"You are Jenny," Karl reaffirmed.

"I don't like her, and I won't be like her."

It was several months before Selena listened to Karl's explanation that the personalities were Jenny's way of helping her, and agreed to cooperate with the integrative process as long as others moved into her, not she into them.

In the process of the integrations, Selena allowed herself to age-progress to Jenny's current thirty-four years. It was getting difficult to remain seventeen, especially with her responsibilities for the house and with Jenny's children's being teenagers themselves. For the first time, Selena saw the few wrinkles around her eyes. She was aware of the extra weight in her middle. She wasn't sure her decision to be over thirty was a good one.

Jenny was pleased to learn about Selena's becoming her age and about Selena's personalities. She didn't even resist Karl's telling her that it was she who created the personalities, as she had created Selena. Jenny mused, "It's like creating something that takes its own shape and own life."

Jenny reasoned, "Selena has to know what I feel. She's the other half. Without her going through this, we would always be separate." Jenny got up from her chair, and taking a blue marker, drew a graceful butterfly on the board. She added many spots on each wing. The wings were she and Selena, she said, the spots, personalities. "Now the two sides can come together."

Aware that many of Selena's personalities had helped her to deal with men, Karl asked both Selena and Jenny to consider reasons why they reacted as they did to men, and why they thought the prostitution had occurred. As they gave their reasons, Rachel listed them on the board. Under Jenny's name she wrote: called me pretty, felt wanted, not alone, afraid to be alone. Under Selena's name: called me pretty, gave money and presents, wanted to get even, hurt them for hurting me.

Karl asked each of them to erase the reasons after he explained why those reasons need no longer exist. For example, friends could help her to feel pretty and not to feel alone. Jenny slowly erased her whole list, but Selena would not remove the last items in her list. "The reason to get even for the hurt never goes away," she said with bitter conviction. Karl and Rachel had some sense of how powerful the motives were. The writings and erasures just symbolized the work to come in uncovering and releasing the considerable hurts.

It was not difficult to lead Selena from the general discussion of men to talking about her father. Though she never acknowledged Gladys Faye as her mother, Selena accepted Jenny's father, Donald Poehlman, as her father too. Karl asked what she would say to Donald if he were there with her.

"I wouldn't talk to him; I'd kill him."

"Why are you angry at me?" Karl took on the persona of the father. "I had to go away."

"You left me with her and went off and married another woman and had a houseful of kids." Selena spewed her disdain.

"I couldn't stay with Gladys Faye. I couldn't live with her."

"You protected her just like everybody else did, so nobody knew she was crazy. If you didn't have the guts to stay, you shoulda taken me with you." Her hand flew out so rapidly that Karl was just able partially to deflect the blow she aimed at his chest. Selena's eyes closed, and her shoulders slumped as she escaped to a deep trance.

Mind surfaced at Karl's request and explained that Selena had run because she could not face the hate. "She has more hate than you'll ever know." Mind's soft, slow speech and the solemnity of her closed eyes made her wisdom seem especially profound. "To get rid of that hate, she will have to forgive."

"How do we help her deal with it?"

"Just keep forgiving her."

The next day, when Karl broached the subject of her father, Jenny ran immediately to deep trance. Mind at first said that Jenny could not be found. But with Karl's continued insisting, Jenny returned, though she refused to talk about her father.

Karl gave permission not to discuss her father. Instead he engaged Jenny in discussion of a hypothetical situation of having a friend who hated her father. Jenny slipped easily into the role of the friend, and as easily let Karl become the father. "I know you hate me," Karl ventured, "but I couldn't live with your mother."

Jenny covered her ears and turned away, but not before Karl saw her tears. He touched her shoulder. To his surprise, Jenny spun around and slapped at him. "Go away. I hate you."

"Tell me more about how you feel, and I will leave you alone." Karl was gentle but insistent.

"How could you hold me and then walk away? You left me with her." Jenny was seeing her father as she looked in Karl's eyes and expressed her hurt and defeat.

"I'm very, very sorry. Could you forgive me?"

"For leaving me, no!" Jenny replied with uncharacteristic force. The flash of anger was brief but definite.

Even such a slight show of anger was enough to generate extreme anxiety for her. Jenny had been taught long before that anger was a sin. She feared immediate, terrible retribution. Karl at once refocused her to the present, reminding her that she was in the office and he was her counselor. He touched her hand to help ground her in reality. Jenny began to weep softly. Karl simply assured her that nothing she had done had caused her father to leave her.

Mind was encouraged by Jenny's showing emotion. Karl was continually impressed with Mind's open pushing of Jenny toward health. "Let Jenny keep expressing the anger and the bitterness," Mind said. "Get her to scream it all out. She must remember all the bad."

Karl shared Mind's statement with Rachel when they talked together that evening. He reiterated also an earlier statement of Mind's that for Jenny, dealing with the emotions associated with her experiences would be more difficult than dealing with the memories. They wondered how much more "bad" there would be for Jenny to remember.

CHAPTER 27

It did not take long for Karl and Rachel to come to expect crises to follow significant progress. Jenny did not just recall events, she relived them with much the same intensity and terror she had experienced as a child. Although Karl mitigated the immediacy of her recall with hypnotic suggestions such as she view the events as if watching on film, and that she need not experience pain, Jenny often felt the pain, both physical and emotional, that marked the original experiences.

This kind of recall not only occurred in therapy sessions but also intruded into her consciousness in flashes of experiences from the past which seemed immediate and threatening. Jenny and her alters experienced these flashbacks awake and in nightmares. She would learn that the flashbacks were an expected response to trauma and that they would continue to surface repressed memories. Eventually she would learn to gain some control over them. For now she felt at the mercy of the memories.

Her response to the surfaced material was to feel ashamed. Rather than feeling the anger and righteous indignation the events warranted, she felt guilt and shame that she was such a bad person to deserve such treatment.

After episodes of recall, she invariably stared at the floor, unable to face Karl. Just as invariably, he tilted her chin with his index finger, gently bringing her eyes level with his own. He wanted her to know she had no need to be ashamed. Over and over again he asked her to see that the events were real but in the past, and that she had no control over, was not responsible for, the abusive things that were done to her. Her faint smile showed her desire to believe him, though she could not bring herself to do so. At times she replied cryptically, "But there were things I did, things I knew were wrong. I was responsible for that." She would not, or could not, explain what she meant. The details were a mystery to her, though she was very sure she had done something wrong, something very wrong.

On the rare occasions that Jenny allowed herself to feel and show anger, the ensuing guilt was even more acute. She saw herself compounding the sins of the past. She dealt with the distress as she always had, by withdrawing into her own worlds.

Jenny's distress and withdrawal left Selena alone and frightened. In her anxiety she enacted self-punishment with drinks or drugs, or by cutting or burning she could not feel. The acts of self-abuse gave some relief for a time from the anxious, terrible feelings.

The relief did not avert periods of depression and inertia in which she spoke about or wrote about wanting to die. Death, she said, was the only way out of the pain and confusion. In death she would find peace and finally would be whole.

The threat of suicide was constant. The desperate feelings were the inevitable response to prolonged abuse. The feelings were expressed more intensely at times, but they never disappeared entirely. The common practice for clients to be hospitalized when they experienced suicidal ideation did not fit for Jenny. It would have meant almost continuous hospitalization, and there was no facility available with staff knowledgeable in the care of multiples.

The therapists had to come to grips with the reality that Jenny might choose suicide, and that they might not be able to prevent it. Death could occur for Jenny at her own hand, or she could become victim of an internal homicide. One personality, unable to accept the truth of having a body in common, could seek to harm or kill another.

Karl and Rachel hoped that they would be able to prevent fatal harm to Jenny. When a personality spoke to them of suicidal or self-abusing thoughts, they asked Mind to increase vigilance in Jenny's interest. The therapists acknowledged the reality of the destructive feelings, but did not place undue emphasis on them. They did not want to give the threats manipulative leverage, nor did they want to dismiss Jenny's distress.

Self-punishment and suicidal thoughts were often followed by self-reproach. She didn't deserve the attention given by the Alexanders. She took up too much of their time. She should stop therapy. She had to get a job, or she would have to return to the streets to pay bills that were accumulating or to get things the children needed. The phone company was threatening to cut off her service. Their refrigerator had to be fixed. She needed to quit therapy.

While Karl and Rachel came to recognize the pattern of behaviors as evidence of her pain and her need to pull back, to resist the momentum of therapy, it was difficult to weather the crises. As much time as they gave her, whatever resources they found for her, she seemed to need more. The awful deprivation of her childhood created needs that seemed impossible to fill. Therapy was demanding for all of them.

The voice on the phone was familiar, but neither that of Jenny nor Selena. Her name was Pam, and she wanted to talk to Karl. Karl shook his head, knowing she could not see the evidence of his chagrin. The relative stability of the personality system after the integration of Selena's personalities had lasted such a short time. Was Pam the last alter personality, or would she be the first in still another series to be encountered?

Psychotherapy often progresses in levels, with traumas being dealt with in turn, as if peeling away the layers of an onion, until the inner core is reached. While the inner core would hold the most significant traumas, like the analogous onion, it would also hold the potential for renewal, for rebirth. Karl wondered how many layers would be encountered for Jenny, peopled with the many fragments of her self, before she could find an inner core of wholeness.

When Pam came into the office, she was agitated and could not sit still. At eighteen, she was skinny at a hundred pounds, and, at five feet five inches, taller than Jenny, and she wore her hair shorter.

Karl did not crowd her. He saw she was too fidgety to sit and talk, so he suggested she might like to draw on the art board. Many of the personalities had been able to express ideas or feelings through drawing. Pam worked quickly, and in just a few minutes had filled the board with a number of pictures.

She was hostile and abrupt, but she gave Karl the interpretations he requested. He let Pam choose the order in which she would describe her pictures. First, the hand with "bad" in the palm showed that every hand had hurt her. The fat woman was for Jenny's hating fat and never wanting to be fat. A crying eye inside a triangle represented Jenny's mind in confusion, and an adjacent spiral meant things inside were getting tighter. A series of small, fuzzy creatures were those Jenny continued to see. Finally, a female figure made of hearts showed how Jenny felt unloved. That was the reason she had come, Pam said, to take the feeling of being unloved. She had many memories of the things Gladys Faye had done that made Jenny know she was not loved.

After talking about the pictures, Pam was calmer. Karl reached his hand toward her but was not surprised to see her recoil, anticipating pain. He expected she might do that after seeing her drawing of the hand, and he had seen this response to touch in several of the personalities. They had been hurt so many times that for them, any touch was painful.

Learning that touch could be caring and that she could have control over how she would be touched would be a part of Jenny's healing. As he had with the others, Karl was able to use hypnosis to take away Pam's pain. He asked Pam to relax to trance, and suggested that touch could be pleasant for her. Out of trance, she experimented with tentatively touching Karl's hand and eventually worked up to an awkward hug. She was impressed with Karl's ability to remove her pain. She became less hostile and more ready to disclose her memories.

The pervasive element of Pam's experiences was water, and the ways the mother had used water in abusing Jenny. Pam told Karl how Gladys Faye — Chunk, Pam called her — punished Jenny for wetting her panties by putting her face in the toilet and holding it there while the flushing made the child nearly choke in the swirling water.

Pam knew about Chunk's putting blood in the bathtub and making Jenny sit in the icy red fluid and listen to screams about evil spirits. She knew, too, about the time Chunk took Jenny out in a rainstorm when she was about six. Chunk threw her into the muddy water where the dirt road had flooded by Aunt Mamie's garden, and held her down until she went limp. The water wasn't cold, Pam said, but it felt as cold and looked as bloody as the tub water had to Jenny. How could anyone be more unloved, Pam pondered, than knowing that your own mother tried to make you drown.

Mind cautioned that the memory of the near drowning would be especially hard and advised that Jenny be allowed to regain Pam's memories slowly. After just a few weeks Pam was agreeable to integrating with Jenny.

As Karl had suspected, Pam was one of several newly surfaced personalities. She told Karl she knew there were others, though she didn't know their names. They were shadowy to her, but would emerge soon. One she drew a sketch of — a creature with one eye, sharp teeth, a crooked nose, and five horns.

In the integration with Pam, Jenny experienced a sensation of wetness on her arms, as Mind let her face some of the memories. She remembered the bath in blood in detail and admitted to Karl that there had been times recently when she was in the bathtub and the water had suddenly turned cold and red to her. Karl assured her that need not happen anymore since she knew the reason.

Karl had been aware throughout the months of treatment that whenever Jenny went to the rest room, another personality, usually Selena, returned. He asked Jenny to go with him to look at the rest room and specifically to watch how the commode worked. Jenny admitted she had not used a bathroom since she was a very little girl, and though she felt somewhat afraid, she thought she might be able to use it now. Nervously she submitted to Karl's instruction. Then, left alone, she triumphantly used the facility. Pam had returned to her a very basic function.

Sometime later, Jenny and Selena recalled the near-drowning incident. It was very painful for both of them. Both were able to cry. Selena became angry. "I didn't want to live then, and I don't now." She tried to run, but Karl helped her to stay and face the sadness. He was not able to stop Jenny's running.

When Jenny returned from her withdrawal to her worlds, she put a name to the creature Pam had drawn. She had fallen away, away from herself, she told Karl, to where swervy walls held her in darkness. On her way back to the real world, she was sucked through doors, and the walls became like melting butter. She burned her hands on the walls. She saw a terrible face and heard the name Blair. Karl asked her to draw what she had seen. Her sketch was identical to the creature Pam had drawn weeks before.

Karl placed paper and pencil on the table. With Jenny in deep trance, he asked if there was a personality who could hear him and speak or write. Jenny's left arm came up to cover her face. Her right hand took the pencil and wrote *Go away*.

"Who are you?"

Blair.

"Are you male or female?"

Male.

"Describe yourself for me."

Ugly. Still hiding his face, Blair pointed to the sketch on the art board.

"Talk to me. I don't mind your looks."

Blair was hard to understand with his arm across his face. He explained that his purpose was to help Jenny not feel ugly. He had tried to get her out from behind the swervy walls. "But she was sucked into the doors of mind time."

"Why do you look as you do?"

"Chunk always told me I was ugly. My eye burns. I can't even see very well."

Karl went into the hallway so Blair could relax without being self-conscious. "Picture how you would like to look," Karl instructed. With hypnosis, Karl had Blair see himself as he wanted to be, six feet tall, blond, and handsome. Then he had him erase the picture on the board because that creature no longer existed.

Blair made himself comfortable in the chair and crossed his legs, happy to have legs to cross. He talked about how Jenny was a pretty little girl, but her mother made her feel ugly. When he learned that the mother was dead, he knew he was no longer needed and integrated with Jenny effortlessly.

In the variety of personalities who emerged along with Pam and Blair, Karl and Rachel recognized a pattern they had observed in Selena's personalities. There were fifteen or sixteen personalities in the group. One of the first to emerge acted as herald or spokesperson for one or more still to come. Functions were divided among the group to include: one to help Selena with whatever she was about, be it prostitution or honest work; a twelve-year-old child, corresponding to Jenny's age at the start of the lost years; a child of seven or eight to play with the twelve-year-old one; an internal self-abuser; one to hold Jenny's bad feelings about herself; an inner-self-helper, who augmented Mind's protective functions; and one or more to deal with issues of the past.

In this new layer of personalities, past experiences recalled were increasingly horrible, and the personalities who embodied them, more extreme. The therapists hoped they had reached the depth of Jenny's abuse and her splitting in response to it.

Selena brushed her cheek and smiled to see the flour that came off on her fingers. The biscuit Michael had thrown still lay on the floor. "Guess he oughta be glad it didn't dent the linoleum," she said out loud to herself, and laughed. She hadn't dared to say anything directly to Michael as he stomped off to work so mad he left behind the lunch she had packed for him.

She had thought to please Michael with the mayonnaise biscuits like Marcie used to make, but she did something wrong, because they were as hard as rocks. Hell, she didn't know anything about cooking, and Michael griped every time she burned the potatoes a little or didn't put enough fatback in the beans. All she could say was that she was trying. She couldn't tell Michael she never had to do the cooking when the others were around.

She missed them, not just Marcie's cooking, but also her taking care of the kids. She missed Nina's making over Michael and keeping him happy. She would even put up with Flisha's uppity ways to have her to take care of business — paying the bills, making appointments, talking to people. She wanted Justin back to keep the kids in line and to help her when she had trouble with the car.

Selena felt that she had it all to do, and sometimes she just couldn't handle it. She couldn't talk to people, not like Flisha could. She didn't have any business trying. She belonged on the streets with drugs, and people who accepted her as she was. With her old friends she didn't have to put on airs. She could be happy in her sandals and jeans, with a drink or a joint or some acid to share.

But that was all messed up now. She wasn't a kid anymore. The streets were fine when she was seventeen. Now she was thirty-four, too old for the scene. She couldn't go back. She had tried to explain it to Karl. The life she knew was on the wrong side of the tracks, but she didn't belong there anymore. She could never be accepted on the right side of the tracks because of all the things she had done in the past. So she just stayed on the middle of the tracks, and trains kept coming along to knock her down. Michael's throwing the biscuit was just another train on the tracks.

When Karl suggested that telling Michael about the nature of her problem and the treatment might make things easier for her, Selena was in the mood to agree. Maybe it would help if Michael understood, if he could understand. So what if he made her stop seeing the Alexanders? It didn't matter to her anyway.

She was a little surprised that Jenny agreed to Michael's being told. She was even more surprised when Karl told her that Jenny's main reason for letting him know was to make things easier for Selena.

Selena felt some real trepidation when the actual time came to tell Michael. She had led him to believe that she was seeing the Alexanders as friends, and that she spent so much time with them to help out around the office. She wanted to stay home while Karl told Michael the truth, but Karl insisted that she be there.

Karl had a nodding acquaintance with Michael, having spoken to him a few times when he brought Jenny to the office. Karl telephoned Michael to inform him that he and Rachel were Jenny's therapists, and that they would like to meet with him. They would watch a videotape of the movie *Sybil* together as a way to begin the discussion.

Michael remained silent throughout the movie. When it was over, he directed his question to Karl. "Do you mean Jenny Lynn has something like that?" He lacked the easy acceptance the children had shown, but at least he was willing to listen.

Together Karl and Rachel gave the same kind of explanation they had given Morgan and Noel earlier about the personalities arising as a response to an abusive childhood. Michael seemed better able to accept Jenny's changeability than to accept that she had been abused. He was aware that Jenny was often depressed, often suicidal. He just ignored it, he said.

Michael grew uncomfortable with the discussion. He acknowledged he did not understand Jenny and seemed almost apologetic in saying that he loved her, when she caused him so much trouble. From his manner and restrained remarks, Karl and Rachel gathered something about Michael's expectations. He accepted as duty the need to provide for his wife and children. In return, he expected that they show respect and obey him. Whatever happened, family was family, home was home.

Selena worried that Michael would be angry after the meeting. He never even mentioned it. His behavior toward her did not change. As before, he wanted his meals on time and his clothes clean. He called her Lynn or Jenny Lynn, and he pulled her hand away and fussed at her if he found her hand in her mouth. But he did not make her stop therapy.

Selena found herself restless. While there was some lost time for her, she was experiencing a continuity she never had before. Rachel's suggestion that she go to school didn't seem like a bad idea. Without Flisha to take over, Selena could study what she wanted, although she wasn't sure what she did want. She knew she was good with her hands, and she wanted to work with people. After going over catalogs with Rachel, to review the possibilities, she decided on a junior college program to become a physical therapy assistant.

Selena was excited about school, but nervous that she wouldn't be able to handle the course work. Her biggest problems were in reading and spelling. She seemed to have some learning disabilities. Rachel administered tests which verified the deficits. However, Rachel was not sure if the deficits represented organic dysfunction or were the result of the dissociative process. Perhaps learning Selena had missed during grade school because of the switching personalities would be restored in the process of integration. But Selena had to function as a student now.

Rachel offered to help. For a time a good portion of the therapy sessions was devoted to offering encouragement and helping Selena to upgrade her skills. Unable to grasp certain concepts and principles, and forced to read slowly and deal with many unfamiliar words, Selena simply had to memorize a great deal. Laboriously she managed to keep up with her classmates. She rejoiced at successes, but approached each test, each new class, with fears she would fail. She could not believe Rachel's assertions that all students are anxious at the beginning of classes and at the time of examinations.

"That's quite good."

Selena couldn't believe her ears. Mr. Rutland was actually praising her work. In his class she tried to make herself invisible. He refused to acknowledge her learning disability and insisted she meet the same standards as other students. She simply could not deal with the man. Now her anatomy professor was taking real notice of her.

Her drawing of the cat's nervous system lay on the desk in front of her. Jenny had done the drawing, and it was good. When drawings were required in class, Selena did the best she could. At home, Jenny could help her. Selena did all the dissection. Jenny couldn't handle seeing the dead animals.

"You did a good job with the cat. I noticed you did all the cutting." Mr. Rutland continued his assessment.

"Yeah, my lab partner's a pansy." Selena grinned and poked playfully at her classmate.

Mr. Rutland returned Selena's smile. "You're the best I've seen in this laboratory in a long time."

Mr. Rutland further acknowledged her skill by asking her to do a special dissection of a human arm for demonstration to medical students and for preparing photographic plates for a textbook. To do the special project meant traveling for the day to a university medical center with Mr. Rutland and working in front of several unfamiliar observers. Selena was uncharacteristically confident. Experiences in the cult had prepared her for what she would do.

The smell of formaldehyde was strong, but it didn't bother her. She made slow, careful incisions, progressing through the layers of skin to the muscles, nerves, and tendons, to their points of contact with bone. Her cuts were accurate and exact as she proceeded layer by layer to expose the intricate mechanisms of the once-living limb without severing a single nerve or blood vessel. Mr. Rutland expressed amazement at her skill. He never questioned where Selena might have learned so much about human anatomy or how she came to handle a knife so well.

School gave Selena, and, vicariously, Jenny, successes that Karl and Rachel hoped would help to improve the severely damaged self-image. It gave a chance, too, for success in a new social setting. She learned that other students liked her when they elected her as class representative to the student government.

Instructors guided her toward more conservative appearance and behavior, insisting that she give up her bubble gum in class, and that she tone down her makeup and manner of dress to project a professional image. Selena accepted their suggestions without seeing them as criticisms.

There were some disruptions for her on and off campus. Occasionally an alter surfaced and left class inappropriately, or stayed, but failed to take notes or to respond to questions. Once a young male alter created a stir by using the men's rest room. But, for the most part, schooling was left to Selena.

Her pattern of illnesses, accidents, and hospitalizations caused frequent interruptions in her schooling. Because professors allowed incomplete work to be continued to ensuing semesters, she was able to make steady progress, although for her, the usual two-year program would stretch to three years and beyond.

CHAPTER 28

Karl knew Selena was often angry at him, but he was not prepared for her suddenly springing at him. The bite was superficial, but her attack was meant to do harm.

Karl deflected her attempts at more bites and blows aimed at his chest. She spun away from him and began to beat her fists against the glass front door of the office, apparently determined to break through. He asked her to talk to him, to tell him what was wrong, but her lips were creased in a tight line. She was small enough that even in her fury, Karl was able to restrain her.

As he got her still, he felt her relax, and as she became limp, Mind's voice began an explanation. Karl had been talking with Selena at the end of a session, and she had casually mentioned that her cousin, Billy Joe, was in town. She hadn't seen him, but had heard from Aunt Mamie that he was there. Karl had noticed she showed no particular emotion at speaking of the man who raped her, but he failed to notice the personality switch. Mind assured him she could control the personality until the next session, and allowed Selena to surface for going home.

Vera Ann Birchausen was young, around sixteen. She saw herself as tall and slim, with black eyes, black hair in braids, and brown skin. Her father was Indian. Her mother was white. Part-Indian, as was Billy Joe, she was wily enough to outsmart him and strong enough to fight him.

Karl had no trouble recognizing her when she walked in for the next session. He had asked Rachel to be there to be sure they could protect Vera or themselves, if need be. There was an animal-like quality to Vera's movements. She moved quietly, almost stealthily, and always stayed ready to escape. She sat on the floor cross-legged, and for nearly an hour responded only in grunts when they talked to her. Rachel finally asked that she let Mind tell her about them, that she could trust them. "Just be quiet and listen to the voice inside."

"Hear nothing. Trust no man."

She sounded so much like something out of an old western movie that for a moment it was hard to take her seriously. Her lunge for the door and a swing at Karl were swift reminders of the hostility and violence embodied in Vera. She was tough and angry, even if Jenny had modeled her from a child's impression of how Indians behave. (The place of fantasy in the development of multiple personality disorder is explored by Young, 1988b.)

Karl restrained Vera. She went limp, and Selena surfaced. Selena told Karl and Rachel that there was trouble at home because Vera couldn't handle the pills and booze she was taking, and had gotten into several scrapes with Michael. Vera had come years before when Billy Joe gave drugs to Selena. Vera was using the drugs now to escape thinking about his being so near.

Selena had heard from Mamie that Billy Joe wasn't well. Mamie said that his color was terrible, and he was thin and weak, probably from drinking all those years. His wife, Rose, had left him years before, and he lived alone in Texas or somewhere. A couple of his children still lived in the area. He had come to visit them and the rest of the family. Selena made excuses about being busy with school to avoid having to see him.

Vera resisted Karl's efforts to gain her trust or to get her to stop the alcohol and drugs. After a few weeks she softened a little, but refused to discuss integration. If he tried to eliminate her, she said she would kill herself and Jenny and Selena. Although Billy Joe had gone back to Texas, or wherever, without her ever seeing him, Vera was still creating havoc and leaving Selena unable to deal with home or school.

The problems with Vera were solved as suddenly as they had appeared. Word came that Billy Joe had died, alone in a veteran's hospital. His body would be sent back for burial at New Hope Church.

Vera's acting-out behavior was replaced at once by the subdued demeanor of a personality whose function was to deal with aspects of a death in the family. Bridgette had not appeared often. Other personalities had the functions of dealing with the deaths of friends or acquaintances or distant relatives, even pets. Bridgette had come first when Jenny's grandmother died. She had surfaced again for the mother's funeral, and returned to dormancy until this new death in the family.

Bridgette stood with the family in the receiving line at the funeral home, accepting condolences. She expressed honest grief for this deceased cousin, having no bad feelings about Billy Joe. She retained her dominance for several weeks, participating with her aunts, uncles, and cousins in their mourning.

While Bridgette presented the appropriate behavior to the family, Jenny pulled far back in her own worlds, leaving Selena feeling alone. Selena was aware of Mind's presence, but Mind did not have the kind of reality to Selena that Jenny did. Although they could communicate by a sort of thought transfer, Mind seemed remote. To Selena, it was as if she had to wind her way through narrow cracks to make contact with Mind. With Jenny in her own worlds, Mind could not keep Selena from feeling alone.

It was Selena's idea for Karl and Rachel to go with her to places she knew as a child. The idea seemed benign enough to them. They were curious really to see how Selena and Jenny would react to the settings where so much abuse had taken place. They hoped to enhance Jenny's sense that what had happened to her was real and in the past.

Jenny directed them to Aunt Mamie's house, but withdrew as they pulled into the dirt driveway. Selena went inside with them. She introduced Karl and Rachel as friends of hers to her aunt, and they chatted about the weather and other neutral topics. After a time Selena went into the basement to get some jars of beans and pickles Mamie had canned and stored just a few feet from the old wooden potato boxes. Selena called to Karl and Rachel to help her carry the jars, so she could show them the boxes out of the view and earshot of her aunt upstairs.

Selena evidenced no distress beyond mild nervousness. Karl and Rachel were much affected. Seeing the rough boxes just as they had heard them described, big enough to hold a child, hit them both with stark, sobering reality. So vivid was Karl's mind picture of Jenny's torture, he nearly wept aloud. Rachel admitted in whispers to Karl that the boxes were proof to her of abuse that had seemed too extreme to be real.

From the aunt's house they drove to where Jenny had gone to school. They walked around the vacant grounds, looking periodically in windows of the low granite building. Selena recounted for them the story of the time in fifth grade when she pulled her bra off to "show real tits to that smartass, Margaret Ann, who was always calling 'em falsies." Selena's easy laughter about the incident in the school yard lifted the heavy feeling that seeing the potato boxes had caused the Alexanders.

The car was cool. They had left the windows down and parked in the shade of two large live oaks. They started to pull away when Selena pointed to a little house across the street from the school. "Chunk moved us there when Jenny was around twelve," she said. "Things were gettin' all messed up, and a doctor told Chunk she had to get Jenny away from Mamie's house."

"How long did you live there?"

"Till Nina married Michael, and they moved into the trailer," Selena responded with studied disinterest.

"Did anything of importance happen in the house?"

"Nothin' that I know of. We went to the state hospital from there was all."

Karl stopped the car to study the house. There was much architectural detail for such a small house. A covered entry to an arched doorway connected with a wraparound porch. Round attic windows accented a peaked roof. More the pity that the house had been so neglected.

They would have driven on, except the door to the abandoned house stood open, seeming to invite them inside. Selena hesitated briefly, then acted unconcerned and walked through the arch of the doorway. For a few minutes Karl studied the detail inside, as carefully done as the exterior and in even more disrepair. He noticed bricks torn from the fireplace and gouges in the walls. There was writing on the walls, a lot of it, but he paid little notice. His attention was drawn to Selena's increasing distress. Her discomfort became evident when she saw the tongue-and-groove walls of the old bedroom, and heightened when she saw the moldering yellow walls of the dining room. She moved her mouth, trying to rid it of some foul taste, and she clutched at her abdomen as she experienced waves of nausea and paroxysms of pain. She knew bad things had happened in the house, but could not recall any details. Karl led her outside and helped her to focus on things in the present, some flowers among the weeds in the yard, traffic on the street, to avert an abreaction until a better time to deal with undoubtedly awful memories and their accompanying painful affect.

When Selena regained a level of comfort, Karl asked her to go back inside just long enough to look at the writing on the walls. Something about the writing made Karl want to look at it again. Selena had not noticed the writing. When it was pointed out, it did not have any particular meaning for her. She showed no emotion as she looked at remnants of playing school, arithmetic problems, and grammar lessons. She read the list of names and saw the childish sketches without making comment. She became pensive only when she read the admonition that was familiar to her: *I must keep my mouth shut because if I don't I will get in trouble.*

Karl saw her sad expression as they left the house; he realized how firmly the warning to silence still held her. He knew, as did Rachel, that Jenny, some part of Jenny, had done the writing on the walls of this little house.

After the visit to the little house, both Selena and Jenny experienced flashes of memory and feelings of confusion about the house. Karl asked Selena if she would return with him there. He would allow any abreaction to proceed this time, and would arrange for extended time in therapy to help her process the memories and emotions. He knew from his experiences with Vera, the angry Indian, that he could physically control a violent outburst if necessary. He returned with Selena the next week.

Selena began at once to move her mouth in response to some foul taste. "Tell me what happened," Karl instructed.

"People I didn't know shut me in a box and threw a yellow powder on me that tasted awful and stung my eyes and smelled like a dead cat. Then I was shut in the box with live chickens clawing at me until I didn't remember anymore."

Before Karl could question her, she closed her eyes, signaling a personality switch. Karl grabbed Jenny's arm just before the fist smashed the windowpane. "Who are you? Let me help," Karl pressed, but the one who wanted to break the glass only stared and remained mute. "Is there someone I can talk to?"

"That's Todd," a small voice answered. "He doesn't talk. He breaks the glass because it hurts us."

"Who are you?"

"Abby. They won't let us play anymore."

Abby was nine years old. She grinned and told of times of playing school when she was the teacher. She showed Karl where she had put lessons on the wall. "Chunk wouldn't get us no blackboard." She became sad and told of times of being hurt. "They hurt us with a funny-looking thing. Chunk would be gone, and they would come and hurt us in the evil room. They had our names wrong. They called us Jenny. They didn't love us enough to know. They made us do bad things little girls shouldn't do."

Karl did not ask for clarification. At this stage of revealing, questioning frightened the personalities away. Going to the house provided access to more layers of dissociated material. Over the next several months a confusing tumble of personalities revealed themselves. Many were children whose only function was to play. A few besides Abby remembered bad things such as having hands slammed in doors and drawers, of trying to hide in corners, of being scared they would be locked away. The personalities were fragmentary, with none having a sense of continuity of time and events in the little house.

As fast as the child personalities were integrated, still other personalities appeared, some with memories from well back in Jenny's past, some with no history but with current protective functions. The newly formed personalities confirmed Karl's suspicion that Jenny was still using the defense mechanism of dissociation to cope with stresses.

Jenny's hold on reality was as tenuous now as earlier in therapy. To Karl, it was as if she were behind a veil, never able to see clearly the things in this world. Jenny said it was like looking at the world through a mirror. It could take hours for her to focus in and have a sense of being in the real world.

Karl talked with Mind about the situation. He suggested there must be some way to cut down on the time and energy required to bring Jenny from her worlds, or to hold her in this one. Karl asked Mind to devise a cue, a word or phrase or behavior that would help to bring Jenny out at once.

Mind told Karl about the top in Jenny's crystal world. Jenny could see herself and the others in the facets of the top, a most prized possession, and sense her connection with the real world. "Crystal top" would be the cue.

Karl was pleased with how well the cue worked. Although Jenny seemed to be unaware of its effect, his mentioning the cue made her more alert.

* * *

It was early October, almost exactly a year since therapy with Jenny began. The colors were dazzling, all the variations from gold to red to violet. The muted tones of fallen leaves served to make those still on the trees seem the more vibrant. No matter how many times they had seen them, the colors of fall in the Appalachians, the great masses of color on the gentle mountains, gave Karl and Rachel wonder anew.

Jenny had wanted to make the trip to the state hospital. The time she was told she had spent there seemed so unreal. She wanted to see the place to convince herself she had been there. Karl and Rachel had agreed, thinking perhaps return to the place Jenny had gone from the little house would help to uncover events of the lost years.

She was uneasy on the drive, alternating between silence as Jenny and nervous chatter as Selena. The mountains made her afraid, and the fear was magnified by the changing leaves. Autumn, red leaves, red sunsets, red blood, came to her in snatches. Bad things, the glint of silver above her face, the feel of a knife in her hand, robes, horrid faces, made no sense in a scatter of flashbacks.

The walk on the expansive grounds of the hospital brought Jenny the desired sense of reality. She saw the swings where Lisa had played. She remembered Marcie's helping to care for the old people and Hilda's washing dishes. Selena remembered the gazebo, and led Karl and Rachel there as she talked about the activities she remembered and pointed at a barred window in the huge brick building to show where her room had been. Together, Jenny and Selena were able to account for the few months in the hospital at age fourteen and the few weeks at age twenty-one, and know that the time had not been years, as it had seemed.

The trip brought no new clues to the lost years. But as the end of October approached, the emerging personalities took on a new and sinister nature. Like the array of children who emerged after the trip to the house, an array of witches emerged after the mountain trip. Most were teenagers, and each had a limited function. Tolanda was fourteen and had endured tortures and kept Selena from making mistakes in the rituals. She said she wanted to be pleasing to Lucifer, and tried to study books about the occult. Autumn, who took her name from the season, resisted. She never wanted to belong to Lucifer, and she never gave in to him.

Jenny began to talk of vague memories of things happening in the cult, flashbacks of herself on the altar, the taste of drugs and blood, the feel of the dagger, seeing animals and people and children sacrificed. Jenny was anxious and ashamed.

Karl and Rachel had trouble processing what they were being told about Jenny's involvement in the cult. They had heard and read about people who practiced witchcraft, making potions and casting spells. Sandy's report of her solo practice matched the opinions they held about witchcraft. They had not heard of groups who worshipped and made sacrifice to Satan, human sacrifice if the personalities were to be believed.

Karl began to search the literature, both popular and scholarly works. It was not a topic to explore through conversation. If the cult did exist and operate in the area, it was a well-kept secret, perhaps a deadly one.

Karl's reading confirmed for him that what Sandy and Selena had reported, and now Tolanda and Autumn spoke of, could be true. There was no direct proof of the events, just the knowledge that others described similar happenings. It gave Karl and Rachel unique appreciation for Jenny's difficulty in accepting her memories as real.

The young witches warned Karl that a powerful demon, Mindoline, would come to possess Selena, so that she would hold to the ways of the occult. Karl asked to speak to the demon.

"Don't look on me. So ugly. From the dark side."

"Tell me what you look like."

Her arm fell away from covering her face. Her eyes closed. Mind explained. "She can't stand to think of how she looks — like raw flesh."

Karl asked that Mindoline return so he could explain how he could help with the way she looked. Using hypnosis, Karl suggested Mindoline take any form she wished, then asked her to go with him to look in the mirror. Mindoline looked at her feet. "Not hooves," she said. She walked with difficulty on unfamiliar feet to the bathroom mirror. "I look like the others," she gasped. "Human." She touched her face and head. "The hair is gone, and the horns. My skin is white, not bloody."

Karl thought of the parallel to Blair, the personification of the ugliness her mother caused her to feel. Mindoline must represent the ugliness the cult caused her to feel. He felt much compassion for Mindoline, knowing that in her own way this hideous demon meant to help Jenny.

Karl's apparent power to make her over in Jenny's image impressed and frightened Mindoline. She saw Karl writing notes with his left hand and muttered, "Evil child," loud enough for him to hear. "Are you from there? Do you know the dark side?"

Karl smiled. "This is the only world I know."

Mindoline looked doubtful. "Don't put me back," she pleaded. "All the screaming souls there."

CHAPTER 29

Although the Alexanders could predict a crisis to follow the progress in therapy, they could not avert it. Selena made good a threat to leave therapy with the Alexanders and convinced Jenny to sign a statement that it was her own decision not to continue treatment. The pace of therapy had slowed with Selena's enrollment in the college program, but the progress that continued to be made brought memories and, with them, shame, pain, and confusion. The surfacing of material about cult involvement was especially distressing.

Jenny began the talk of how bad a person she was, not deserving the time the therapists spent with her. How could they truly care about such an evil person. Selena echoed the feelings. Her defiant I-don't-need-you-to-care attitude contrasted with Jenny's humble, defeated one.

Selena shifted the emphasis to routine problems — the bills, Michael, the children. She just couldn't cope with the house and Michael coming down on her about the bills. She was behind on her bill for medications and the payments on the refrigerator. Nobody would help. Ezra was pressuring her to return to the streets.

When the therapists did no more than listen to these

complaints, Selena shifted emphasis again. She hinted, then asked outright, for more time in therapy. She needed more time, more attention, so did Jenny. Selena wondered if it would help to go in the hospital.

The Alexanders did not think hospitalization was indicated, nor did they see the need to extend the already considerable number of hours they spent with her each week. The therapists saw the manipulation in this pattern of behaviors repeated time and again, but were frustrated in attempts to break the pattern. Neither Jenny nor Selena seemed able to see the paradoxical thinking in the attempt to control getting what she wanted. She was totally unworthy. She was totally deserving. She should have nothing. She should have everything. She took either stance, whichever seemed likely to get results.

Karl and Rachel could not escape some feelings of hurt that the trust they so carefully built was being tested again. They knew Jenny had to manipulate to survive in an environment where she could trust no one. But they had done nothing to betray her trust. It was frustrating to deal with her. But the therapists had to admire her skill. She was a master at manipulation.

Selena resisted returning to the streets. She contacted several ministers, but could not establish an ongoing counseling situation with any of them. Selena talked often with Dan Burke, a family counselor. Dan suggested she call the mental health clinic. She delayed that move for a time.

During the year she had operations on both wrists for treatment of carpal tunnel syndrome. After each surgery a personality tore open the incision, to inflict self-hurt, to offer a blood sacrifice, to let evil out; Selena didn't know the reason. Her feelings were hurt by the surgeon's anger at her. She could not tell him how or why the damage was done.

Selena knew she was not actually entitled to treatment at the clinic because she no longer resided in the county. But she was so persistent with the telephone calls, and so insistent that only he could help her, that Mr. Mooreland agreed to see her.

Mr. Mooreland was now program director at the clinic. A

lot of years had passed, twenty-two in fact, since he first saw Jenny Walters. He was a staff social worker when he recommended admission to the state hospital for her as a very disturbed fourteen-year-old girl. He noted then in the summary for hospitalization that she expressed thoughts of suicide, that she spoke of "a world of her own," and that she had "a rather unsettled childhood."

Ironically the notes Mr. Mooreland made after seeing Jenny at age thirty-six had striking similarities to the opinions he noted when she was a child. This time he wrote: "She describes herself as depressed and states that she wants to die." He wrote in some detail of her explaining that she was Selena, not Jenny, and telling him about her various personalities, and showing him diaries with different hand-writings. He noted: "She told how these different personalities live in various worlds, for example, in crystal worlds or behind mirrored walls. She appeared frankly psychotic, but seemed to have all of the various personalities structured in her thinking." His diagnostic impression that "this person is a severe paranoid person . . . who experiences ideas which are delusional" failed to acknowledge her as multiple, although Selena tried to tell him as much as she understood of it. Mr. Mooreland recommended hospitalization, as in the past. This time Selena declined.

The day after she saw Mr. Mooreland out of county, Selena was at the mental health clinic in her county of residence, talking about being multiple and saying she wanted to die. Mrs. Buxton, the senior staff member who saw her, insisted she be hospitalized because of suicidal feelings. If she would not go voluntarily, Mrs. Buxton would initiate involuntary commitment.

Somehow Selena was able to convince her to wait. Selena said she had to take care of some things at home before she could be away for any period of time. Mrs. Buxton agreed as long as she could be assured the client would return to the clinic by one o'clock in the afternoon prepared to enter the hospital.

Selena went to school and gave an oral presentation of a paper she had written for psychology class. Half the grade was based on the oral report, and she would not have been able to make that up if she had missed it. She made an A on the report. She was on time at the clinic.

She spent three weeks on the psychiatric unit. It was a relief to be away from the pressures of school and the pressures of taking care of the house and dealing with Michael and the children. The first day on the unit she broke a glass and cut her wrist, just scratches, but enough that she was placed on the locked unit. She liked the privacy of her own room and not having to attend the group meetings required on the open ward. She took most of the medications they gave her, but flushed some pills down the commode because they caused her face to twitch. When she was released, she telephoned Karl and asked if she could return to therapy.

For nearly a year she had stayed away from the care offered by the Alexanders. She, however, kept them aware of her reaching in every direction to relieve the pain, psychic and physical. She telephoned them many times, daily for a period. Neither of the therapists insisted she return. They were available if she chose to return to their care.

They had told Jenny as well as Selena that they believed leaving therapy was not in her best interest, but they acknowledged it was her choice. Their easy tolerance was pushed to the limit when Dan Burke telephoned to say that he was concerned because Selena had been very hurt by their rejection. Within a few days the hospital chaplain called to voice his concern at their rejecting a client in need.

Rachel was more angry than Karl. She felt her professional reputation could be threatened by the circulation of such erroneous information. Karl reminded her that Jenny Harris was well known in the area, certainly to most of the health care, religious, and mental health agencies. Whatever accusations she might make would be tempered by long-established opinions the community had of her. Still, the therapists were not happy to be so misrepresented. They would have to deal with the issue as soon as there was time to assess how well Jenny, with her system of personalities, was functioning.

When therapy resumed, Karl broached, with some trepidation, the subject of her talking with others. From what he could understand, Selena had been the one to instigate the interruption in therapy and to seek out other counselors and doctors. At the risk of reactivating the manipulative pattern of self-pity, self-reproach, self-justification, or the pattern of running from problems, he asked Selena about the hospital chaplain.

Selena looked quizzical. She hadn't spoken to any chaplain. It must have been some other personality. Karl could not be sure if this was her true perception or conscious disavowal. He did not accuse her further. He talked about how, although she perceived herself as one of many, she was one person. He let it be known that he assumed Jenny could hear what he was saying to Selena. He told her he believed her to be responsible for all the current behavior done in the name of Jenny Harris.

Karl did not fail to understand Jenny's dilemma. All of her life, she had run from physical and emotional pain, managing her escape through alter personalities. By refusing to acknowledge alters as part of herself, she could avoid accountability for their actions. She could run and not be blamed for running. When she needed to escape the psychic pain activated in therapy, she had run in her usual manner, effecting not only literal avoidance, but dissociative evasion as well.

Early in her therapy Karl and Rachel had made videotapes of sessions with alters to provide undeniable evidence of multiplicity to Jenny and her personalities. They continued periodically to record sessions for over a year. After that time they discontinued the cumbersome recording process, finding this kind of evidence no longer necessary.

Most of the alters accepted their being a part of Jenny, often requiring no more proof than the therapist's explanation or internal communication with Mind. Jenny and Selena admitted the multiplicity at times, but would hold to denial of responsibility by treating the personalities as separate.

Jenny could never gain control of her life if the pattern of denial and evasion continued. Karl hoped that letting her know that he held her accountable would help her to move toward control and toward changing her pattern of responses.

The Alexanders' taking Jenny to Chicago was as much for their benefit as for hers. Her therapy was the most demanding they had ever encountered, and they felt isolated at best as her caregivers. They recognized their limitations in caring for such a complex client, but not being able to refer her for appropriate treatment elsewhere, they felt committed to caring for her.

They had read all they could find in the literature, and had managed to have the diagnosis corroborated by psychiatrists, but they lacked the support of their colleagues and would have liked direction from therapists with experience in treating multiple personality disorder. Knowing that the lack of knowledge and acceptance of multiple personality by the health caregivers in their area was no different from that in most parts of the country was of little comfort.

Jenny's need to continue to exploit every available resource from ministers to medical doctors to mental health workers served to scatter energies and frustrate the Alexanders' efforts to maintain progress in therapy. They lost ground each time she was hospitalized in facilities not familiar with working with such clients. The antipsychotic drugs and major tranquilizers often prescribed for her seemed to aggravate her symptoms rather than to calm them. Diagnoses of psychoses, schizophrenia, or borderline personality were still seen by many as more accurate for Jenny than was the designation of a dissociative disorder.

The Dissociative Disorders Program at Rush-Presbyterian-St. Luke's Medical Center was established in 1984, a year after the Alexanders began working with Jenny. However, the Alexanders were not aware of its existence until 1986, when their inquiry to the National Institutes of Mental Health elicited information about the program. The center was at some distance, but could reasonably be reached by automobile. They wrote at once requesting a psychiatric evaluation for Jenny and consultation with an experienced clinician.

The meeting with Dr. Walter Young had a salutary effect for all of them. He met with Jenny alone, with the Alexanders alone, then with all of them together. His evaluation of Jenny confirmed the Alexanders' perceptions that she presented symptoms of classical multiple personality disorder. With careful explanation of his findings, Dr. Young expanded their understanding of the condition and suggested strategies for working with Jenny. He commended them for the significant progress made and encouraged them to continue to work with her, advising them to have patience in the process and optimism for the outcome.

For the Alexanders, validation by a professional colleague, an expert in the treatment of dissociative disorders, helped to counteract the effects of nearly three years of feeling ostracized, or at least being considered mavericks by their peers. For Jenny, it was enough to be believed and acknowledged as multiple, not crazy. They all gained from Dr. Young's warm acceptance and his pragmatic insights. Karl had to smile, though, when Dr. Young pointed out some symbolism in Jenny's journal. She consistently misspelled "else," writing "elfs." Karl couldn't believe he never noticed her simple message of plural entities in a mixed-up self.

Selena was nervous. Her efforts not to show it made it the more obvious. She wore too much makeup and had dressed in a low-cut, fuzzy sweater and tight jeans. Staccato smacks of her gum punctuated an otherwise uninterrupted string of chatter. "Morgan won't help clean up the house and acts like she'll die if she has to cook supper for her daddy (smack) and the kitchen floor is piled slap full of dirty clothes and half of them are hers (smack) and all Noel wants to do is run around and play soldier with his buddies like he ain't got nothin' to do like mow the yard or wash that nasty dog (smack) and if the damn kids don't help out around there I can't keep up with school (smack) like it does me any good to study anyway (smack) like the other day Mr. Rutland said we had to be able to name all the bones and muscles and nerves in the face (smack) then he didn't give us the test after I learned all them damn words (smack) hell (smack) I'll forget them before he ever gets around to askin' us about them."

Rachel thought of how Selena had talked in the past about hiding behind walls. It seemed so literal now with Selena's gobs of eye shadow and blusher and her virtual wall of words. She had to admire Selena though, knowing how scared she must be, yet she trusted enough, or wanted to be well enough, to make this trip with them.

They were hoping to find the meaning to at least some of the repetitive dreams that were troubling Selena. Although pictures were incomplete, bits and pieces of scenes recurred in her nightmares: being chased by robed figures, a waterwheel, bonfires. Asleep and awake, she saw faces of monsters, demons, and children — hurting, terrified children.

One image was just shapes. She sketched what she saw. In the foreground was a large rectangle topped by a triangle. In the background were several curved, upright forms.

Karl studied the drawing, so like a child's simple drawing of a house. But it had no windows for a house. It could be a barn, with haystacks behind. Selena agreed it could be a barn. She knew the cult used old barns a lot for the rituals. Karl drew big barn doors in the picture.

He asked Selena to enter trance and remember more if she could. She knew it was a place something important happened. He asked if she knew how to get there. "Highway Thirty-seven. I can see the sign."

As they drove along the highway, Selena recognized side roads that she said led to houses where they used to pick up people for the meetings. One led to a campground that she recalled the cult had used for up to a week at a time for several summers. They passed a number of barns. Many were old, but none was familiar to Selena. She began to settle down. The things they were finding posed little threat to her.

Karl was paying particular attention to her reactions to

the countryside and the buildings they passed. Right away he noticed her discomfiture as they drove by Marsden's Cold Storage. The small white building looked fairly old. Its modest sign offered low prices for meat processing and freezer locker rentals. It seemed no different from the dozens and dozens of meat lockers so common in areas where people raised their own cattle and hogs, or bought meat for home freezers by halves or quarters.

Selena began to shiver as if she were very cold. Her lips turned slightly blue, and her face went pale. Karl parked the car and asked Selena to relax in her seat and remember.

Selena remembered the sharpness of the cold, the hardness of hands slapping her, and the harshness of bright lights in her eyes as she found herself in a place of pure white, cold white torture. She remembered seeing Gladys Faye's face under a hood and the mother's carrying her to a dark place where she was made warm. Black-robed figures crooned to her, "White to black. All the good is gone." She was six years old.

While Rachel waited with Selena, Karl went inside. It could have happened here as she said. Cold air gently swirled against stark metal tables and white-painted walls. Karl figured it must have looked much the same thirty years before. "Can I help you?"

"I just wanted to know your price for half a beef."

Back outside, Karl looked at the sign with a sad, new understanding. The sign promised SLAUGHTERING TO ORDER.

Karl and Rachel talked with Selena for a long time to sort out the memory, to assure her it was real and in the past. She seemed comfortable enough, so they decided to drive on a few more miles before turning back. If they found the barn, they could talk about it later in sessions in the office.

Karl heard Selena suck in her breath. They were in town. There were no barns in sight, just a large brick church, and next to it, a cemetery filled with large, modern-looking grave markers. Karl pulled into the parking lot. Selena got out of the car and turned away from the church. She fought back waves of nausea, denying any knowledge of what had happened here, then she ran.

Louann was twelve years old. She remembered this place well, and began to half tell, half show the Alexanders what had gone on here. She led them in a triangular path through the cemetery, where they saw that the modern markers encircled an older graveyard with stones dating back to the 1700s. She took them to a stone topped by a statue of an angel and told how the children were made to curse God and the angels.

"That proves this is a place for children of Satan." She was pointing at a large rectangular stone with a triangular top. As they walked to the stone, Louann extended her hand to touch it reverently. Beyond the stone were rows of very old markers. Black mold obscured the inscriptions on the classically curved marble stones. They had found the "barn and haystacks" of Selena's drawing.

Louann showed them the grave where she said she was placed for demons to be called through her. She described being drugged and tortured, then giving way to Selena when the pain of passage of the creatures overwhelmed her.

Days later, in sessions in the office, Selena remembered the incidents in that cemetery. She had to go back, she said, to let the demons return to the pit and to put the children at peace. She was convinced that the faces she saw were those of demons loosed on the world when the ones who summoned them failed to control them, and those of children tortured and sacrificed to invoke Satan and his demons.

Already Karl and Rachel had overstepped the usual bounds of therapy in working with Jenny. They saw much value in returning with her to sites of abuse and other significant events; however, they had some doubts about outside-the-office therapy.

Rachel had a chance to pose questions about many concerns about their therapy with Jenny at the Third International Conference on Multiple Personality/Dissociative States in Chicago. The conference, attended by some five hundred professionals working with multiples, interested others, and a few victims of multiple personality disorder, provided invaluable input for Rachel that she would share with Karl.

Rachel was able to address her question about out-of-office work to Dr. Cornelia Wilbur, the psychiatrist who had treated Sybil, and who was a pioneer in treating multiples. The exchange was reassuring.

"Would going to the cemetery put your client or yourselves in any danger?"

"None that I know of."

"Then do what you need to do. Just don't do anything that could cause harm to or embarrass you or your client."

Rachel learned firsthand that many others felt as isolated from their colleagues in their own communities as did she and Karl. She learned that overinvolvement, especially in first treating a multiple, was so common as to be almost unavoidable. Many of these clients presented so much distress, had histories of such extreme abuse and deprivation that caring professionals were prompted to extend the time and energy they made available to these clients or to extend the relationship with them beyond a client-therapist one. Rachel made note of the studied attention required to set the necessary limits with such needy, often cleverly manipulative clients.

Questions concerning client cult involvement were raised in general sessions by others as well as by Rachel. The questions were not addressed in the general meeting, but an ad hoc meeting of interested persons was called.

In the short, tension-filled session, Rachel heard brief accounts of ritual abuse and human sacrifice. One attendee made the point that as Halloween approached, she knew there would be many more deaths in the name of Satan. Rachel was faced again with evidence that what the personalities said about Jenny's experiences was true.

Karl and Rachel reasoned that returning to the cemetery might help Selena and Jenny to accept the events there as real. Too, if Selena could find some relief from the hallucinations even for a time, it would do no harm. Karl worked with her to set limits that she not cry out or feel pain, and that she would know she was in the here and now when he spoke the words "ultimate reality." The phrase, like Jenny's "crystal top," would help Selena stabilize in the real world.

Selena retraced the path Louann had shown them and sat down on the grave facing the old marker. Her breath quickened, and her hands clenched to fists. Her eyes began to flutter, then to close. Her face looked sad, then registered fear as rapid eye movements gave Karl and Rachel the awareness that Selena was indeed seeing her horrors. In a few minutes her hands relaxed, and a tear ran down each cheek. She fell into deep trance.

"You have lain on the grave, and all the demons have gone through you back to the pit. All the curses of the children have been lifted, and they are returned to be whole and integrated. The faces will be seen no more. When I count to ten, you will know the ultimate reality of what happened, that it was real and it is over."

"Free," Selena whispered as she returned to conscious awareness. She looked briefly quizzical, then said, "Father." Karl and Rachel weren't sure what she meant until she pointed to the marker. Once they knew what it said, Karl and Rachel could read the weathered inscription, "FATHER," barely legible across an open book of stone. Selena knew the inscription from memory.

The experience at the cemetery left Selena feeling dirty. She continued to feel the blood and dirt and filth from the grave. It increased her sense of shame and guilt. "Gotta take a bath." She couldn't sit still for the therapy session. Karl suggested she could use imagery to take a bath in whatever way would feel right to her. He had her relax into trance and tell him about her cleansing as it took place.

Selena told of walking through a forest with wildflowers, where an opening revealed a high-backed tub filled with lavender water that felt like satin. She undressed and sat down in the warm water. The water began to move, like a rushing wind touching her body. As the water circled and vibrated, the dirt started coming away, except from her face and chest. "Find a sponge," Karl told her.

She couldn't find a sponge, but found a flower that looked like thousands of tiny fingers. She washed for a long time. She washed her eyes, ears, tongue, and chest with the flower. The hurt was worst in her heart and head. She felt the water become still. She felt lighter. She pulled the plug to let the dirty water down the drain, leaving the tub as sparkling clean as the air. The air was clear and fresh, and it made her skin feel warm and prickly. She dressed and came back through the forest path, knowing that for a time at least, the dirt, shame, and guilt were gone.

Part IX

Darker Secrets

A deep, deep fear,
One that's way down deep inside.
One I can't reach.
One that can't be let out.
A deep fear,
One which no one cares to know.

Jenny's Journal

CHAPTER 30

Kecia's thumb made a moist "pop" as she pulled it out of her mouth. She needed both hands to pull at the shoelaces. Even using both hands, she couldn't pull the laces tight enough to make Noel's size-eleven basketball shoes stay on her feet. To wear them, she had to shuffle her feet along the floor. The shoes were fun for a few minutes, but they didn't make the play shoes she had hoped to find.

"Whatcha doin' in my stuff?" Noel made his voice sound gruff, but Kecia could tell he wasn't really upset this time. She hadn't meant to get caught in his room. Sometimes he got really mad if she bothered his things. But she had been so engrossed in the tying operation that she hadn't heard him come in from school. She giggled and did her best to run from him, falling in a heap over the much-too-big shoes. She pushed her lower lip out in a pout as Noel reclaimed his property. "I need these right now myself," he said, but she was not mollified.

Noel left her holding the shoes and went out of the room. He returned momentarily, winding the music box inside a cuddly cloth doll. A mechanism made the doll's head and arms move in a sleepy rhythm with the tinkling lullaby. Unable to resist, Kecia let her pout give way at once to a grin. She dropped the shoes and reached for the doll with one hand, the other having found its way to her mouth at the first sound of the metallic notes. Noel changed his shoes and went to meet his friends, leaving the little girl who was also his mother happily occupied.

Kecia would not be satisfied with the little leather flats, or worse yet, the high heels she kept finding herself wearing. At the first opportunity she invariably took them off, much happier to be barefooted.

"What's the matter with your shoes?"

"Too tight." Though he didn't recognize her, the piping voice let Karl know he was dealing with a child. He had been seeing Selena out the door after a session when she stopped abruptly, looked down at her feet, and kicked off her shoes. Karl knew there had been a switch. The child looked around the room, then eyed the drawing board.

"Want to draw some?"

"Uh-huh." Kecia's sudden disarming grin made Karl think of Lisa. Since the integration that ended Lisa's separateness, a whole array of children had come and gone. They, too, had been integrated with others once their memories were revealed and their purposes were served. Still, it seemed there had always to be a child. Often the child was about seven or eight. Perhaps Jenny needed the child to continue the childhood she herself had given up at that age. Karl would not be in a hurry to seek Kecia's integration.

Kecia reached eagerly for the pens and began to draw a scene in varied colors. She drew gentle green hills and trees, and behind them, brown-peaked mountains, the valley between them made orange by a setting sun. She added a blue lake to the scene which became background for the portrait of a man. The man's eyes were black and had a wild, evil look. A violent slash of red marked his throat. The same red dripped from a large knife in his hand.

Karl asked the child to tell him about herself and her picture. Kecia giggled and slipped her thumb into her mouth, self-conscious as she told him her name and that she was eight years old. She giggled again and answered, "I reckon," to Karl's asking if she was pretty.

Any lightness vanished as she began to tell about the picture. Words rushed out in her need to tell it all at once. "They told the man to cut his own throat with the dagger and he did but when the blood started I got scared and ran off in the woods but the people chased me and I couldn't run good because the rocks cut my feet and they had dogs so they caught me and brought me back to the fire and told me to cut my arm with the dagger but I didn't."

In recent weeks Selena had told Karl about a recurring dream of being in the mountains and running through the woods away from something evil. After Kecia's story, Mind confirmed Karl's hunch that the dream was about running from watching the suicide. When Kecia had been caught, Mind told him, Selena had been the one to cut her arms and to burn herself with embers from the fire to prove by hurting herself her renewed obedience to the cult.

"Is that why she hurts herself now?"

"It could be part of the reason." In her emotionless monotone, Mind agreed to let Selena recover the memory.

Selena jumped as if startled and turned away from the drawing board, afraid of the picture and its message. Only by relaxing to trance was she able to talk about the memory of seeing the suicide and being made to use the same knife on herself.

When they finished talking, Karl asked her to get up and erase the board, letting the feelings of fear and hurt be gone as she removed the picture. Selena deliberately wiped away the mountains, trees, and lake in turn, and finally erased the figure of the man. She left, however, his hand holding the knife.

"Go on," Karl encouraged her. She began at the hand with the knife handle but hesitated at the blade. "All of it," Karl said, and saw the deep sadness in her eyes as she wiped the board clean. How much more to remember?

Remembering was only half the problem for Selena and Jenny. Getting along day to day was nearly as difficult. Selena feared the changes she saw in herself—the emergence of emotions and the experience of physical pain. Although she could "put up walls" against the emotions and "numb out" the pain with little effort, the fact of their reaching her awareness at all was disturbing. She saw herself becoming more like Jenny, and she would not be like her.

Rivalry, with concomitant bad feelings, surfaced often. There was dissension in something as simple as buying a sweater. Selena wanted her favorite color, purple. The color distressed Jenny as a symbol of pain, so she insisted on blue. Selena liked hamburgers and beer; Jenny preferred fried chicken and iced tea.

They competed for time. At home Selena wanted to sunbathe or study; Jenny, to draw or play the piano. Selena resented Jenny and the others in therapy. Jenny resented Selena's going to school. Selena claimed she needed school so she could get a job. Jenny never intended to work.

As much as Jenny and Selena had feelings of anger and jealousy one toward the other, each had a need for the other. Selena needed Jenny's presence not to be alone. Jenny needed Selena's ability to cope, to manage in the real world.

Karl suggested they try a temporary "merger." He used the term to differentiate the process he was suggesting from the eventual lasting union he hoped would occur for them after enough of the past was dealt with and enough issues were resolved for them to come together in a final integration. The merger would allow them to experience coming together as one whole person, for a time, in a safe place.

Karl and Rachel set up the guidelines. The merger would take place in the safety of the office with Karl's and Rachel's support. They would address the one new person as Jenny. Either Jenny or Selena could end the union at any time. During the merger neither could use the opportunity to invade the other's own place. Selena must not enter Jenny's worlds, nor Jenny venture behind Selena's walls.

Karl assisted Selena to achieve a moderately deep trance and suggested that at the count of ten, the merger would occur. He would continue his count to fifteen to allow feelings of fullness and confusion to dissipate.

At the end of the count Karl could see that she was having

trouble surfacing from trance. He used the key words for each of them to speed entry to the real world. "We want to reach the ultimate reality and have things become as clear as a crystal top," he said. She blinked her eyes and was very alert.

"What is your name?"

"Jenny."

Karl and Rachel were fascinated with what they saw. The "new" Jenny appeared to be at ease, almost outgoing. Her hands were relaxed, and her voice was forceful. Karl asked her to look in the mirror and describe what she saw. She seemed pleasantly surprised. "I'm as pretty as Selena, but my face is more thin, and my hair is more blond."

"Do you feel different?"

"Crowded. Selena's inside."

"Do you feel strange?"

"I feel sad, lonely."

"She'll always be here."

"But she's not out here like me. I don't see her with me."

"You can feel her, though."

"I'm scared. She's not here. I don't know if I like this or not."

"Because you are in control?"

"All of it, going to school, the house, and Michael and the kids."

"To deal with them, you might have to think like Selena."

"It's like I buried my best friend." The force was gone from Jenny's voice. She closed her eyes and slipped into deep trance.

Mind told Karl and Rachel that Jenny had felt stuffed and confused and very lonely. Selena had felt lonely, and she did not like the loss of control. Although the merger was short-lived, Mind assured the therapists that Jenny and Selena would continue to practice coming together in a safe place. Each feared to be, yet longed to be, reconciled with the other.

Later, Jenny characterized the experience of the merger with good humor. "It wasn't so bad," she said.

"What did it feel like?"

"You know," she responded as if she expected they really did know, "like a butterfly with boots on."

A few weeks later Karl and Rachel accepted the invitation to her baptism. They were aware that Jenny had an abiding concern with Christianity, a concern manifested by several personalities. Barbara, Marcie, and Flisha had all been involved with churches and religion. With all of them gone, Selena held on to the desire to be Christian. Minor personalities surfaced from time to time with religious purposes, but it was Selena who sustained the interest.

Karl and Rachel knew it was an act of courage for her to seek baptism when she had been taught for so long that the church was the place of the enemy. They understood her need to affirm a faith in God as she moved in the shadow of the memories of Satan worship. They realized it also affirmed a desire for wholeness when they heard the minister say, "Jenny *Selena* Harris, I baptize you . . ."

Selena was somewhat shaken by the communion service that followed the rite of baptism. She accepted the wafer and drank the wine, all the while fearing she would be struck dead. As she was leaving the church with the Alexanders, Jenny came out to look at the stained glass window in the front of the church. The minister walked up behind her and touched her shoulder as he spoke. Jenny jumped, so startled that with Selena upset, Kecia was left facing the minister.

Karl caught her eye as she started to put her thumb in her mouth and stopped her with a shake of his head. "It was a very nice service," he said to the minister.

"Let us walk you to your car," Karl said as he piloted Kecia away from the minister. "Get Selena or someone who can walk in those shoes," he instructed her.

"I don't know where they are."

"Just take the shoes off, then."

"Selena'll be mad if I wreck her stockings." Kecia looked so forlorn that Karl didn't press. He took Kecia's arm. With Rachel walking on the other side of her, maybe no one would notice how she wobbled in the high heels. He hoped

Selena would surface once they were safely away from the church.

Crises followed progress right on schedule. During a heavy spring rainstorm Selena skidded her car into a stalled vehicle. No one in the other car was hurt. Selena was kept overnight in the hospital for observation and released when she was found to have only bruises.

Short of two months later she was back in the hospital for surgery to correct bladder dysfunction. Her postoperative course was complicated by infections. Her physicians could not account for the delay in healing and the recurrent problems on the basis of the relatively simple surgical procedure. Still, she did not get better.

Karl suspected that self-abuse might be involved. After several weeks he discovered a personality fragment who was purposely causing harm by dissolving granules of a drain cleaner to burn her urethra and perineum.

Karl governed his feelings with difficulty. Of all the frustrating aspects of Jenny's illness, the self-abuse was the hardest for him to accept. So many people had hurt her so many times. How could she hurt herself? No matter that he understood the action as part of her illness. He was angry.

Karl knew that Selena could sense his strong feelings, so he spoke them. "I can't help but get angry when you hurt yourself."

"You don't need to yell at me. I didn't do anything." Selena defended herself loudly against Karl's soft-spoken disapproval. Her defensiveness made Karl wonder how much Selena might know about the self-harm. Did he want to accuse Selena to find a target for his anger? Was Jenny not one person who had to be held accountable for all her actions? Or must he admit that Selena, like Jenny, was victim of a hidden part of herself who was compelled to do harm?

There seemed to be, in the complex system of Jenny's personalities, many fragments with limited purposes. They were opportunists who remained dormant, ready to resume their functions when some external event called them from whatever mind space they occupied.

This self-abusing fragment gave up her function when Karl convinced her that Jenny had suffered enough. Recovery from surgery, which should have taken a few weeks but dragged on for months, was completed.

The physical problems effectively stalled progress in therapy. With so much current distress, the Alexanders could not continue to help her uncover the past. An unnamed voice, a personality or fragment, let Karl know the nature of what was being avoided. She spoke cryptically and would not be questioned. "Everybody has a deep dark secret that they don't tell anybody. There is something deep deep down and very frightening that can never be shared."

Karl was sensitive to her great fear. "It could be that if the secret is shared, is out in the open, Jenny would feel better about herself. We won't press you or any of the personalities. But no matter how deep or bad the secret, our caring about Jenny, and you as a part of Jenny, will not change."

CHAPTER 31

Karl was not quite sure what to make of it when Selena appeared at a session wearing a silver ring embossed with a winged Satan. She acted coy at first, saying that she just happened to find the ring at home and that it must have belonged to Sandy. Karl asked if there might be someone else there who would know about the ring.

"I know about a lot of stuff." The voice was cynical, almost hostile.

"Could we talk about it? I'm a friend of Jenny."

The usual disbelief in offered friendship was followed by the usual willingness to talk about other personalities, especially Selena. The voice identified herself as Amanda, age seventeen, dark and attractive, and a witch. She said she planned to return to the cult. She thought Selena might be going back, too, but she wasn't sure. Amanda seemed scornful, doubting the sincerity of Selena's desire to return.

Amanda reported that she had seen Selena at home burning incense and candles on the coffee table. Selena had placed a brass candlestick and an inverted cross on her makeshift altar, and was chanting words to a spell to control a person, Michael probably.

She was collecting books again and had begun entries in a new grimoire, a compilation of personal chants and spells. New catalogs to order objects for spells and worship had been coming in the mail. "Maybe she does mean business," Amanda finally surmised. "I saw Selena reading in *The Necronomicon*." When Karl looked puzzled, Amanda explained that Selena was studying a book of the dead, how to reach them, how to use them to please the master.

Her mentioning pleasing the master turned Amanda to reflection. "You had to do things right in the ceremonies. You couldn't break the rhythms, even when you were just a kid."

"What happened if you did make a mistake?"

"Oh, a lot of things, like they'd make you prove you were worthy of the master. They'd tie your hand to a limb or a board and make you say the chant or count numbers. A man stood there with a dagger to cut your finger off if you messed up. They had to do it. You had to be worthy, or you could ruin the sacrifice."

"Would they always do this for a mistake?"

"Naw, sometimes you didn't get the chance to prove worthy. They'd just take a pair of pliers and yank out your fingernails."

Karl felt his hands coil protectively to fists at the thought of such cruel punishment. Amanda went on. "We'd keep our fingernails bit off so they couldn't get ahold of them."

Karl hadn't given much thought to the nail-biting habit he had observed over the months of therapy. One personality or another would try to grow her nails out, often protecting them with artificial ones while they grew. But always, before much progress was made, a personality, or Jenny herself, would bite her nails back to the quick.

As Karl consciously relaxed his hands, he thought of Jenny's hands perpetually in tight fists. He wondered if the now-forgotten threat of the cult's punishment was what kept her unable to open her hands. He had hoped that her remembering events in the potato box would help her change the fist-clenching, but it had not.

At least two reasons for the clenched fists had arisen in the potato box. First, she had to conceal the damage she caused by trying to claw her way out of the box. Second, she had squeezed rats to death in the box. Jenny had recalled both these things, but continued to keep her hands in fists. Karl asked Amanda if she would share her knowledge of the nail pulling with Jenny and Selena. Amanda agreed.

After a period of quiet, inner communication, Jenny came out staring at her hands. "Open your fists," Karl instructed.

"Bloody," she whispered. She pulled back, just barely in touch with the real world. Karl reminded her to let things be as clear as a crystal top. With great effort Jenny talked about the punishment. Karl used his index finger to tilt her head to face him as many times as she dropped it in shame. The abreactive nature of her recall meant that she not only saw the blood and felt the pain of the original experience, she experienced the shame of having failed to please the master. At Karl's reassurance that she was not responsible for the terrible things that were done to her, Jenny said, "But I've done things I knew I was doing and knew were wrong— things too bad to tell." She held on to her shame.

Selena's response was somewhat different. Karl asked her to concentrate on her fingernails and to tell him why they hurt. She clenched her fists, thumbs in, as Jenny did. "No," she said, with a touch of anger and defiance in her tone. She remembered times of finding herself with her hands bloodied from the pliers. Her hint of anger gave way quickly to a sort of resigned acceptance. It would take time to get at the anger.

As Selena seemed about to be finished with talking about her hands, she stopped, opened her hands again, and stared at her palms.

"What do you see?"

"Holes."

"What caused the holes?"

"Nails." She began to cry softly. "We were nailed on a cross. We were to suffer and die and rise in Satan. Water — cold — mountains . . ." Her voiced trailed off. She inclined her head and was gone.

* * *

Amanda's appearance was herald for a new series of personalities, mostly witches and children, who held memories of specific events in the cult. Karl began at once to effect integrations of those with memories with Amanda. She had knowledge of the whole time period of the events that were being brought to the surface, events that happened when Jenny was very young. Amanda would organize and record the memories so she could later help Jenny and Selena with them.

Amanda took her role seriously. She was patient with the difficulty the Alexanders were having accepting the new information they were hearing. The therapists had been told that Jenny was introduced to the cult at age five or six. While the child had been subjected to very early abuse by the mother, she had not, they thought, experienced ritual abuse until she was school age. What Amanda was suggesting put Jenny's cult involvement much earlier and with much more intensity than the Alexanders could have imagined.

Amanda kept notes as bits of information were revealed by other personalities — place names, highway numbers, details such as ropes, cold, ice, father. She brought in old photographs and postcards she found in a box at home. The cards and photos were of places in the mountains where, according to Amanda, Jenny was involved in rituals. She asked the Alexanders to examine her hands and see the scars left from the crucifixion Selena had partially remembered. There were barely perceptible marks on her hands, in the center of the backs and palms. Karl had to tilt her hands just right in the light to see the shine of the small raised curves of scars that could have been made by nails driven in the hands of a young child.

The impingement of the memories was terrifying to Jenny. She came out only at Karl's insistence. Her hands were still balled in fists. When Karl asked her to look at her palms, she saw no scars.

Selena became equally withdrawn, pulled back behind her walls. She left Amanda to cope with home and school for days at a time. She was troubled by dreams of being put in a small black box. She had a sensation that there had been a terrible pain in her heart.

Amanda told Karl and Rachel that she knew about the box and the pain. In time she would help both Selena and Jenny to remember. "But," she cautioned, "they will have to understand what happened, what came before. We have to start back with the first ritual."

"For now, tell us about the black box."

Amanda told her story dispassionately, but with confidence in her own knowledge. She spoke of a very special occasion.

Hours were spent preparing Jenny. She was bathed. She was rubbed with the precious oil rendered from the bodies of unbaptized babies, killed earlier in ritual sacrifice. She was injected with potions to purify the blood. She was robed in white, led into a great round room, and made to walk a path formed by many people robed in black. The path was lighted by torches, and Jenny was led by two figures walking before her. One carried an inverted cross; the other slowly rang a large brass bell.

Jenny was brought to stand by the altar on which a man lay naked. Her mother stood near her at the altar, but neither looked at her nor spoke to her. Jenny watched the dagger come down and cut the man's throat, and the blood be caught in a chalice. She saw his heart cut out and placed on a platter and passed among the people for them to touch. She saw the heart cut in pieces and offered with the blood to the people to eat and drink.

After the dark communion, someone removed Jenny's robe and lifted her to the altar. Her legs were strapped down, and her head was extended over the side. She tried to lift her head to stare at the pentagram above her on the domed ceiling, but a priest held her in a taunting sexual assault.

As frantic chants of the excited crowd filled her ears, Jenny saw the master himself stand before her at the altar. A black cape covered his hairy body, but did not hide the horrible claws or the hideous goat's head. He raised his arms, and the cape billowed open to reveal the shining silver rod he would thrust into her as he straddled her on the altar.

The crowd quieted as the master spoke. "Now we will be as one, to have the power of the universe. All your desires will be for me and me alone. I alone love you, and will hold you with me forever." Amanda wasn't sure of the exact words, only that they meant she was the desired of Satan.

Jenny felt triumphant. She turned her head to face her mother and smiled. She wanted to scream out, *You don't love me. But somebody loves me. It's me he wants, not you. I have the power. I am wanted. I am the one.*

She turned her head in time to see the dagger above her. The blade was very thin and sharp and engraved with the outline of the locust.

At the moment she knew she would be sacrificed, the blade came down. She closed her eyes. She could hardly breathe. She could feel the cutting, the warm blood on her skin. But something was strange. She felt the blade be jerked from her chest. She opened her eyes to see that the priest's hands were shaking as he dropped the knife on the altar.

He gave orders to take her away. She was picked up from the altar and put in a small black box. In the coffin, lined with black satin, she was carried through the throng of people and out of the round room.

The next thing she knew, she was in a pea-green room. She was lying on a table, and had a big bandage on her chest. A man, the doctor, knelt beside her, and she heard him say something like, "Hail, Princess of Darkness, they will surely fear your power now."

Karl and Rachel were stunned. They had let Amanda speak without interrupting, without asking questions, as much as they would like to have shown her story to be imagined. Rachel asked now, "How could it be that she was not killed?"

Amanda wasn't completely sure, but she offered some possible reasons. Maybe the high priest never meant to kill her, but just meant to draw blood and make a show. Chunk was friends with the high priest. Could be she worked some kind of deal, though Amanda doubted it. Chunk had little power in the cult.

The high priest could have made a mistake. He was

obliged to do things exactly right. He should have cut out her living heart in a single sweep. Failing to do so, he could not show his error by cutting again. Acting as if the child were dead would have saved him, and her as well.

"What did they do with her then?"

"They kept her away for a few months until she was all healed. Then they brought her back into the cult, and said she was her own twin. I don't know who all believed it, but they couldn't talk against what the high priest said. They knew anyhow that Jenny Walters had some kind of power. They started getting her ready to be a bride of Satan."

Karl did not probe into the new issue Amanda had raised. "When did the cutting happen?"

"Jenny had just turned five. It was in October, I think, of 1954." The date had no special meaning to Karl. He would realize its significance later.

"There must be some kind of scar."

"Yeah, below one breast. She was just a little kid."

"Would you show me?" Rachel asked. She went with Amanda to the privacy of the rest room. Without self-consciousness Amanda opened her blouse. The scar was very faint, but in the bright light the shine of the scar tissue could be seen beginning in the lower half of the breastbone and extending left under her breast.

Neither Jenny nor Selena could see the scar. It did not exist to them. Mind cautioned Karl and Rachel, much as Amanda had done, that Jenny and Selena would have to understand what had gone before the sacrifice. Jenny and Selena would see the scar when they could remember and accept the memory as real.

CHAPTER 32

"I knew somethin' was up when I came out with my hand up a turkey's butt." Selena was in a fine mood. The family had had a good Thanksgiving with all the trimmings. They had some friends over, and some of Michael's family. Everybody got along fine all day.

It was pleasant relief from the week before, when Morgan had gotten into a huge argument with her daddy. He had threatened to ground her for a month for being a few minutes late coming in from a date. Morgan bridled at the threatened restriction, and made a threat herself to move out of the house and go live with her boyfriend. She wouldn't speak to her father for three or four days, and she began packing her things.

"Jenny was so tore up, she went zapping off in her worlds, and I was just left with the mess. Hell, I don't blame Morgan. Michael acts so strict and uppity sometimes. Morgan's got a job. She ain't no little kid anymore. I figured to just let them handle it. I'm not sure what settled things down."

With Mind's help, Karl discovered what had calmed the situation. Marcie had resurfaced when she somehow perceived that Morgan was distressed. Although Marcie had integrated with Jenny over a year before, it was apparent that she was able, with the appropriate stimulus, to return to a separate status.

Both Karl and Rachel had mixed emotions about seeing Marcie. She had been a gentle, helping personality. However, her return pointed out how fragile was the stability gained for Jenny. They realized that even when Jenny achieved full integration, it could never be viewed with complacency. Given sufficient stressors, the oneness would likely give way again to many selves.

The returned Marcie was as cheerful and compliant as she had been when the Alexanders first met her, and just as protective of Jenny. She resumed her role at home and her place in therapy. She cooked special treats, including a pair of squirrels that Michael had got hunting, and Selena didn't know how to prepare. She did a thorough housecleaning. Right after Thanksgiving, she decorated for Christmas. She made gifts for the children, and took them to shop and to enjoy the lights of Christmas.

In therapy sessions Marcie again good-naturedly chastised Karl for simple errors. She came out as before if she felt he might be pushing Jenny too hard. She didn't need to appear often. Karl kept the therapy light and supportive during the holiday season, keeping as much stability as possible.

When the holidays ended, Marcie saw that Morgan would not be leaving. She spoke to Karl of going herself. She would go back, she said, to the farthest corner of Jenny's heart. Karl asked if Mind could help, and Marcie's leaving was as gentle as her reappearance had been.

Selena's good moods were interspersed with feelings of depression. She continued to have disturbing dreams, and spoke of them with Karl. She was aware of vague discomfort along her whole left side, especially in her head, shoulder, and hip. She kept seeing place names but couldn't give them meaning. She knew that there was something especially important about one place, Fontana.

January was not the best time to travel in the mountains, but Mind, Selena, and Amanda were all insistent that they needed to go there. Amanda had continued compiling notes of the cult memories and looking for evidence in photographs and souvenirs from Jenny's childhood.

Amanda knew what had happened at Fontana. "It was the beginning," she said. She would help Jenny and Selena to remember, but they would be very frightened and would try to say it was unreal, it never happened.

The long drive to the remote corner of the Smoky Mountains was starkly beautiful. An unusually large and widespread snowfall covered the hills, bearded with the gray of bare trees. Snow clouds allowed brief spates of sunshine, but held their dominance, giving a steely tint to the whole landscape.

Traffic was light, and surprisingly the roads were clear the whole way up to the visitors' parking lot at the entrance to the usually busy tourist attraction. A sheet of ice and ripples of snow covered the pavement in the direction of the dam. There were no other cars or people in sight.

They didn't need directions to find the way to go. A soft roar from the dam deepened and grew louder as they made the short downhill walk to the visitors' center. Karl tried the door and found it unlocked. They walked into the warmth of a circular, nearly all-glass observation room.

The view was awesome. The great concrete dam, nearly four hundred feet high, held back a ten-thousand-acre lake as gray as the day's sky. The wall of the dam dropped straight for a distance, then flared to widen toward the base for strength. The wide walkway atop the dam was bordered by steel guardrails as big as a man's leg and studded with lights. Great funnels beside the dam led to the penstock for driving massive turbine generators at the base. There was a sense of power here, of nature and man, cold, gray power.

Karl asked Amanda to go over again what she had told him about the place. Mind would let Jenny and Selena hear as much as they could tolerate. Karl would ask each of them to come out at least to see that the place was real, and to remember as much as she could for now. Amanda would take control at once if either Jenny or Selena tried to break away or to harm herself.

It had been night, Amanda told them, and Karl and Rachel could almost see the eerie blue she said the lights cast on the water and the dam. First there was a ceremony in the round room. Then the people marched to the center of the dam, carrying Jenny above their heads. The child was bound head to foot by ropes. One end of a rope was tied to the guardrail, and at the high priest's command, the child was thrown over the edge.

Amanda could not be sure if they meant to hurt her or just to cause terror. But the child swung too low and slammed into the flared wall of concrete, striking her head and shoulder and hip. Stunned and in terror, she dangled there for some time before they hauled her up to care for her as a child "dammed" to Satan. "Jenny was only two," Amanda said, "when it all started."

Karl and Rachel did not question the accuracy of recall. The event was surely real to Jenny, whether the recall was augmented by having been told later of the event, or whether she remembered from such an early age.

The remembering was very hard for both Jenny and Selena. Amanda maintained control most of the time, with Jenny and Selena making only brief appearances. Jenny surfaced at Karl's request in the round room. She sucked in her breath and cowered away from the sight of the dam. Karl sat with her on the floor and insisted that she look at the dam and say the name of the place and know that it was real. She did as he asked and wept briefly and was gone.

Selena was almost as subdued. However, after talking for a time, her curiosity overcame her fear. She asked to walk out on the dam. Karl agreed only if she would walk between him and Rachel and would talk about her feelings. She admitted she had a strong urge to jump. She repeated the story Amanda had told them. "We've come to the place it all started," she said.

Selena seemed to understand that the pain she experienced in her side could be caused by memories of that time. Body memories, physiologic responses of taste, smell, or sensation, are common to people who undergo dissociative states. Body memories are insistent, often being the first indicators of repressed material. They are persistent in generating sensations from the past which are hard to distinguish from those arising in the present. It is as if the body repeats its pain or discomfort waiting for the mind to remember and to integrate the sensation with thought in a unified whole experience.

Not long after the trip, Amanda brought a small cardboard box of photographs to the office. Karl and Rachel sifted through the pictures with Amanda. They noticed three pictures among the others because they were discolored similarly, as if they were made with the same faulty film. The pictures had been dated on the back by the film developer. The first photo was of flowers on Jenny's grandmother's grave. The other two were dated two months later. One showed a distressed two-year-old Jenny standing next to her smiling mother. The other was of Fontana Dam.

The old photographs provided other clues to Jenny's past. In several of the photographs Jenny was shown wearing a dark cape. "Did the cape have any particular meaning?" Karl asked.

"She was a little princess," Amanda explained. She handed Karl a picture of Jenny in the cape with one hand extended upward in salute. "See, she's saying, 'Hail, all power to Satan.'"

Amanda said that after Fontana, Jenny had entered a kind of training. Her mother did some, but much was done by Mavis, an old woman who lived in the mountains. Jenny was sent for weeks at a time to stay with her and be taught.

Jenny liked Mavis. She was old, but she had a pretty face and had glasses like Grandma and wore her hair in a bun. She would hold Jenny on her lap in the rocking chair and sing little songs to her and tell her stories about mushrooms and hoppy toads. She'd get Jenny to make up stories, too, and would praise her for her good imagination. She gave Jenny special teas to drink so she could imagine better and see the magical worlds that Mavis told her about. Sometimes she let Jenny have sips of her moonshine or a taste of her snuff. While her mother beat her for seeing things and called her evil, Mavis told her she was smart and fine. Jenny didn't realize that Mavis was getting her ready, just as her mother was, for a special place in the cult. Jenny wished she could spend all the time, not just summer, in the mountains with Mavis.

It was winter when Jenny was returned to the mountains. Small wooden crosses were laid out along a stream bank, stark against the snow, cold and distant from the fire. There were more crosses than Jenny could count, and more children. As were the other children, she was stripped of her clothing and laid on a cross. A robed figure tied her hands to the top, then splayed her legs to secure them to the ends of the cross member.

She made no sound as a second robed figure drove nails into the center of each small hand. She lay in silence with the others and listened to the rhythmic chants of the ritual. After the proper words were said, each child was immersed head down in the stream, living blasphemy to the crucified Christ, to receive baptism in the unholy spirit.

The needlelike pain brought out Selena. Struggling to regain her breath, she lay on the cross. The water was freezing in her hair, on her lips and eyes. She was there a long time, listening to the whimpers and gasps of the other children. Finally someone came to wrap her in a blanket. Selena peered beneath the hood to see the face of the old woman gently tucking warmth around her. It was Mavis, and Jenny returned to reach out to her.

Jenny didn't understand what Mavis was saying. "Why," Mavis asked no one in particular, "must they risk you at the feast? Don't they know you have more power than we have seen in a long, long time?"

Amanda's recall of Mavis's words helped her to put things together and see that the dam, the lessons, and the cross were all in preparation for Jenny's sacrifice. She told Karl the name of the celebration observed every twenty-eight years to honor Satan on his return to his people. Jenny had been stabbed at the Feast of the Beast in 1954.

Selena continued to process some of the memories. She remembered Fontana and spoke of it with Karl. She cried a little. "Did they hurt me like that just because Mama didn't love me?"

"It was part of a plan. Can you tell me about it?"

"I dreamed about a pine box lined in black in a round room. A child was put in the box, but it's too bloody to tell who it is." She drew in her breath. "It looks like me." The memory had become current reality. Selena ran.

Mind suggested that Karl tell Selena the whole thing from Fontana to the Feast in the form of a story, so she could hear what she was ready to hear. Karl countered that Selena was dealing with the memories well enough. Perhaps Jenny would write a story.

Karl made no mention of anything specific to Jenny. He just asked her to write a story for him about anything that came to mind. Jenny seemed pleased at the suggestion. She fell to the task, and in just a few minutes handed Karl her story. "Read it to me," he said. Jenny grinned, slightly embarrassed, but read her story at his urging.

"There once was a little girl who lived in the Forest of the Beasts. The only friends she had were the animals and trees and flowers. But she was not free to play in the outer walls of the kingdom. She was to be loyal to the inward walls of the old king and queen.

"Then one day her father, who loved her very much, had to go off to fight the beasts of the forest. He never returned to his little princess. The wicked old queen then gave in to the beasts of the forests. She sold the princess for precious gold, and to spare her own life.

"The little girl had to withstand the beasts' rules and do all that was demanded of her. Her frail little body was smaller than any other girl's in the kingdom, and her long golden hair turned from golden blond to red. They saw great power in her and so they were to offer her to the Greatest of Beasts.

"She was bathed in the finest of oils and her hair was combed until it glowed like the sun. But she was so unaware of the death that was to come.

"They came with robes. She wore white; the beasts wore black. They marched in two rows, and the princess walked between them, very brave, to show that she wasn't afraid, and to show the beasts that she was truly a real princess.

"The table was already prepared for her to lie upon. As she stood before the table, the Greatest of the Beasts told the other beasts to unrobe her and lay her on the table. She walked up to the table, sat down, then turned and lay down. She was ready to face the Great One.

"He unrobed and climbed on top of her. He had a golden sword which glistened as rays of flickering firelight hit it. It shone with an eerie feeling as the words were spoken. 'Here is the offering I offer to the Prince of Darkness.' And the princess saw the sword come down and strike her between the breasts. No more did the eyes of sadness cry for the lack of love."

As Jenny finished her story, she gently inclined her head. She had shown no emotion beyond a resigned sadness. Karl would not let her slip away. "What would happen if the princess didn't die?" he asked.

"She would have to face the Great Beast or the queen. She would never be happy."

"How could she be happy?"

"Maybe the trees or animals and flowers took her to a place to be safe, maybe to a crystal world. Then one day a prince came, but he didn't know how to break the crystals. The princess had to come out, had to trust. But she was afraid because she knew nothing of the world he came from. So she went back, and the animals told her things and how not to be afraid. But there was still something deep and black inside her. The princess is so afraid that someday the Beast or someone will shatter her whole world, and she will die a lonely and sad death. Sometimes she wishes that the little girl on the table really died. That would be the end, no more running, hurt, or tears."

Jenny's fantasy tale of the past had become current reality for her. "You know the whole story," Karl said.

"I was just a child," Jenny said, "and it was my pain. It wasn't even Selena's." She cried and hugged herself and gently rocked back and forth. This time Karl could not stop her leaving.

Mind emerged to verify that Jenny knew about the Feast of the Beast but to caution that there was still much she did not know. "Let whoever needs to come out, come out," Karl requested. When Amanda emerged, Karl asked her about Jenny and Selena.

"They need time alone. There is so much hurt. They are together right now." Apparently the two had merged for a time to combine their strengths in an act of self-comforting.

CHAPTER 33

Karl thought he was ready for the encounter with the mother, but the actual events of the first meeting and the meetings that followed were some of the most unsettling of all his experiences with Jenny's personalities. He had been warned by Amanda to expect the mother's appearance when Amanda gave her presence as explanation for Selena's finding herself wearing one of Gladys Faye's old dresses.

Karl could understand the existence of a mother personality. In the process of growing up, all children internalize their parents. For Jenny, internalization took the form of creating an alter personality. The personality must have evolved over time, taking on the thoughts and traits that Jenny ascribed to her. Jenny learned the traits for her parent alter through her own interaction with her mother and through what her mother told of her own past.

Another way to think about the mother personality was in terms of ancestral possession. In his work with multiple personality clients, Adam Crabtree encountered the spirit, or essence, of parents seeming to reside after death in the being of their children. They could be regarded as alter personalities, or as the parents themselves remaining in this plane to resolve issues, to find forgiveness perhaps, before being able to move to a new plane of existence. (See Crabtree, 1985.)

While the language of ancestral possession did not suit Karl in this instance any more than did that of demonic possession when he encountered personalities of witches and demons, he studied the concept. Theories of possession could be disregarded out of hand, or examined for relevant issues. Karl looked for the issues.

In his experience with Jenny, the entities Karl encountered had their origin within her and were not imposed from some external source. The witches and demons were alter personalities requiring reconciliation with, not expulsion from the being they inhabited. Karl expected he would find the same phenomenon in the entity of the mother.

Understanding aside, it was difficult for Karl to keep in mind that with the mother, he was dealing with an alter personality. Because of his feelings of anger at the abuse she had committed herself and the abuse she had subjected her child to, Jenny's mother seemed a very real and separate entity.

She emerged brash and hostile, self-centered and indifferent to Jenny. "Could you not turn off the lights?" The sarcasm that seemed to question his intelligence was reminiscent of Hilda's, although it was more cynical and lacked any suggestion of humor.

Karl ignored the implied "stupid" in the question and managed not to wince at her contempt. He had never experienced such raw, cold anger as he saw in the eyes she flashed at him before she squeezed them shut and clutched her head. Karl turned off the fluorescent fixture. "Why does your head hurt?"

"It has always hurt. The doctors didn't know for a long time. Now they say it's from hemorrhages and high blood. Makes my nose bleed too."

"Would you be more comfortable if it didn't hurt? I could try to help you stop the pain if you would trust me a little."

"I trust no one. The doctors thought they could help me, but they couldn't." With more unspoken contempt she let him know she found his audacity ridiculous, to think that he thought he could help her.

Unlike other personalities who accepted Karl's help, this representation of the mother held on to her distrust and anger and would not let Karl make her more comfortable. She consistently evidenced disgust with her appearance and resisted Karl's repeated requests to describe herself to him. "You know what I look like," she responded as if he were taunting her by asking. She used the nickname Chunk, as if to emphasize its derogatory connotation.

At times Karl had to ask for Mind's help to keep Chunk calm enough to talk with him. Without Mind's influence, she was vicious in her opinions of Jenny and would strike out violently at Karl with screams of "Leave her be. She is the seed of Satan."

She told Karl she had no choice. In the cult she had to turn the girl child over to them. "It wasn't like it was easy. It was a twenty-four-hour job to train her, to turn the Scriptures around, to teach her chants, to have her ready so men could use her by the time she was three."

She showed ambivalence about Jenny's place in the cult, proud that the leaders recognized power in the child, and jealous of that power. She described Jenny as pretty and sensuous and bright, able to do more than any of the other children. "But I had to punish her always because she is evil, Satan's seed. I hope she dies before I have to kill her. She has to die."

Karl tried to draw Chunk to a positive feeling about Jenny. He called her attention to the ring on her little finger. He spoke of how Jenny told him her mother had bought the baby ring.

Chunk interrupted with "It used to be hooked to a bracelet, but I stomped it one time when she was being a snot."

Karl persisted. "Could it be," he asked, "that deep down you really loved Jenny?"

Chunk threw him a snide glance, as if she was thinking about it. "No, not really," she concluded.

* * *

Chunk dabbed at her nose with a tissue. The way she held her head and peered at the tissue, Karl could almost see blood himself. At his suggestion she lay back on the couch briefly, and when she opened her eyes, Karl could see that cold hatred had been replaced by pained guilt.

As she picked up the conversation, the difference in tone was remarkable. "Jenny is so like her daddy, same kind of eyes and smile, and she is as gentle as he is." She smiled slightly as she spoke of the child with no evidence of jealousy or anger. She spoke of Jenny's musical and artistic talents. "She could pick out tunes on the piano when she was no more than four or five and couldn't read a note, and she would draw the prettiest little pictures."

Chunk was definitely changed. Karl could not tell if the sadness that came into her eyes was for herself or for the child. Perhaps both. "I never had it," she said. "There was too many of us. They didn't care if I could even read or write. Jenny always had somebody to take care of her."

She went on, as if thinking about things she hadn't thought about in a very long time. "Sometimes I'd look around and find her hurt, and I didn't even know how she got hurt. I'd call her to me to tell her I loved her, and she would run away from me, or stand there and scream and cry."

"Did you ever hurt her?"

"Oh, I beat her butt sometimes. We'd be real sick and she'd get on my nerves so bad. I had such headaches. But if I yelled at her or slapped her or had to beat her, later I would brush and curl her hair and tell her I was sorry."

"What is your name?"

"Gladys Faye Walters."

Karl noticed her reference to "we" and realized that she was not a changed Chunk, but rather a second representation of the mother. There was no way to prove or disprove that Jenny's mother was multiple, although it was now clear that Jenny experienced her as at least two distinct personalities.

He called Gladys Faye's attention to her hand. "Did you buy her that ring?" he asked, and pointed to the baby ring on her little finger. Her hands clenched into fists, and she began to cry. "Deep down you loved Jenny?"

Gladys Faye continued to cry as she nodded and whispered yes, then she clutched her head in pain.

"Relax and breathe deeply and let whatever happens happen. There is a reason for the headache." Gladys Faye's hands relaxed as she followed his instructions.

"Mama," Jenny cried. She clenched her hands to fists and looked puzzled. "I dreamed of Mama. Mama hurts. I can't help her, and she hurts."

"Your mother is dead. She can't hurt anymore," Karl reassured her. He would let her think for now the experience was a dream. He helped her to focus on the present. It was time to end the session.

Karl anticipated a time when Jenny could face the personifications of the mother within her, a time perhaps when there could be reconciliation. But for now, with the cult memories impinging, both Jenny and Selena remained unaware of the Gladys Faye and Chunk whom Karl encountered.

In the two aspects of the mother, one was a hostile, hating woman who had given her child over to the cult to save her own life, she said. The other was guilty and defeated, ashamed that she had failed to protect her child and to love her as she needed.

After two months of working with the personalities, Karl again considered making Jenny and Selena aware of them. Mind was convinced that they could not deal with the essence of the mother at this time. There was too much hate toward her. Selena had been terribly upset by seeing herself in the mirror wearing one of the mother's old dresses. She accepted Karl's explanation that a new personality must have found it in the closet. She did not want to know more.

Selena was experiencing again a dream she had had many times as a child, from the time she was small until the mother died. In the dream the child came home from school and was locked outside as usual. After a time the door opened by itself, and she went inside. She saw blood on the floor. As she walked from room to room she found body parts — a hand, a leg, a torso — all bloody. She was terrified, but she had to keep looking. She knew somehow that they were the mother's hands and feet, but she had to be sure. She ran up the stairs to the bedroom she shared with the mother. The head lay on the floor beside the bed. The mother was dead. In the dream Selena smiled. She was sure.

Rather than the confrontation Karl envisioned between Jenny and the mother, an internal reconciliation was effected. Karl continued to work with both Chunk and Gladys Faye for some time. Chunk remained hostile, although she became gradually less violent. She felt old and tired and of little use. She agreed to integrate with Gladys Faye to avoid the continual headaches and to escape having to deal with Jenny.

Gladys Faye weathered a period of confusion and mixed feelings after accepting Chunk, but she consistently maintained her desire to somehow make up for failing to protect Jenny. Gladys Faye felt that to make herself known to Jenny would bring on anger and hatred that she deserved but could not face. She responded with much relief to Karl's suggestion that she could have another chance. She could become an inner-self-helper, giving Jenny any sense possible of a mother's love.

There were few pleasant memories, but Gladys Faye caused Jenny to think of a time that she sat on the porch steps and tossed a ball to her, and a time when she picked her up after she fell and skinned her knee. Gladys Faye reminded her of the pretty dresses she bought for her, and of a birthday party she gave for her when she was six. She stayed close to Jenny to help her deal with the cult memories and agreed to come out at once to stop Jenny if she tried to harm herself.

Amanda continued to focus on the cult memories, compiling notes and finding pictures of significant events still secret to Jenny and Selena. She asked for, and Mind confirmed a need for, still another excursion into the Appalachians to complete the partial memory of rituals there and to help Jenny and Selena recognize them as real.

Karl and Rachel agreed that going to the sites could help. The trip to Fontana Dam had opened up a whole new level of awareness. It was as if a dam burst and let the memories flood out.

After the trip to the dam Karl had instituted the use of a key word to halt reactions that threatened to become violent or overwhelming. Although he had been able to restrain Jenny physically in any of her personality states when he had to do so, he hoped to supply an internal restraint to protect her from harmful or embarrassing actions, especially when they were away from the privacy and safety of the office. He used a technique suggested by Dr. Young, who had evaluated Jenny in Chicago and consulted with the Alexanders about her treatment.

Karl worked with Mind to establish the word "close," pronounced klōz, as the stimulus to bring behaviors or feelings to a close when they were inappropriate for the time or place. Although Karl was aware that the stimulus word might not always be effective, he developed confidence in the technique when he used the word to calm Chunk's violent outbursts and to stop some of Jenny's running to her own worlds when she became frightened by feelings or memories. Generally when Karl said "close," the personality he was working with would relax to a deep trance and be able to resurface and focus on the here and now or allow another alter to surface at Karl's request.

The Alexanders believed past behavior to be the best predictor of future actions, and did not expect Jenny to become uncontrollably violent or carry her self-hurting to the extent of suicide. In the past Jenny and her alters had been trusting and responsive to them and had followed their requests to settle down or had reacted favorably to their gently holding her. The internal restraint of the key word was added assurance of keeping her safe.

Using clues from partial memories, and with Amanda's help, Karl traced a route for them on the map. Interstate highways and generally improved roads would make the travel far easier than it had been when Jenny was a child.

The day of the trip Amanda was calm and businesslike. She was dressed in casual slacks, a short-sleeve knit top, and comfortable low-heel shoes. She was prepared to deal with the memories, to help push Jenny and Selena to remember but to take over when the recall became too difficult for them.

Selena was nervous and chatty, resorting to reading aloud from a diet booklet when she ran out of things to say. Jenny was frightened and silent, coming out for short periods in the car, attracted and then repelled by the early autumn beauty of the mountains. Kecia was excited about the trip. She brought her doll with the music box, and cuddled it while she sucked her thumb.

Karl and Rachel both laughed at Kecia's expression when she first put her thumb in her mouth. She quickly extracted it and examined it to find why it didn't feel or taste right. Karl explained that Selena had put on artificial fingernails the night before. "It's okay, Kecia," he reassured her, "maybe Selena will take them off after while." Kecia eyed the long pink nail on her thumb, then shrugged and popped the thumb back in her mouth, accustomed to the minor inconveniences of sharing her body with adult personalities who were concerned with fashion.

The reflection of the old mill in the picture-perfect pond seemed to gainsay any possibility of black rituals here. There were a few other visitors admiring the colors of the leaves beginning to change as Karl, Rachel, and Selena walked the path by the mill pond, and heard the gentle squeak of the slowly turning waterwheel.

Inside, the restored grist mill did not seem quite benign. There was a musty smell from the grain about, and the whole building shuddered as the stones turned. Selena, mesmerized by the turning stones, solemnly reached to put her hand between them. Before Karl could say "close" or grasp her hand, it snapped back out of danger. Apparently Gladys Faye had kept her promise to protect Jenny. Karl led her outside.

They sat in the shade of a huge old oak, and Amanda

surfaced to tell Rachel and Karl that Jenny had been brought here as a child and had been threatened with having her hand crushed if she failed in summoning demons. Karl asked, puzzled, "Weren't demons usually summoned from graves?"

"Oh, yes," Amanda assured him, and led the therapists along a path they hadn't noticed to a small fenced family burial plot behind the mill. The cemetery could not be seen through the surrounding trees, but was simple to find if you knew it was there.

Karl and Rachel were well aware that just being in the mountains was difficult for Jenny and Selena. Seeing an increase in the discomfort level of either was an indicator of their being near a place where cult activities occurred. With gentle questioning and exploring the sites, the therapists got a picture of what happened.

It was hard to accept the truth of what was described to them. However, the Alexanders could not otherwise account for the intimate knowledge of the areas, of knowing the whereabouts of such things as obscure paths and hidden crevices. Jenny must have been to the places before.

At a place not far from the old mill, a section of rounded mountaintop took the shape of a reclining Satan. At one end was a columnar stack of stones; at the other, a huge stone face. From a distance both the face and the phallic feature could be seen. Up close the outlines were lost in the general plant growth and rock formations. Amanda remained the dispassionate reporter as she walked around with the therapists and told what had happened.

It was evening, and a fire was built at the base of the huge "Satan's rod." The children were made to wait some distance away, huddled under a rock outcropping. As the full moon rose, Jenny was called with the other children to take part in sexual rites, where adults danced naked and prepared the children with smaller rods. The adults marched in procession across "Satan's back," carrying the children to the head end of the mountain. Jenny was tied with ropes and lowered over the edge to dangle at the mouth of the great face. She was told that if she were a true child of Satan, the mountain would not open and consume her. She passed the test that justified her place in the devil's cult.

Karl and Rachel talked with Jenny and Selena about how as a child she was trained in the ways of the cult. Her teachers, seeking to control her mind, body, and soul, continually put her in double-bind situations. To do well, the child had to prove she was evil. The only way for her to have any sense of worth was for her to learn the lessons as they were taught.

If you thought of her experiences as schooling, it was apparent that the whole Appalachian Range provided her teachers with a vast source of field trips. Caves, waterfalls, streams, odd rock formations were considered sources of power or conduits to the source of all power, The Father, Satan. The children were taught at all times to fear, yet to seek, that power.

To the Alexanders the lessons they were hearing about seemed often to be random acts of brutality with no purpose apparent except to terrorize and debase children. What they heard at Bridal Veil Falls reminded them that the acts were part of a plan to tie children, at least some chosen ones, irrevocably to the cult. Jenny was one of the chosen.

Soft mist from the falls felt refreshing on their faces in the warmth of the day. However, Karl and Rachel had no trouble imagining the night chill of late autumn that Amanda described, when five-year-old Jenny was dressed in a sheer white gown and placed on an altar behind the falls. After an injection of drugs, she was anointed with oils, and Satan was summoned to meet his bride-to-be. Through a drugged haze she saw a horned and winged creature come to claim her.

The actual chill of approaching evening reached them all. They walked back toward the car to begin the trip home. Karl assured Jenny and Selena that they need not remember everything the trip suggested to them at once. There would be plenty of time in therapy sessions to review and process the memories and the feelings associated with them. Both he and Rachel again reminded her that whatever was remembered would not change their caring, and that they understood that she had no control over what was done to her in the cult.

Back in the car, Kecia kicked off her shoes and reached for her music-box doll. With her thumb in her mouth she quickly fell asleep.

Selena awoke a few minutes later and absently wound the music box. As the lullaby played, the mechanism made the doll's head and arms move. Rachel turned at the sound of the music and saw the surprised look on Selena's face.

It was as if the doll had come alive. Selena looked tenderly at the baby squirming quietly in her hands, then laid it on her knees. Her face registered sadness and fear. She looked up when she heard Rachel ask Karl to stop the car.

"What is it?" Rachel asked. She touched her hand to Selena's knee next to the now-still doll.

Selena began to cry, and made no move to stop the tears, nor to wipe them away. "She was so pretty, black hair and blue eyes, and she cried so hard." She cradled the doll in her hands to look squarely in its face while tears continued to wet her own.

"What happened to her?"

"Satan got her." Selena's look of distress was compelling.

Rachel could feel a tightness in her chest when she realized the meaning of what Selena was saying. Selena had watched a baby (could it have been her own?) be taken from her by the cult. Rachel's response was automatic. Her mind raced with thoughts. "They may have told you that in the cult, but that baby is safe. God protects innocent babies," she said comfortingly.

"How old were you?" Karl asked.

"Twelve, I think. I had my baby, but they took her." Selena went limp as she escaped to a deep trance. Karl and Rachel let her rest.

The therapists were stunned. Rachel tried to hold to disbelief, yet she knew, as did Karl, that it was truth. Jenny had been made to give over a child of her own to the cult. The lost years had begun at age twelve. As much horror as she had endured, Jenny, even with Selena's help and with the other personalities, could not withstand the taking of her own child.

Mind emerged to tell them that things were very heavy. Then Mind let Kecia surface to continue her nap.

Jenny remembered the baby in much the same way as Selena. In an office session she emerged from trance as if from sleep. While in trance she had moaned and pulled her legs up and clutched her abdomen, apparently reliving the pain of childbirth.

She was calm as she told Karl that she had dreamed that someone was having a baby. "They let me hold her," she said. "But then in a couple of weeks I couldn't find her."

She became agitated as the past event became immediate. "They have her. I scream, but they hold me — and they cut her in two."

Before Jenny ran to deep trance, Karl was able to ascertain that she had been pregnant when her mother moved her to the little house across from the school. She had given birth in the house, and had seen the baby sacrificed.

When Jenny ran, Kecia came to suck her thumb and rest.

As Karl and Rachel glimpsed the events of the lost years, they understood more than ever Jenny's need to forget, to deny the horrors. Still, they had to bring her to reality.

At the next session Karl reminded Jenny that the baby was not a dream. It became real and present for her again. "Stop, stop, don't do it," she yelled.

"What can you do?" Karl questioned.

"I hate 'em. My baby. They're hurting me." Jenny went limp.

"I know you hurt," Karl told her, believing that she could hear him wherever she had run. "It was out of your control. Just know that we understand."

After a review with Mind, Karl spoke with Selena to let her know that Jenny had remembered about the baby. Selena looked sad. "No hiding from it really," she said philosophically.

"Maybe you and Jenny could merge for a few minutes to help each other with this." Selena was agreeable and effected the merger at Karl's words "Do it now, please." Jenny sat up and held her head. She took a few minutes to sort her thoughts.

"What are you feeling?"

"All mixed up. The thoughts are different, all guilty, all hurting, all hating." She hugged her arms around her shoulders. "Nobody loved me enough to hold me. I don't know which hurts worse, the hate, or the hurt of not being loved."

Without prompting she remembered the baby and began to cry. "I had somebody to hold that was mine, and it was destroyed. Oh, God, it hurts." Her hand flew out so quickly that Karl was caught off guard. She nearly knocked him off his chair as she screamed, "The crystals are breaking!"

"Close," Karl said, and watched her relax. As he left her to rest in deep trance, Karl wondered if Jenny had, with daring to be angry, destroyed her crystal world so that she might come to live in the real one.

Part X

Promises

It takes a lot of courage and brings much pain, but I am being born again. This time as myself.

I opened my eyes this morning and saw the future for a change. Been looking behind far too long. It was about time I learned that the past can't be changed. The future is what really counts.

Jenny's Journal

CHAPTER 34

Ayla introduced herself to Karl without prompting. She was a religious young woman who denied any knowledge of the events recently remembered. She gave no details of her childhood except to say it was a pleasant one. Her denial of any abuse or knowledge of the cult was genuine. She had no history. She knew nothing of Jenny's background. Ayla was blond and pretty and a good Christian.

Karl made no effort to explain his role or to prolong the contact with Ayla. He asked to speak to Jenny, instructing Ayla to close her eyes and relax. He was relieved to see the rash appear above the collar of her blouse and her hands ball into fists. Jenny had been in her own worlds for several weeks since she remembered the baby, her baby, being taken by the cult.

Jenny's head was bowed. She gazed at the floor. Karl tilted her chin with his index finger. "Look at me. You have no reason to be afraid or ashamed." He repeated the assurance he had given countless times, then requested, "Tell me about Ayla."

"She's a good person, not bad and evil," Jenny responded. The guilt in her eyes added, *Not like me.*

Karl knew that Jenny experienced shame over having

created alter personalities. He questioned her gently to allow her to admit that she had newly created Ayla.

"She is good. She never did bad things. She can live in the real world."

"Jenny, you are a good person. You are not responsible for the bad things done to you in the past. You had no choice then, but you have choices now. Let us help you learn to live in the real world." He tilted Jenny's chin again, so she would look at him. "What happened with the baby was real. You were a child yourself, doing what you had been programmed, trained almost from birth, to do." Karl noted incredible sadness in her eyes before she turned away from him. But she did not run.

"We don't need Ayla," Karl said. "You made her. Can you take her away?"

Jenny turned back to face him. She nodded her head.

"Do it now, please."

Jenny focused into deep concentration. Her brow was furrowed, her muscles tense with effort. For several minutes she engaged in her struggle, her face showing beads of perspiration although the office was comfortably cool. When she turned attention back to Karl, she said simply, "She is gone."

Jenny's conscious removal of a personality was significant. At times she admitted being multiple, at others she denied it. Her active response in undoing the new alter denoted a new level of acceptance, and perhaps a new level of control.

The pattern of personalities changed. Amanda, Gladys Faye, and Kecia had completed their roles in helping Jenny with recall. They had covered with her a time span from her initiation at Fontana Dam at age two to her giving over her own child at age twelve, the start of the lost years.

Gladys Faye faded away. Amanda remained to deal with home and school until Jenny and Selena stabilized, then, with Mind's help, integrated with Selena. Kecia integrated with Jenny. It was no longer necessary for Karl to facilitate integrations with imagery or structure. With issues at rest or purposes completed, personalities found their own resolution.

Karl had forgotten a threat made some months before that the father would come for Jenny. Selena reminded him when she pointed out this entry in Jenny's journal: *Watch out, old man. I am going to get her — in her mind where you can't get at. I know the heart's weak, but I will get it.* The entry was signed *The Father.*

Karl had been told to expect that Satan himself would come for Jenny. He knew Jenny believed she deserved to be taken. Selena told him that Jenny was very upset by seeing what had been written in her journal. As for herself, Selena affected resignation. She could not fit into the world Karl offered. Perhaps she should return where she belonged.

Selena said she has seen The Father. He was old, with skin that was gray and claylike. Sometimes he had the head of a goat, at others, a fleshless skull. He could be seen only in dim or flickering light. Selena showed mild surprise when Karl turned off the fluorescent fixture and asked to speak with The Father, but she complied without comment.

"What in hell do you want?" The voice was gravelly and angry.

"To find out what you want." Karl's belief system acknowledged the possibility of physical entities of good and evil. He could not avoid sensing fear when he allowed himself to think that Satan could materialize here if he chose.

The thought was brief. The personality he faced made no claim to be Satan. He was not the master, but the likeness of one of many spiritual fathers who had taught Jenny in the cult. No more than a representative, he had come to reclaim her for the master.

Agent or not, he spoke with authority. "I want her. I will have her. I have all except one, and I will get her."

"Who is she?"

"Jenny, the birth child."

"I don't believe she is yours."

"The others are mine. I will have her." With that declaration, The Father was gone, leaving Selena rubbing her aching head.

While Selena relaxed to ease the pain caused by the rapid switching, Karl had time to think. Others, witches and demons, had focused their attentions on other personalities connected with the cult or on seeking Selena's return. This was the first direct bid for the real Jenny.

Rachel joined the session just as Karl began to describe for Jenny his encounter with The Father. Jenny gave a helpless shrug. She had been a victim for so long. "You can stand against him," Rachel said.

Jenny showed disbelief, but asked, "How do you mean?"

"I guess you could think of it as divorcing Satan."

"But divorcing is wrong." Jenny looked sad. She pulled back to let Mind surface.

"How is it done?" There was strength in Mind's familiar monotone.

Karl gave the answer. "I don't know that much about it, only what I've read. From what I understand, you need only to say, 'In the name of the Father, the Son, and the Holy Spirit, Satan begone.'"

Mind went limp. The therapists watched a redness appear on Jenny's forehead in the shape of a cross, like that traced recently by the minister at her baptism. The redness could be explained as a body memory, a recall of the touch originally associated with the words. The therapists were moved nonetheless.

Selena surfaced to tell what she had seen and heard. The words had been screamed inside by everybody together. Things had seemed dark, hazy, and confused for a time, but now the room seemed light and very real. Selena was more peaceful than Karl and Rachel had ever known her to be.

The same sense of peace was evident in Jenny when she surfaced. She smiled gently when the therapists pointed out the mark now fading on her forehead. She described essentially the same experience as had Selena. Jenny had taken a stand. The Father would not return.

* * *

Kayla had to be coaxed even to tell Karl and Rachel her name and that she was five years old. She cast her eyes about the office as if trying to see if someone was watching or listening. When her desire to please overrode her fear, she accepted the pencil Rachel offered, and drew left-handed a picture of a roundish creature with what appeared to be a child inside.

As Kayla stared at her own drawing, she became again shy. Her grip on the pencil changed to the awkward fist of a toddler. She scribbled at the paper for the few seconds that it held her attention.

"How old are you?" Rachel asked.

Kayla studied her hand, then laboriously held up two fingers. Speaking in short phrases, she could tell the therapists little. Karl told her to close her eyes, to let him speak with Mind.

"Kayla is an inner part of Jenny," Mind interpreted, "a part who was always there, who experienced everything. Kayla is the little one, the lost child. The picture shows the time when she was little, and they cut out the insides of a goat and put her in it — you know — a symbol of Satan's child. Kayla came then to always be with Jenny."

Karl thought with horror of the two-year-old child "born" in the bloody, still-warm body of the dead animal. "Let me talk to her, Mind, let her be five years old."

When Kayla surfaced, she looked past Rachel to Karl. Her eyes showed respectful recognition as she asked, "Did I do good? Did I do like you told me?"

Karl nodded, but did not speak. He realized Kayla was reliving a past time. She saw Karl as the high priest, and she was desperate to please him. "I made the pieces like you said," the child continued. "I made pieces of the baby like you said." Her small hand held the imagined knife, while her eyes sought his approval.

"You did fine, just fine." Karl played the role long enough to see her relieved expression before he pulled her back to the present. In real time she again looked around the room, afraid to speak.

For a period of several weeks Karl made brief but frequent

contacts with Kayla. She began to trust enough to tell them that she had to be careful of the spirits in the trees and in the wind, lest they hear her speak. Karl showed her there were no trees or wind in the office. She could be safe there.

Consistent with what Mind said about her, Kayla knew about most, perhaps all the early times in the cult. She described for Karl the sacrifice at the Feast of the Beast. "He got up over me and pierced me to make the blood start. He pushed it in, and it hurt real bad."

Karl noticed her choice of words. A five-year-old child would not say "pierced," except as she mimicked those who taught her in the cult. Karl saw the angry glint in her eyes. She blinked the anger away as she said, "It seemed like daylight would never come. Then I didn't remember if it did or not."

Daylight had come, Karl thought, but it had come for Selena. Kayla had the company of several alters, including Selena, when she lived through the experience at the Feast of the Beast.

Kayla's anger was so near the surface that Karl hoped she would release it. She would come close, would almost say it, but she would bite the words back, saying instead, "It is wrong to be angry. It is wrong."

Kayla shared many of her memories. She told of times of waking up with snakes in her bed. If she screamed, she'd be put in the box. She didn't scream. She told of a time of being put in a kind of hole. It was dark. She could feel snakes crawling, and she could touch parts of bodies, hands and arms all sticky, slimy. Again she waited for daylight. Again she held her anger.

With Kayla's disclosure of memories, Karl was faced squarely with an issue he had known for some time, but wished he could avoid. Jenny had spoken often of being evil, not just because of the things done to her, but because of the things she had done.

Kayla made Karl aware of how the cult made her victim, then made her victimizer. As young as three years old she was made to use the knife on others as it was used on her. She could not be angry with the cult. She was one of them.

The brainwashing had been thorough. Kayla followed the rules. She wanted only to please. She did not get angry. She kept the secrets.

Jenny held the limp, soft body of the little bird in her hand. She had found the pet, one of a pair of finches, lying on the floor of the cage. Its partner was unharmed. Jenny wept as she wrapped the little body in tissue and placed it in a small cardboard box. She'd ask Noel to dig a hole for it in the backyard when he got home from school. For now she held the little package and cried.

Selena told Karl about Jenny's being upset about the bird, although she had no idea what had happened to the creature. "It just died, I reckon. It was just a dumb little bird. Shit, it's nothin' to get upset over." In the space of a sentence Selena changed her concern for Jenny to contempt.

"I believe it bothered you a little," Karl ventured. "Jenny's not the only one with feelings now." The flicker of an almost apologetic smile let Karl know he had touched truth before Selena hurried to deny it.

"Naw, it's bad enough I have to see her face sometimes when I look in the mirror. I sure as hell don't act like her."

Selena seemed unaware that she had let slip a new admission that she and Jenny were moving closer together. She had admitted some weeks before that she didn't like her old miniskirts anymore. She could no longer eat onions and didn't much enjoy country music. Her new preferences for things Jenny liked frightened her. She had managed to avoid Jenny's control of her through integration, but she feared Jenny might have some new power. Selena had seen her get rid of the newly created Ayla, just made her disappear. "I will never be like her. I will fight. I will always fight her," Selena assured Karl and herself, although not with the same bitterness and conviction as in the past.

Karl and Rachel were aware of times that they could scarcely tell Jenny and Selena apart. Their voices, ways of moving, and mannerisms were so blended at times that the therapists had to ask a name.

Jenny was tolerant of her own assumption of Selena's

characteristics. She no longer took the bubble gum out of her mouth when she surfaced. She could smack it almost as well as Selena. An occasional "shit" or "hell" found its way into her conversation, and she looked relaxed when she sometimes laughed Selena's laugh. She did not mind that sometimes when she looked at her hands, she saw Selena's.

The next time Karl saw her hands they were covered with burns, small round sores made by a lighted cigarette applied to the flesh. Jenny admitted she had caused Selena to do the burning. Selena could do the self-punishment without feeling pain. If Jenny had new control, she had used it to harm herself.

Neither Jenny nor Selena would admit to anger associated with the recalled abuse. Neither could see the self-hurting as turning the anger on herself. If Jenny came close to sensing the anger, she escaped at once to near-catatonic trance. Selena stayed aloof from her anger, untroubled, she said, behind her wall.

Karl used hypnotic suggestion to remove a portion of Selena's wall, and assured her he would not let her harm him or herself. Selena's impassive expression changed. She slammed her hand into one of the cushions Karl had placed around her. She beat the cushion until she was tired.

"I hate them. I hate them," she screamed over and over.

Karl assumed she made reference to the people of the cult. He spoke quietly of the incident at the dam and of the crucifixion. Selena's mind was on more than strangers in the cult. "Mama hurt me," she said when she finally quieted. Her nearness to Jenny let her touch pain she had avoided for over thirty years. Then she escaped to deep trance.

After a few minutes Karl asked for Mind. "There's so much anger to deal with, but they run from it." Karl posed the problem for Mind's consideration.

"They are afraid they will hurt someone, hurt you or Rachel, like Kayla with the bird."

"Maybe I should talk with Kayla."

Kayla gave her explanation, complete with her child's logic. "I killed it so it wouldn't grow up and get killed."

"Were you mad at anybody?"

"It's wrong to get mad." She had closed the issue, although anger danced in her eyes.

"Trust your feelings, Selena," Karl counseled. "Don't put yourself in a bad situation." He was responding to her concern over her aunt Mamie's asking her to go to a church homecoming in the town of Baldwin. Selena didn't even know where the place was, but the mention of it made her feel sick and frightened.

Selena avoided the trip with her aunt but could not put the place out of her thoughts. Her dreams became more troubled with flashes of rituals. She dreamed a familiar dream of fleeing from some threat, running up a staircase only to have it end abruptly at the ceiling.

The therapists decided to go with her to Baldwin. As other places had done, perhaps this town would release new, important memories for her.

As before, Karl and Rachel took their cues from her reactions. She pointed out streets where she remembered picking up members for meetings. In town she remembered the jewelry store. She was taken there, she said, to choose rewards when she did the rituals well.

They followed a road out of town some ten miles, making a turn into a section of farms at Selena's direction. Less than a mile from an intersection where she directed they turn left, they found a big, old two-story house. The house needed paint. It had a tin roof, a wraparound porch, and an irregularly shaped section, like an oversize bay window that extended to the second story. A For Sale sign was surrounded by a yard overgrown with weeds and shrubs.

"We can look through the windows," Rachel offered as Karl set the brake.

Selena was quiet getting out of the car. Karl and Rachel moved close to her. As Selena turned toward the house, she stopped, began to shiver, and fell backward. Karl caught her and eased her to the ground.

A personality new to Karl and Rachel emerged. Her name was Melissa. She was ten years old. She did not seem at all surprised to be at the old house. She continued toward the porch with them, holding her right arm out at an angle to her body.

Rachel moved close to her when she started up the steps. "My gown, my gown," Melissa cautioned, a mild irritation in her voice. Rachel moved aside for the imagined fabric. Karl reached for the door. It opened with a turn of the knob. The locks were so old, no one had bothered to secure them.

Melissa swept through the doorway into a large living room, and moved at once to a stairway on the right-hand wall. The arrangement of the steps gave the appearance that the stairs ended at the ceiling. Karl took Melissa's arm. Rachel found a light switch. The light came on, although Melissa did not need it. She knew her way.

Melissa moved with ceremony, repeating for the therapists a procession she had been part of years past. She paused briefly on the landing where the stairway turned, before she continued to the second floor.

To the left a hallway appeared to lead to upstairs rooms. Melissa turned right toward a small door. The door was constructed of boards placed vertically and had no knob. A small piece of wood rotated on a nail to secure the door to the jamb.

"Secret room," Melissa whispered. She turned the rough latch and stepped without hesitation down two steps into a low-ceilinged space. "We have to wait here until it's time," she explained.

The bulb Rachel had turned on in the hallway cast just enough light for them to make out the irregular shape and unfinished boards of a space between the floors of the house. Karl stopped Melissa from moving deeper into the unlighted room. "Tell me about your gown," he said, guiding her back to the door.

Her face showed the pleasure of touching soft, silky fabric. She stroked the remembered gown, caught up in the telling. She described an elegant garment, long, all white, high at the neck, and decorated with jewels and embroidery.

She touched her chest. "There's a star here inside a triangle, and a big triangle down the front." Her hand moved to her shoulder. "See, here's a star at the top," she said as she let her hand slip toward her opposite forearm, "and a cross down on the sleeve." She stared at her hand and wiggled her fingers. "This netting on the hands is like a spider web, and the red jewels are like shining drops of blood." She alternated effortlessly between past and present, sharing her experience, aware that she could see things the therapists could not.

"Where will you wear the gown?"

Melissa straightened her shoulders and moved up the two steps. "The master is ready," she said, and walked in remembered procession to a door off the upstairs hallway. She pushed open the door to a five-sided room, walked to a window opposite the door, and stood as if waiting further command.

"Tell me what's happening," Karl instructed.

"All the people are here to summon the master. I must wait at the altar until he comes for me."

Melissa had nothing more to say. She had told them all she knew, had shown them the limits of her existence. She had nothing more to do but stand and wait.

"Let's go now," Karl said. He touched her arm, and Melissa walked with him and Rachel back down the stairs.

Near the still-open front door, Selena surfaced. She turned to face the stairway, her eyes following the steps to where they disappeared at the ceiling. "The steps in my dream," she said, incredulous. She hurried up the stairs with Karl and Rachel at her heels. She made the same turns as Melissa, taking them again to the secret room. Quicker than Melissa, Selena moved to the far corner of the room by the time Rachel got to the light in the hall. When Karl got to Selena, he could see her hand on the latch of a small square door connecting the room between floors to another like it. He stopped her before she could crawl through.

"It's too dark in here. Let's go back outside and talk." Selena did not resist, although she paused on the stairway, feeling the rails, as if to assure herself they were real.

Once they were outside the house, Karl questioned her about the gown Melissa spoke of, and about the secret room. Selena asked for paper and pencil. She sketched the gown as she described it, elegantly adorned with pentagrams and inverted crosses. Her description matched Melissa's, but was broadened to include the elaborate headpiece.

A veil, tight across the forehead, bore a pentagram within an inverted triangle. The tip of the triangle met an inverted cross at the bridge of the nose. The base of the triangle balanced goat horns at the top of the head. Lacy streamers came down over eyes dark with makeup.

Selena described the ritual room, complete with candles, dagger, chalice, and an inverted cross. She spoke of the robed figures who watched her be lifted to the altar (from the spot Melissa had stood and waited) and the lovely gown be cut from neck to hem, as the high priest began the sexual assault that would offer her as bride to Satan.

The secret room was a waiting place where the children stayed. Sometimes they were called to the rituals. Sometimes they just waited until they were taken home. Talking was forbidden. Even with many children in the space, each child was alone.

"What did you do all the time in there?"

Selena looked puzzled that Karl should question that there could be more to do than wait. "Oh," she remembered, "there was a knothole to look through where you could see the stars and watch them."

Selena's statement seemed benign and a good signal to move the discussion back to the present. There had been enough clues found, enough remembering, for one day.

Selena's knowledge of the secret room made it possible for Karl to seek tangible evidence that the old farmhouse had been a site of cultic rituals. He went back the next week.

Alone in the house, Karl sensed an eeriness he had missed when his attention had been focused on his client. The house creaked in the wind of an approaching storm. Twigs dropped from trees onto the tin roof, making Karl hurry to be done with his solitary observations.

The living room was as bare and uninteresting as before. The ritual room yielded little more, except for a single dark knothole an inch or so in diameter in the tongue-and-groove wall boards a few feet above the floor.

Making an effort to ignore the snaps and creaks of the old house, Karl stooped to enter the secret room. He shone a powerful flashlight into the corners of the room to see only bare, rough boards. He looked carefully, if quickly, around the empty space. The room was small, but would have seemed spacious to a child. Karl found nothing to make note of except some writing. The numbers one through nine and the letter X were written in white, chalk perhaps, on a board above the door.

Karl moved to the far corner and opened the square door to the other between-floors space. Before he could play his light into the room, a small beam shining through a hole in the wall caught his attention. He lighted his way to the spot, then turned off his flashlight. He pressed his eye to the hole and looked directly into the ritual room. Karl could see a window across the room. He watched the early afternoon sky darkening and leaves blowing in the storm gathering outside the second-story window.

Karl had assumed he would find the peephole Selena spoke of in an exterior wall. Now he realized that he had found exactly what she described. At night, with the lights off in the ritual room, Selena could easily have seen the stars. Karl had further assumed she had referred to the stars when she said she could watch them. Now he knew she meant she watched the rituals. There was nothing to see but the activity in the ritual room when light from candles obscured the view of the stars.

Knowing that the child had stayed in this space to watch previews of horrors she would later endure made the little room seem suddenly stifling and filthy. Karl heard the patter of rain on the tin roof as he hurried in a stooped-over walk to the door near the top of the stairs.

Karl had plenty of time on the long drive home in the rain to think over the meaning of what he had found. Jenny had surely been in the house as a child, perhaps many times. Although Jenny herself had not surfaced at any time during the first visit to the house, Karl would talk with her about it the next time he saw her.

Jenny acted as if she knew about the existence of the secret room and the place of rituals. She knew about the house, although she insisted it was Selena who lived through events there.

"You and Selena are one," Karl said, wondering to himself how many times he had made that statement. "What happened to her happened to you."

Jenny did not speak her usual argument to the contrary, although Karl could see her tense with resistance to the notion. He went on with his premise that Jenny had the experiences. "There's something written on the wall of the secret room, can you tell me what it is?" he asked.

"I was never there," she said, fully believing the truth of her statement.

Karl did not contradict her again. He handed her a pencil and moved a writing pad in front of her. "Just write what comes to mind, what you think might be there."

Jenny was thoughtful just a moment, then wrote the numbers one through five in a line, and six through nine on another, separated by the letter X. The writing seemed to have no relevance for her. For Karl it was tangible proof of her past presence in the house in Baldwin, where, as a ten-year-old girl, she was made bride of Satan.

CHAPTER 35

The invitation to an all-day conference introducing a new treatment center for multiple personality disorder within driving distance offered the Alexanders an opportunity to seek input from experts in the field. They didn't get such an opportunity very often. There would be formal presentations as well as unstructured time to converse with colleagues. One of the presenters would be Chris Costner Sizemore, the Eve of *The Three Faces of Eve*. Rachel had seen Chris in several television appearances and was impressed by her advocacy for the mentally ill.

Sizemore's presentation was dynamic and informative. She spoke of her own experience, of achieving integration many years after she was pronounced "cured" by Drs. Thigpen and Cleckley, the psychiatrists who first diagnosed her problem. Their best-selling book about her introduced the phenomenon of multiple personality both to the mental health care community and to the lay public. The disclosure she allowed gave credence to and popular awareness of the reality of multiple personality.

Twenty years after the original publication of her story, Chris co-authored with her cousin, Elen Pittillo, her own account of her story, as she identified herself in *I'm Eve*. An additional ten years later, she stood before an audience of professionals and an interested public to address issues relevant to those who were currently coping with or had dealt in the past with mental illness. She spoke of the need for proper diagnosis and treatment and of the right of the mentally ill to be free of stigma. She spoke of tolerance and optimism, and the need for the community to be concerned with providing support so that each person suffering from mental illness would have the chance for a successful outcome. If others could not achieve a successful outcome as she had, she insisted they still have respect and protection in the community.

When Chris completed her well-received presentation, she moved into the audience to take a seat directly in front of the Alexanders. At the first break in the program, Rachel spoke to her. "I really enjoyed your presentation."

Chris turned to reveal up close her open face and warm smile. She chatted easily about her background, and about her current efforts through appearances and interviews to work for the mentally ill. Both Karl and Rachel were struck by her self-confidence and sense of purpose. Rachel commented on the fact that Chris could be more effective than some because she was such an important role model for those still struggling to overcome mental illness. "We have a client who could surely use the encouragement you offer." Rachel shared her thought with Chris. "Do you ever meet with multiples and their therapists?"

"I have many times. I'd be happy to meet with your client."

"We'll check it out with her, but I can't believe she would miss an opportunity to meet you. We'll call you to arrange a time convenient for your schedule." There was just time to exchange phone numbers and for Chris to introduce her cousin, Elen, who was seated beside her, before the program resumed.

Jenny was eager, if somewhat nervous, about meeting Chris Sizemore. Selena tried to act as if it made no difference to her, although she was first to greet Chris at the arranged meeting.

Chris was a gracious hostess, greeting Karl with a hand-shake and Rachel with a hug before extending her hand again, with "You must be Jenny."

"Actually"—Selena grinned—"I'm Selena, but I'm used to answering to her name."

"I'll use your name. I know how important that is." Chris smiled a sense of camaraderie that made Selena feel understood in a way she had not experienced before. She was ready to hear whatever Chris had to say to her.

Chris was deliberate and unhurried. She directed her comments to Selena; however, she glanced often at the therapists and made brief exchanges with them, so that all were included in the conversation. Taking her cues from information the Alexanders had, with Jenny's permission, shared with her, Chris focused on telling Selena things she thought would be meaningful to her.

Chris talked about the place and importance of all the personalities, knowledge she gained from having to find resolution for nineteen more than the original three who were first identified. She asked Selena not to fear integration. "You do not die," she said, "or go away. You are not lost. No one dies. Everyone becomes a part of the whole person."

Chris acknowledged that the process of final integration was tumultuous and frightening for her. She had loving support from her husband and her cousin during the confusing process that spanned some six weeks. She felt at times that she was going crazy or even dying as her life passed before her vision. She did not need to relive the events, she said, only to remember them, for them to become her own. After she saw each event, it became hers without reservation. When all the personalities went together, all their abilities were still there, and all their experiences, but for the first time in her life, Chris had control.

She admitted she could not access all the abilities immediately, that it took time to learn to use the skills available to her. "For a long time I couldn't sew, even though the Turtle Lady and others could sew beautifully," she said. Chris laughed. "I guess I never really liked sewing to begin with."

It seemed that she described her own experience so that Selena could see that a period of confusion, perhaps even chaos, could be expected, but that the process was not one to make personalities die, as Selena feared. She did not minimize Selena's feelings, and showed a genuine liking for her. She gave her a hug, saying, "You'll always be there. Jenny would never want to be without you."

Chris turned to Karl to ask if Jenny was ready to talk with her. Jenny surfaced at the therapist's request, smiling shyly and staring at the floor. Karl made the introduction, and Jenny's eyes registered an instant recognition of Chris. Her hands relaxed their fists without Karl's asking.

Chris reviewed her experiences for Jenny. While she acknowledged that she had not been abused, as she understood Jenny had been, and had not had experiences with the cult, she was well aware that those kinds of things were all too real. She communicated that the similarities they shared in being multiple were more important than the differences in the experiences leading to their illnesses. She hoped for Jenny that she would achieve full integration as she had done. Chris focused on the positive aspects of becoming whole, the joy of being in control of her life, the comfort of being normal.

Jenny expressed reservations about integration. "Did you have personalities you didn't like?" she asked.

"Of course I did, but all of them are still a part of me. I can choose the actions of a party girl or a housewife. I can be proper or curse if I want."

Jenny smiled and nodded understanding. Still, with her usual self-effacement, she expressed doubt that she could manage total integration.

Rachel raised a question to turn attention from Jenny's doubts. "Chris, do you use your ability to dissociate now, to cope with pain, for instance?"

"Never." Chris was adamant in her response. Dissociation was part of her past. She believed it important to put all the experiences of being multiple in the past and to behave always in a normal manner, staying to face problems, not running from them. She emphasized that she did not want to be different, did not want to align herself solely with multiples. She had the right and ability to be normal. She urged Jenny to reach for such a status for herself.

Both Jenny and Selena wrote letters to Chris thanking her for the meeting. Chris responded with a note.

August 26, 1987

Dear Jenny and Selena,

I ask that you two please share this note. Time does not permit me to answer both of your letters.

Let me stress that I have really good feelings about your integrating, remaining one, and having a good, productive life. You have everything working for you. Your therapists are knowledgeable, caring people who will see you through this. That makes you one of the very fortunate MPD patients! And your attitude is positive, that is a plus for you.

I felt good when you left. Inside of me the feeling that all will be fine, you will get well, existed. And that made my day. I really care about you, and want you to know the peace that I have. And you shall!

I will be thinking good thoughts for you. God bless —

Love,
Chris

Jenny was surely affected by her contact with Chris Sizemore. She evidenced more hope than Karl and Rachel had ever known her to allow herself to feel. Within a matter of weeks Mind announced to Karl that the final integration process had begun for Jenny, and could not be stayed by anyone.

Mind said that first Selena would get the memories, then Jenny would get them. Mind would fade away when she was no longer needed to keep things stable. There would be a fight at the end between Jenny and Selena. But Jenny would soon function with one mind, although she would still try to deny the awful things in her past. "I want to warn you now" — Mind added a caution to her disclaimer — "if some real stressful thing happens to her, she may dissociate again. You know she's done it before."

Karl did nothing that might detract from Jenny's intent. He did his best to suspend judgment. Her motivation could well be wishful thinking, a flight into health to avoid facing her past and dealing with issues. Or it could be acknowledged as a sign of her sincere desire to be well. Karl would believe the latter and supply support for her efforts. In four years of therapy he had seen her make remarkable accomplishments.

Selena began to report an increase in nightmares. She dreamed of her aunt's house, the house in Baldwin, the little house across from the school. She thumbed through stacks of old pictures, fixing the places in her mind.

As diligently as Selena searched the pictures for memories, Jenny avoided them. Mind reported that Jenny was pulling far back into her worlds, and that Selena was getting too upset, remembering too slowly and feeling the others' pain. Mind proposed to speed the process by giving Selena all the memories in one night. "She will get no sleep tonight and will be depleted tomorrow. But it will be done."

Karl could not be available the next day, but Rachel agreed to make time for Selena. Selena came to the office, looking tired and drawn. "It was like my mind exploded into hundreds of minds," Selena told Rachel.

"Tell me what you remembered."

Selena began a lengthy report of what she had learned, beginning with her belief that she was unwanted at birth and proceeding through abuse by the mother. She recalled the cult abuse from Fontana to the Feast to the little house and the lost years. "I heard all that Mind told me, but she said I couldn't cry or scream."

"I think you need to scream. You can do that here with me. You can just relax on the couch and go back in time as far as you need to go." With Selena relaxed to trance, Rachel gave suggestions that Selena would remain still on the couch, but she could cry or scream as she needed.

Selena turned to her side and drew her feet up under her

hips. Her hands curled to fists. She rooted her face into the cushions of the couch and began to make sucking motions.

Even noting the fetal position, Rachel was surprised when the cries began. Rachel had expected angry screams. She heard unmistakable cries of a newborn, a kind of primal scream.

Rachel offered reassurance and positive suggestions as Selena remained for a time regressed and vulnerable. "You are a good person. Others were responsible for the bad things in your past. It is okay to have feelings. You are gaining control of your life."

After surfacing from trance, Selena said, "It feels like my head is together. I don't feel anybody's pain."

With Selena comfortable, Rachel asked to speak with Jenny. "What do you think of Selena's remembering?"

She stared at the floor, deep in thought. She raised her head to face Rachel and share her insight. "The wounds are beginning to heal," she said. "The scars will remain."

Jenny's shared insight held more truth than she wanted to admit. The memories were just the beginning. Not only did she have to remember the past, she had to accept that she had lived it, that she was one with all of her alter personalities. Beyond that she had to resolve issues that adversely affected her life in the present.

The problems were complex and interrelated. Many attitudes and behaviors once vital to her survival now hampered her functioning. Jenny could not just give up these exceptional survival skills. She would have to replace them with ones appropriate in her recovery.

Reluctance to own or experience the anger associated with the abuse kept her tied to the past. She could not seem to accept that anger, even rage, was an appropriate response to what was done to her and what she was made to do. Whether she held to childhood admonitions against anger or feared she would lose control and cause harm to someone, she resisted discharging the anger.

Holding in her anger kept Jenny from grieving over her

past. She was not only terribly hurt, but also was deprived of a real childhood. As she held to her anger, she held to an unrealistic hope of recapturing a childhood. Only by grieving her losses would she be able to turn loose of the past.

Trust also continued to be at issue. Certainly as a child, she had every reason to trust no one. Now the therapists asked her to base responses on new experiences, to see that they and others in her current environment did not betray her trust. Jenny tried to trust, but was at best tentative, never fully giving up the expectation of eventual harm or abandonment.

Manipulativeness sprang from the inability to trust. Because she could trust no one to respond to her needs, she developed exceptional skills of manipulation to have her needs met, or at least to respond to what she thought she needed. Many who found themselves manipulated — doctors, ministers, counselors, friends — responded with anger, the natural reaction to feeling used. Once angered, they pulled away from association with or caring for Jenny, actualizing the abandonment she feared.

Jenny continued to exploit whatever options she saw open to her. With one hand she held on to what she had — for instance, therapy with the Alexanders. With the other hand she reached for something more — for instance, ministerial counseling from one or more churches. If a counselor said he could not see her while she was in the care of another because of rules of ethics, she felt the rules should be broken for her. She evidenced a sense of entitlement common to many traumatized individuals. She did not expect to operate within limits she assumed were meant for others. (Entitlement seen in multiple personality victims is discussed by Kluft, 1988b.)

Jenny tried to hold on to the level of involvement the Alexanders allowed early in therapy. She bridled each time they set limits on time spent with her. She questioned their caring, demanded more time, threatened to leave therapy. All of these actions stalled progress in therapy on other issues. However, the Alexanders knew that her sense of entitlement had to be challenged, and that she had to learn to accept the reasonable limits meant for everyone.

The entitlement issue was especially knotty because it could be seen as originating from at least three sources. First, as an abused person, she could feel that she deserved compensation for past mistreatment. Second, she had been brought up in the cult, a little princess groomed to be high priestess. While she suffered abuse at the hands of the cult, she was taught that she was special, an exception. Third, her ability to dissociate meant that she never had to live within the rules. Whenever a circumstance was beyond Jenny's tolerance, she gave the situation over to an alter personality. That alter could, in turn, give way to another. Through dissociation, by becoming multiple, Jenny managed to avoid all limits.

For Jenny to deal with the issues, she would have to give up her ability to escape to safe places, an ability that had worked so well for her in the past. For her to learn from her present experiences, she had to stay in the real world and let her therapists help her find new ways to deal with her life.

"But," Jenny protested, "if I admit the past and believe that I am multiple, it will be like pulling the wings off a butterfly."

Her metaphor let Karl and Rachel know how fragile she felt, and how difficult it was for her to give up her means of escape. They wondered if Jenny could find the help in a hospital situation that they could not provide her. They had learned that in hospitals not accustomed to treating multiples, Jenny seemed to profit from getting away from stresses at home, but was so effective at manipulating the system that she made no meaningful changes. Perhaps in the safety and structure of a treatment center knowledgeable about multiples, Jenny could be helped to release the anger she was so reluctant to face with them.

Jenny had had good feelings about the Dissociative Disorders Program at Rush-Presbyterian-St. Luke's Medical Center in Chicago since her evaluation there two years before. She agreed readily to the Alexanders' making application for her admission. She felt she could manage the trip alone to the center if she was accepted for treatment. As the therapists expected, Jenny reached eagerly for this new option.

Rachel completed the application forms, extensively describing Jenny's background and treatment, and outlining the hoped for goals for the inpatient treatment. The therapists received notification that Jenny's name had been placed on a waiting list for admission.

CHAPTER 36

Jenny became more vulnerable to memories. The Alexanders continued to encourage her to stay out in the real world, at least with them when she could feel safe. But formerly innocuous places began to trigger responses in her. For instance, algae on the little pond in the park where the therapists walked with her reminded Jenny of a slimy pond in a farmer's field where she had been made to drink the vile water as part of a ritual.

Not all the memories were bad. A bed of daisies in the park reminded Jenny of picking daisies with her grandmother. Jenny recalled for the Alexanders how the old woman chose flowers with tall, straight stems, some fully open, some just starting to bloom, to make the best bouquet. The therapists could not be sure if the details of the story came from memory or from fantasy. They could be sure that Jenny saw her grandmother as wise and loving, her only protector.

Jenny turned to look again at the daisies, to find in them more time in pleasant memory. Any reference to the cult was difficult for her. She would make brief admissions, but if pressed would escape to trance or switch to an alter. When she acknowledged events in the cult, she denied their happening to her.

Selena had become increasingly curious about the cult. She wanted to remember, but more than that to make some sense of the horrors she had known there. She remembered incidents isolated and out of sequence. She could find no pattern, although she knew that the cult was a source of pride and power as much as a source of fear and pain.

Selena looked in bookstores and libraries for books to read, but found little to give her the information she wanted. She expressed to Karl that she felt somehow if she could recapture the scenes and know the rituals in exact detail, she could put meaning to her experiences. Karl suggested they review together what they knew so far, and try together to find meaning. They could keep notes and revise them as necessary to put events in order. Karl did not question Selena's almost obsessive need to understand the cult experiences. No matter what other personalities were involved, the experiences always caused pain, and with the pain Selena became part of every cult experience.

Karl and Selena began their review with what they had learned in recent months about Jenny's being given over to the cult at age two in a "damming" ceremony at Fontana Dam. As Karl went over the circumstances with Selena, he encouraged her to see the paradoxical nature of the cult abuses. At Fontana the child was attacked emotionally and physically by cult members, directed by the high priest. Immediately she was given relief by the same high priest, who directed she be comforted and given care. To the helpless child the high priest was omnipotent, holding over her the power of cold torment and warm protection. From the very beginning she was inexorably caught in this paradox.

A period of intensive training followed the initiation at the dam. Mavis, the old woman in the mountains, played a central role in the early training. Mavis used stories and play and praise to teach lessons to a bright and eager pupil. Jenny learned chants as other children learned nursery rhymes.

She played at concocting potions from herbs as other children played at serving tea.

Seen in the light of training, even the abuse by the mother had purpose. Whether Gladys Faye was directed in her actions by the high priest or by the demands of her own nature, her methods were brutal. Her declaring the child "spawn of Satan" was a statement of truth that Jenny had to recognize early. Making the child drink urine, bathing her in blood, assaulting her sexually, all were preparatory, to ready her for ordeals far more severe and far more important.

Once initiated, Jenny had a place with other children in the formal structure of the cult. For long periods the children's place was peripheral to the cult's functioning, although even during those periods the training continued. The children were frightened to silence and debased in relentless conditioning. They were confined with snakes and spiders and objects of horror. They were made to watch killings and given flesh to eat and blood to drink. Ability to reason was altered with drugs and mind-numbing chants. In such ceremonies as the mock crucifixion, the children were used in groups to pay homage to Satan, their collective terror somehow adding power to the worship.

Jenny's grooming for special status in the cult became manifest at the Feast of the Beast. Although she had interpreted the event as a missed attempt to kill her, it was more likely a death/rebirth ritual intended to convince her, along with members of the cult, that she possessed some special powers. The high priest had plans for her. She would be made a bride of Satan, and when she came of age would serve as his high priestess.

Her return to the cult at age twenty-one was probably programmed. She was of age. Although she had left the cult, she was compelled to return and take the place for which she had been prepared.

Selena recalled the marriage rituals, one at age five at Bridal Veil Falls, another at age ten in the house at Baldwin. In remembering these she thought of another that occurred on her thirteenth birthday. "Could it be," she questioned

Karl, "that the marriages were to make the baby legitimate that they took from me?"

Karl assured her that while he could not speak with certainty of the cult's motives, it was evident that they used symbolism and tied their practices to Christian ethics to increase their influence over their followers and victims. Selena verified for Karl that much cult activity corresponded with the church calendar. As the church celebrated life, the cult celebrated death. She had seen, she said, when she was a very little girl, a child cut from its mother's womb at Easter time. "How could they do such evil things? How could they make me do them?" she asked, expecting he could answer.

"Selena, they had to believe that what they were doing was right." Karl's answer touched the basis for understanding what went on in the cult. Selena's answers would not be found by moving close to examine details of the years of her involvement. She needed to move back and see the overall design.

Her mother, the high priest, Mavis — all of them believed in what they were doing. They looked for power or status or control in the worship of the devil. For them it was right. Once this premise was accepted, the acts they did to make Jenny one of them were understandable.

Gladys Faye gave her over to the cult, either in an act of free devotion, or as a requirement of her own belonging. Once a part of the cult, the child was conditioned, systematically brainwashed. The abuse was neither random nor senseless. It was deliberate and intelligently planned to tie her to the cult. Repeatedly she was made victim by the cult and rescued by them. The bond was meant to be complete when she made others victim, even her own child.

There was no means of escape. The terror began when she was too young to tell anyone, and the sanctions against telling were incredibly powerful. She was brought into contact with the mental health system when she was very young, damaging her credibility nearly beyond repair. When she was able to risk telling, the bizarre nature of what she had to tell could only add to the impression that she was markedly disturbed. If she would not be loyal to the cult, she could not betray its secrets.

Karl pointed out to Selena that she succeeded at times in convincing herself that what she did in Satan's name was right for her. But she could not avoid doubts. At some level she always knew the cult was very wrong. Through her personalities Jenny managed to appear to be the child the cult wanted, but she could never accept the evil. When pushed to give up her child to them, her system of personalities broke down, unable to cope with acts so contrary to her nature. She gave up her hold on reality, lost two years of awareness, was thought to be crazy. Somehow she must have known it was the only way she could remain alive and escape the cult's hold on her.

At that age she was not able to make the escape lasting. The conditioning as a child made her vulnerable to being lured back to the cult. She would return to find power, to avoid stresses, to find belonging or understanding. Problems in her life were inevitable. And it was inevitable that she would seek solutions, among them, reacceptance in the cult.

As an adult Jenny could no more endure the practices than as a child. Even with an alter, Sandy, whose sole purpose was in the worship of Satan, Jenny could not countenance the atrocities. Knowing she would be made again to harm others, Sandy fled the cult. Selena even tried to put herself in front of a moving train. The attempted suicide made her again thought to be crazy.

It was probably no coincidence that within a few months of the "accident" with the train, she was in the hospital for a hysterectomy. Crazy and barren, she would be of no more use to the cult. She made complete her physical escape.

The emotional hold of the cult was undeniably stronger than the physical one. Throughout her time of involvement, Jenny held to Christian beliefs. As an adult she chose to renew her baptism. When confronted by an alter self who would reclaim her for the cult, she invoked the words of baptism. She could be free emotionally and spiritually as well.

* * *

During the weeks Karl spent in review with Selena, he made frequent contact with Jenny. She was aware of Selena's recall, but persisted in denying that the experiences happened to her. "Do you remember Fontana Dam?" Karl questioned.

"I dreamed about it," Jenny replied, adroitly avoiding acceptance.

"What do you remember about the house across from Hamilton School?"

"I dream about it, too, sometimes."

"It is not a dream." Karl spoke, realizing she would no more accept his words than she did her own recall. Perhaps returning to the house with her would overcome the denial.

Saturday afternoon the school was deserted. Karl parked the car in the shade of the big live oaks. The house stood unchanged since they were last there, but was perhaps a bit more rundown.

The three of them started toward the barn, but Karl veered off to call out to an old man and woman busy in a nearby field of collard greens. "Hello," Karl called, "do you folks happen to own this place?"

"Naw," the old man answered, stuffing a handful of coarse leaves into a sack he carried. "We have the place yonder." He pointed to the adjacent property. "The people own this don't live around here."

"Ever hear of it being for sale?"

"Naw. Reckon they want to keep it in the family."

While Karl kept the attention of the neighbors, Rachel and Selena walked into the old barn. Long unused, the building still held the musky smell of animals.

Selena spoke softly. "They made us do stuff with animals here, sex stuff, and they'd laugh at us, and they'd kill the animals and make us drink the blood."

"Really bad things happened at this place, didn't they?" Rachel kept her voice low, and she kept close watch on Selena.

"Yeah, a man was hung over there one time." She indicated a cross beam near the door. "He was drunk, but they cut him up, and he was still alive."

Rachel felt bile rise in her throat. She watched Selena grasp her belly and swallow back nausea.

"The altar was here," Selena said, her mind already on thoughts of a different time. She stopped at the spot as if the altar stood there still. "It was raining, and we watched from the window of the bedroom for a long time before they took us to the barn. It was raining hard, just pouring down, and thundering and lightning. But when they killed the baby, even with the thunder, I could hear it crying and crying. Then it was still."

"Let's go now." Rachel led Selena outside to sunlight. Selena had begun to shiver. Rachel also felt the chill.

Karl joined them to walk to the house. The neighbors had gone, but not before insisting Karl take enough greens to "cook a mess for supper."

Inside the house Selena inclined her head, and Jenny surfaced strong and alert. She looked around, intent on detail. She walked through the house to the enclosed back porch, where she ran her fingers along letters written on the wall, opposite a list of names. "Help." She mouthed the word. With a look she communicated that when the word was written, no one had noticed.

Jenny led the way into the small bedroom that had been hers as a child. She stood by the window, then began to trace the pattern of imagined raindrops on the glass. Tears filled her eyes as she stared through the window to the barn in the distance.

"What is it?" Karl asked.

"The baby — the altar — the crying." She whispered the words, then fell silent. She stared at hands she held palms-up in front of her.

"What do you see?"

"Blood," she said. She balled her hands to fists and slammed them against the window. With astonishing control she avoided cutting herself. She broke the glass, but stopped her hands before they could be harmed. Shattering glass released her from the memory.

* * *

Back in the office Jenny sat silently staring at her fists. Karl and Rachel were quiet also, thinking of how to bring closure to the events of the day. Finally Karl spoke. "Of all the things that happened in the two years in that house, what was the worst?" He wondered what torture, what threat to herself, she would choose to have escaped.

"Killing the babies," she answered.

Jenny had paid a tragic price to survive, yet she did not think now of herself, but mourned those who did not live. She seemed to Karl to change, to appear more substantial than she ever had. Her shoulders were square, her hands relaxed. Karl wondered if he had failed to see a personality switch. "Who am I talking to?" he asked.

"Everybody." She spoke the single word, then escaped to deep trance.

CHAPTER 37

"Does that thumb taste good?"

"Uh-huh." Kayla's reemergence, seeking the comfort of her thumb, signaled the end of the fragile wholeness. The short duration did not diminish the importance of the integration. Jenny's being one, if only for the few minutes in the therapists' office, gave promise of an eventual lasting unity.

Karl allowed Kayla to be out for a time, and chatted with her playfully before asking for Jenny to return. Jenny surfaced, subdued and relaxed.

"Tell us what happened, what you felt."

"It was like I looked through a crystal to a mirror and saw all the personalities, hundreds of them."

"What did they look like?"

"They all had my face." Jenny acknowledged with a gentle smile this admission of being multiple. She closed her eyes and gave way to Selena.

Selena was calm. If she had been frightened by the integration, she gave no evidence of the fear. Karl questioned her. "What do you think about what happened?"

"It was okay, I reckon," she replied without any hint of

sarcasm. She stopped to think for a moment, then affirmed, "It was okay."

"We accomplished a lot today," Karl assured her. "But there's still a lot of work to do."

Jenny received notification that she would be able to enter the Dissociative Disorders Inpatient Unit at Rush within the month. Dr. Young, who had done her evaluation two years before, was no longer in Chicago. He had left to become medical director at Columbine Psychiatric Center in Denver, Colorado, where he would also direct Columbine's Center for the Treatment of Dissociative Disorders. As did Rush, this center would offer treatment for persons with MPD or other dissociative states, and for survivors of ritual abuse.

Karl and Rachel shared with Jenny their optimism that she could make good progress during the planned thirty days at Rush. They encouraged her to express her feelings in that safe place. They built on her already positive feelings about the center with their observation that the staff there were considered expert in the care of multiples. State-of-the-art knowledge and techniques should be available for her care.

Once Selena got past the initial anxiety of the plane trip and settling into a new place, she liked being on the Dissociative Disorders Unit. Never before, outside the Alexanders' office or the brief time she spent with Chris Sizemore, had she felt she could be herself unguardedly. She did not have to respond to Jenny's name or be concerned that she might have to cover gaps in her awareness if other personalities surfaced. She was in a place where she could be accepted as she was.

Jenny remained in her crystal world, a sanctuary she had rebuilt. She had told Karl she would talk with the doctors or other staff members if they asked for her. But they did not ask, nor did they make contact with Mind.

The Alexanders had provided full descriptions of Jenny, Selena, and Mind in the extensive application for her being placed on the waiting list for the program and had indicated that Jenny and Mind surfaced only when asked. However, they did not reiterate this information in writing at the time of her admission almost two years later. The break in communication was unfortunate. The staff at Rush did not interact with the birth personality or with the primary inner-self-helper. Selena was left in control.

Selena enjoyed the attention. Unlike the times in the Alexanders' office when she had to give way to other alters as they disclosed their memories and purposes, she remained central in the sessions on the unit. She told what she knew of the memories and the history of her illness. She was the one examined for medical evaluation and tested for psychological evaluation. She interacted with the staff and other patients, happy to have someone to talk with whenever she became upset or just needed not to be alone. Even at night, always a difficult time for her, she could find relief from her nightmares in the reassurance of a staff member.

While Selena maintained her dominance in the personality system, she began to lose control, as something about the setting or something about revealing past abuses and cult involvement triggered the reemergence of many alters, mostly children. Kayla became more active. Kecia returned, as did Penny, Todd, and Abby, children from the lost years at the little house.

Selena was encouraged by the staff to take a parenting role with the child alters. She was to read stories to them, to comfort them with a kind of internal holding, to give them time in the playroom on the ward. While Selena had always shown tolerance for the child alters, she felt somehow oppressed by being instructed to take that role in the hospital. She had trouble being held responsible. At home she could buy things for the children, Jenny's children, Morgan and Noel, as well as for the alters, but they weren't her children and she didn't have to answer to anyone about them.

In the hospital she was being asked to look out for the children, to try to control the frequent switching, and to encourage communication among the personalities. To meet these obligations, Selena had to maintain awareness and not escape as she was accustomed to doing. She felt inadequate to the tasks, but was unwilling to give up her central position.

Selena could not hide the fact that the situation was difficult for her. She evidenced distress verbally in confessing to much internal confusion, and physically by cutting her wrists. Kayla became distressed and turned anger and frustration on herself, beating her arms against the wall on several occasions before falling into deep trance.

In spite of the turmoil and increased scattering, Selena reported to the Alexanders in telephone calls that she liked the hospital and wished she could remain beyond the thirty days insurance coverage allowed. Jenny liked the hospital as well. Although she did not interact with doctors, staff, or other patients, she stayed near Selena and knew of her interactions. She shared Selena's pleasure in meeting other patients who were like her. Jenny came to know through Selena not only other multiples, but others who had experienced abuse in cults.

The experiences in common made both Selena and Jenny feel less alone, not so different, not so ashamed. Validating the experiences with others made them more acceptable and more real. In the safety of the hospital, accepting the reality of the cult was not so frightening. Jenny wished she could stay there and not return to the stresses at home, with the reminders of her past so near to her.

Karl and Rachel had difficulty assessing the effects of the hospitalization. They had learned prior to her admission that the emphasis would be on evaluation, that only limited therapeutic goals could be addressed in the one-month time period. Still, they hoped that some resolution of anger might be reached, and that Jenny could be helped to function with less dissociation.

Jenny returned to them regressed and more fragmented than they had seen her for some time. With the resurfacing of formerly integrated personalities and the emergence of many child personalities, some twenty alters peopled the system. Distress and confusion were understandable in light of the increased numbers.

Several factors could be involved in the scattering the therapists observed. Incomplete resolution of issues prior to the integration of some fragments or alters could account for their reappearance, indicating that more work needed to be done. Too, if Jenny experienced stresses in the hospital environment, she would likely renew familiar defenses.

The personalities that emerged did not seem to represent a new layer of repressed material to be surfaced and resolved. They seemed to respond to current stimuli. Children came to play because play was allowed in the hospital. It was as if Jenny responded to an environment that accepted her multiplicity by giving in to her dissociative patterns.

When Jenny returned to the environment that required her to be functional, to behave normally, she responded with some control and a desire to gain more. Karl worked with her for weeks to reduce the number of alters and relieve the confusion.

The report of the psychological examination gave strong support to what the Alexanders had learned about long and severe trauma in Jenny's life and about extensive cult abuse. Much as it was helpful to Jenny to know that others had experiences similar to hers, it was helpful to the therapists to have such strong corroboration concerning memories of Jenny's they had struggled to recognize as truth.

The summary of findings was sobering but not surprising. Based on three days of psychological testing with Selena as the subject, she was described as "a very disturbed individual who copes with stress through dissociation and multiplicity in the context of an underlying schizophrenic disorder." In every instance of psychological testing over a number of years, a diagnosis of schizophrenia was suggested. It would remain to be seen if the hallucinations she experienced and the difficulty in reality testing she evidenced would resolve as she moved toward full integration.

A treatment plan was suggested in a follow-up letter to the Alexanders signed by Dr. Bennett Braun, Medical Director of the Dissociative Disorders Unit. The letter noted: "It is recommended that the primary goal of outpatient therapy be to assist the patient in creating a strong adult personality who could take responsibility for the chores of everyday living and, ultimately, acquire a job which would provide health insurance for continued treatment as needed. It was suggested that this be done by strengthening existing adult personalities and facilitating internal support and increased communication." The letter further noted that Jenny "has the option to be considered for rehospitalization on the Dissociative Disorders Unit in the future."

It would take time for the Alexanders to evaluate the benefits and drawbacks of this hospitalization for Jenny, and to decide whether to encourage her return there. They had about exhausted the possibilities of seeking help for Jenny when they petitioned her insurance carrier to cover the stay at Rush.

During Jenny's hospitalization, the Alexanders had made the trip to Chicago for an opportunity to consult with the doctors and staff there. In the consultation with Dr. Braun, he focused primarily on the recommendation that they pull back from overinvolvement with Jenny so that they could more effectively confront treatment issues. He reiterated the recommendation in the follow-up letter.

The Alexanders appreciated the encouragement to continue the limits they had been gradually imposing on the therapy. They were struck, however, with the irony that it had been a quote by Dr. Braun in a newspaper article they read early in Jenny's treatment that had validated for them the need for the hours they spent with her. Dr. Braun's position had certainly evolved with his experiences during the eight years since the newspaper interview.

The Alexanders' work with Jenny had paralleled the work of many others in the relatively new area of clinical treatment of multiple personality disorder. Clear guidelines for treatment had only recently begun to emerge. These would be refined by individual therapists, by researchers, and by staff in treatment centers around the world.

The Alexanders continued therapy with Jenny, seeing her twice weekly for two-hour sessions. Jenny spoke often of wanting to return to the unit at Rush. She said she had been told there that she needed to be in the hospital several months a year for a number of years in order to get better. She had felt safe from the cult there and free from the stresses at home. "I didn't have to try so hard to be normal there," she said to Karl.

"What do you mean?"

Jenny looked wistful. "They didn't help me learn to live in this world," she admitted. "But they made it more comfortable to be in my worlds."

This had not been the goal of her treatment at Rush. The focus had been on evaluation, but it was also intended that they help improve her functioning. Jenny had managed to remain insulated from the guidance offered for operating in the real world.

Karl could understand her wanting to escape the awful pain and effort of remembering her past and learning to live in a world that had been for her always hostile. But she had to stand fast if she would learn that the world could be kind. Hospitalization, or any therapy, that allowed her escape did not seem appropriate for Jenny.

In the more than five years of working with Jenny, the Alexanders have encountered over four hundred personalities of varying strengths and influence. The personalities, some fully developed with a range of knowledge and responses, others fragmentary with limited knowledge and functions, revealed themselves to the therapists in groups. When Jenny was ready to confront certain memories, certain segments of her past, the personalities with knowledge of that time surfaced to make those memories available to her.

With each group, as the memories were disclosed and the purposes of each personality examined, individual personalities integrated with others to eventually leave only Jenny, the birth personality; Selena, the primary alter personality; and Mind, the highest center or inner-self-helper. Jenny and Selena moved close in temporary mergers, being able for a time to think and act as one person.

Each time a group of personalities was resolved to the

three, Karl and Rachel hoped that enough abuse had been remembered, that enough abreactions had been experienced, that enough feelings had been worked through to allow a time of stability. Each period of stability, however, was short-lived. As one layer of material was resolved, another moved quickly to the surface, evidenced by the appearance of a new group of personalities.

After her return from hospitalization at Rush, and after the minor personalities were again integrated, Karl and Rachel hoped that a period of stability would last. Jenny had shown that she could be whole when, after remembering the killing of babies, she accepted all the personalities as her own. Her not being able to maintain the unity meant that there was more work to be done.

For most of her life Jenny's past was as hidden from her as it was from the rest of the world. The personalities, who made possible her escape from a painful world, kept silent about its secrets. One wrote the message of the shattered child on the wall of a little house. *I must keep my mouth shut because if I don't I will get in trouble.*

Jenny and all her personalities were held by the mandate to silence. Some tried to tell doctors, or ministers, or counselors, as children, of the horrors in Jenny's life, but they were not understood. They resumed their silent suffering.

To make possible Jenny's return to the real world, the personalities had to break the silence. They revealed their existence and their memories to the Alexanders, who accepted and believed them. In that atmosphere of acceptance and belief, Jenny herself began to know the secrets of her past.

The Alexanders cannot gauge how much more time will be needed for Jenny to achieve full integration. They believe that most of her past has been revealed. Still, there might be more alters to surface, more memories to be recalled, more secrets to explore.

In the process of integration, Jenny will need guidance and support to adapt to the diverse feelings, thoughts, and abilities that once were separated among her many personalities. She will need help in learning new ways to behave as she accepts her past and sees the world as no longer hostile.

Perhaps for a time Jenny will need to function with Selena in a cooperative existence. Perhaps there will be some other pattern. But, ultimately, the Alexanders believe, Jenny can achieve wholeness. If the stresses in her environment are not excessive, and the supports are sufficient, she will be able, if she chooses, to maintain control in a new level of functioning without the use of dissociative escapes.

As a child Jenny had no choices. In order to survive what was done to her and what she was required to do, she gave up awareness and gave over control of her life to alter personalities. For the first time Jenny has choices. As an adult daring to regain awareness and remembering her past, she can take back control.

REFLECTIONS OF JENNY
AND SELENA

After Jenny read the final version of her life's story, I asked her to share her thoughts directly with the reader. Because she and Selena are not fully integrated, "both" of them decided to speak. They move close at times in mutual acceptance of the past and cooperation for the present. At other times, their unique qualities predominate, and Jenny seeks her crystal world; Selena holds to her youth. The honesty is the same.

From Jenny:
I'm not sure how to begin. Only five years ago, I woke up here again, after nearly thirty years, not knowing anything. The world had changed — people, places, and things. For me just to start over again is very hard, and then being told that I'm MPD, and that I've been here through someone else, other personalities who are parts of me. This is very hard to understand and believe. It is very confusing, and fear within is great.

I have so many dimensions, and time pushes on me real

hard. I lose so much time each day — like going to sleep, but don't rest. Like closing the window to my soul.

I still can't tell what reality really is at times, and it hurts trying. Being abused when I was small was a real bad, unbearable thing. I only hope through this book, people will stop and listen to the children.

As children, you must stand up and be not afraid to scream out all the pain you are going through. Hold on to each other, become strong within yourselves, so that the adults will hear you. And adults, listen, because the reality of pain caught within the soul of a child is as the depth of the night. Fear lives within the soul, mind, and heart of the child that is abused.

Maybe someday the crystal will be whole. I'm forever tired. All my essence has gone to the others. The crystal is clear sometimes. Other times, it is tinted by depression, and the rays of the colors are the others. When the others are all gone, will there be no color? Will there then be only tinted crystal? Then who will I be?

I can only hope, and through therapy and the pain of remembering and working hard at putting broken pieces together, that someday I will know what being near whole is. For I am not sure that I want to be totally whole.

I still can't face this world and the people. But maybe someday me and Selena will work together. Selena is very good at the world thing, and someday I would maybe like to be more like her. She sees the world as it is. It see it as still a painful place to be. And many of the people I have seen still hurt us because they don't understand us and MPD, and so they don't try to understand us or get to know us.

I look to the world with real eyes and feel with real feelings, and I'm touched with real deepness. I search with dreams and I long for love.

I hope someday that people will understand us, and that doctors and Mental Health will not be against us and abuse us anymore. I have formed strong bonds with the others of me, and I am not alone. And I have met other MPDs, and *we are all* not alone.

* * *

From Selena:

The book was a hard part of this whole thing of trying to understand ourselves. Which is very hard to try to talk about it, because I was seventeen when I first found out about MPD. I was free and wild and me. As therapy went on, I found out I was really thirty-four. But it was only a small part of finding out that I am not really me, but supposed to be someone else, or I'm a part of someone else.

Now as I wake up as many others have been integrated, I have a lot of confusion. The things I liked and did. Now I find myself liking so many other things, and can't make my mind up. I feel so different in so many ways.

The book also tells of things I didn't remember and things I feel I didn't do. There is still such a separate division of us, and I still feel as *me*, Selena, and not anyone else.

It is hard trying to tell just how I feel, because I'm real confused. It has been real hard trying to take care of the house and kids that I never had to before.

Letting go of myself to be someone else, I can't do. Maybe I'll never know what whole is because there has never been one. There has always been someone there for us at all times. If oneself has to give up themselves to be a *self*, I'm not sure of it at all.

Trying to live with one feeling and pain and abuse is living hell. But to be told that there is more pain and abuse that one does not remember as it being themselves, and to take on those other memories of the others is pure hell.

Someday we will stand, but on a different ground, giving others hope and strength.

REFERENCES

Bliss, Eugene L. *Multiple Personality, Allied Disorders, and Hypnosis.* New York: Oxford University Press, 1986.

Braun, Bennett G., ed. *The Treatment of Multiple Personality Disorder.* Washington, DC: American Psychiatric Press, 1986.

Caul, David. "Group and Videotape Techniques for Multiple Personality Disorder," *Psychiatric Annals,* January 1984, 43-50.

Crabtree, Adam. *Multiple Man: Explorations in Possession and Multiple Personality.* New York: Praeger, 1985.

Crabtree, Adam. "Dissociation as a Way of Life: A Phenomenological Examination of the Experience of Multiple Personality Disorder." A talk presented at a conference sponsored by the American Society for Physical Research, New York City, October 10, 1987.

Greaves, George B. "Multiple Personality: 165 Years after

Mary Reynolds," *The Journal of Nervous and Mental Disease,* October 1980, 577-596.

Kluft, Richard P. "The Postunification Treatment of Multiple Personality Disorder: First Findings," *American Journal of Psychotherapy,* April 1988, 213.

Kluft, Richard P. "Clinical Corner," *ISSMP&D Newsletter,* February 1988, 4.

Putnam, Frank W. "The Psychophysiologic Investigation of Multiple Personality Disorder," *Psychiatric Clinics of North America,* March 1984, 31-39.

Ross, Colin A., and George A. Fraser. "Recognizing Multiple Personality Disorder," *Annals RCPSC,* July 1987, 357.

Ross, Colin A., and G. Ron Norton. "Multiple Personality Disorder Patients with a Prior Diagnosis of Schizophrenia," *Dissociation: Progress in the Dissociative Disorders,* June 1988, 39-42.

Young, Walter C. "Psychodynamics and Dissociation: All That Switches Is Not Split," *Dissociation: Progress in the Dissociative Disorders,* March 1988, 33-38.

Young, Walter C. "Observations on Fantasy in the Formation of Multiple Personality Disorder," *Dissociation: Progress in the Dissociative Disorders,* September 1988, 13-20.

RECOMMENDED READING

ABOUT MULTIPLE
PERSONALITIES:

Bliss, Jonathan, and Eugene Bliss. *Prism: Andrea's World*. New York: Stein and Day, 1985 (Onyx Edition, 1986).

Schreiber, Flora Rheta. *Sybil*. Washington, DC: Regnery, 1973 (Warner Paperback Library Edition, 1974).

Sizemore, Chris Costner, and Elen Sain Pittillo. *I'm Eve*. New York: Doubleday, 1977 (Jove/HBJ Edition, 1978).

Thigpen, Corbett H., and Hervey M. Cleckley. *The Three Faces of Eve*. New York: McGraw-Hill, 1957 (Popular Library Edition, 1957).

ABOUT IDENTIFICATION
AND TREATMENT:

Bliss, Eugene L. *Multiple Personality, Allied Disorders, and Hypnosis*. New York: Oxford University Press, 1986.

Braun, Bennett G., ed. *The Treatment of Multiple Personality Disorder*. Washington, DC: American Psychiatric Press, 1986.

Crabtree, Adam. *Multiple Man: Explorations in Possession and Multiple Personality*. New York: Praeger, 1985.

Kluft, Richard P., ed. *Childhood Antecedents of Multiple Personality*. Washington, DC: American Psychiatric Press, 1985.

ABOUT SATANIC CULTS:

Kahaner, Larry. *Cults That Kill*. New York: Warner Books, 1988.

Smith, Michelle, and Lawrence Pazder, M.D. *Michelle Remembers*. New York: Congdon and Lattes, 1982 (Pocket Books, 1983).

Stratford, Lauren. *Satan's Underground*. Eugene, Oregon: Harvest House, 1988.

Terry, Maury. *The Ultimate Evil*. Garden City, NY: Dolphin Doubleday, 1987.

PERIODICALS:

There are increasing numbers of articles concerning multiple personality in the professional literature. These journals devoted complete issues to the subject.

American Journal of Clinical Hypnosis, October 1983.

Psychiatric Annals, January 1984.

Psychiatric Clinics of North America, March 1984.

This is the official journal of the International Society for the Study of Multiple Personality and Dissociation. The journal began March 1988.

Dissociation: Progress in the Dissociative Disorders
c/o Ridgeview Institute
3995 South Cobb Drive
Smyrna, GA 30080